Praise for *Unlocking Financial Data*

Financial analysts with the best command of information have an edge over their peers. In *Unlocking Financial Data*, Justin shares step-by-step instructions on how anyone can gain that valuable advantage.

—Thomas Majewski, Managing Partner,
Eagle Point Credit Management

Unlocking Financial Data is an essential tool in the information-intensive business of financial analysis, and an invaluable guide for professionals who want to leverage today's technologies to enhance decision-making and gain a competitive advantage in the market. Justin Pauley is a leader in the Structured Finance space. His insights are always well grounded in empirical data that he produces by harnessing today's technologies.

—David Trepanier, CFA, Head of the CLO/Structured Products
Business for a leading US financial institution

Among the small universe of truly talented financial analysts, only a small subset really understand how to harness technology. Justin Pauley is one of the very few people who excels at both aspects. Justin is top in his field in his ability to efficiently harvest and manage data, and then use the data to present clear and concise analysis.

—David Preston, CFA, Managing Director, Head of CLO and
Commercial ABS Research, Wells Fargo Securities

The importance of thoughtful, technological tools cannot be overstated when performing financial analysis. Justin Pauley has become a leader in the structured product market, in large part as a result of his firm grasp on technology. In *Unlocking Financial Data*, Justin curates valuable lessons in accessing financial data that aren't found anywhere else. This book will benefit almost any analyst, regardless of their technology expertise.

—Dylan Ross, Partner, Brigade Capital Management

Unlocking Financial Data
A Practical Guide to Technology for Equity and Fixed Income Analysts

Justin Pauley

Beijing · Boston · Farnham · Sebastopol · Tokyo

Unlocking Financial Data

by Justin Pauley

Copyright © 2018 Justin Pauley. All rights reserved.

Printed in the United States of America.

Published by O'Reilly Media, Inc., 1005 Gravenstein Highway North, Sebastopol, CA 95472.

O'Reilly books may be purchased for educational, business, or sales promotional use. Online editions are also available for most titles (*http://oreilly.com/safari*). For more information, contact our corporate/institutional sales department: 800-998-9938 or *corporate@oreilly.com*.

Editor: Brian Foster	**Indexer:** Ellen Troutman-Zaig
Production Editor: Kristen Brown	**Interior Designer:** David Futato
Copyeditor: Octal Publishing, Inc.	**Cover Designer:** Karen Montgomery
Proofreader: Dwight Ramsey	**Illustrator:** Rebecca Demarest

November 2017:   First Edition

Revision History for the First Edition

2017-10-06:   First Release

See *http://oreilly.com/catalog/errata.csp?isbn=9781491973257* for release details.

The O'Reilly logo is a registered trademark of O'Reilly Media, Inc. *Unlocking Financial Data*, the cover image, and related trade dress are trademarks of O'Reilly Media, Inc.

978-1-491-97325-7

[LSI]

Table of Contents

Preface

If you're opening this book at a bookstore and trying to determine if it's for you, let me help:

- This book will help you combine your views with financial data from Bloomberg —you don't need access to Bloomberg, but it is highly recommended—and IHS Markit, analyze the results, and generate professional reports using Microsoft Excel without any programming or assistance from your IT department.

- This book will show you, step by step, how to quickly produce professional reports that enhance your views with market data including historical financials, comparative analysis, and relative value.

- For portfolio managers, this book demonstrates how to generate a professional portfolio summary report that contains a high-level view of a portfolio's performance, growth, risk-adjusted return, and composition.

- If you are a programmer, or potential programmer, this book contains a parallel path that covers the same topics using C#.

- I am not an academic, and there is a reason "Practical" is in the subtitle of the book. All you need is a basic understanding of finance and Excel. You don't need to know any programing, VBA, or advanced math.

To understand why I am writing this book, it helps to understand my background. I've always loved computer science, and it was no surprise that my first job was programming for Wachovia (now Wells Fargo). However, very early in my career, I realized something important that would lead me down a very different career path. I realized that my ability to use technology for accessing and analyzing data is more valuable in other fields, particularly finance, than as a programmer in the IT department.

After spending three years as a programmer, I moved over to the bank's research group and used my computer science skills to tap into the vast wealth of market and internal information that would be otherwise inaccessible. These skills gave me a big advantage over other analysts, and I left my research role as a director at the Royal Bank of Scotland to become a senior structured credit analyst at Brigade Capital Management, an asset manager based in New York. At Brigade, I still use my technical skills to get an advantage in valuing investments.

Over the course of my career, I have taught many colleagues a useful subset of these technical skills. In teaching them, I've learned that you can do a lot of useful analysis that goes above and beyond Bloomberg screens, all without knowing how to program. All you need is something most people who are employed in the finance sector already have: analytical minds and Excel experience (and this book, of course).

For my fellow programmers, this book has you covered as well. Instead of trying to track down API documentation and reinventing the wheel, this book contains a lot of useful C# examples on how to access market data from Bloomberg and IHS Markit, perform financial analysis using Math.Net open source libraries, and use SQL Server Reporting Services (SSRS) to automate professional reports.

I wanted to write a book to teach these skills to a broader audience and help people use technology to move their resume to the top of the stack.

Conventions Used in This Book

 Many of the code lines in this book have been broken across multiple lines because of the display limits of the page. These breaks are not needed if you are running the code on your system.

The following typographical conventions are used in this book:

Italic
: Indicates new terms, URLs, email addresses, filenames, and file extensions.

`Constant width`
: Used for program listings, as well as within paragraphs to refer to program elements such as variable or function names, databases, data types, environment variables, statements, and keywords.

`Constant width bold`
: Shows commands or other text that should be typed literally by the user.

`Constant width italic`
: Shows text that should be replaced with user-supplied values or by values determined by context.

This element signifies a general note.

This element indicates a warning or caution.

Using Code Examples

Supplemental material (code examples, exercises, etc.) is available for download at *http://bit.ly/unlockFD_examples*.

This book is here to help you get your job done. In general, if example code is offered with this book, you may use it in your programs and documentation. You do not need to contact us for permission unless you're reproducing a significant portion of the code. For example, writing a program that uses several chunks of code from this book does not require permission. Selling or distributing a CD-ROM of examples from O'Reilly books does require permission. Answering a question by citing this book and quoting example code does not require permission. Incorporating a significant amount of example code from this book into your product's documentation does require permission.

We appreciate, but do not require, attribution. An attribution usually includes the title, author, publisher, and ISBN. For example: "*Unlocking Financial Data* by Justin Pauley (O'Reilly). Copyright 2018 Justin Pauley, 978-1-491-97325-7."

If you feel your use of code examples falls outside fair use or the permission given above, feel free to contact us at *permissions@oreilly.com*.

O'Reilly Safari

 *Safari* (formerly Safari Books Online) is a membership-based training and reference platform for enterprise, government, educators, and individuals.

Members have access to thousands of books, training videos, Learning Paths, interactive tutorials, and curated playlists from over 250 publishers, including O'Reilly Media, Harvard Business Review, Prentice Hall Professional, Addison-Wesley Professional, Microsoft Press, Sams, Que, Peachpit Press, Adobe, Focal Press, Cisco Press, John Wiley & Sons, Syngress, Morgan Kaufmann, IBM Redbooks, Packt, Adobe

Press, FT Press, Apress, Manning, New Riders, McGraw-Hill, Jones & Bartlett, and Course Technology, among others.

For more information, please visit *http://oreilly.com/safari*.

How to Contact Us

Please address comments and questions concerning this book to the publisher:

O'Reilly Media, Inc.
1005 Gravenstein Highway North
Sebastopol, CA 95472
800-998-9938 (in the United States or Canada)
707-829-0515 (international or local)
707-829-0104 (fax)

We have a web page for this book, where we list errata, examples, and any additional information. You can access this page at *http://bit.ly/unlockingFinancialData_1e*.

To comment or ask technical questions about this book, send email to *bookquestions@oreilly.com*.

For more information about our books, courses, conferences, and news, see our website at *http://www.oreilly.com*.

Find us on Facebook: *http://facebook.com/oreilly*

Follow us on Twitter: *http://twitter.com/oreillymedia*

Watch us on YouTube: *http://www.youtube.com/oreillymedia*

Acknowledgments

This book is dedicated to my incredibly supportive and amazing wife, Emily Pauley. Very special thanks to those of you who have been especially generous with your time and support; I couldn't have done this without you (in no particular order): Alex Belgrade, Scott Moore, Jeana Curro, Dan Bleicher, Matt Perkal, Sumit Sablok, and Tom O'Shea.

CHAPTER 1
Introduction

In a nutshell, the role of any financial analyst is to develop a view on how much a security—such as a bond, loan, equity, or even a securitized portfolio of commercial real-estate loans—is worth. In other words, an analyst must determine the price at which he would buy or sell a security. There isn't a uniform method, model, or formula that analysts use to determine worth, because every investment is different. However, the valuation process generally consists of two important steps:

- An analyst needs to know each potential investment inside and out, identifying the different nuanced ways and probabilities of losing or making money.
- The resulting risk-adjusted return is measured against other potential investments to determine if the given investment is cheap, rich, or fair valued.

Valuations aren't simply performed once per security; investments must be continuously valued. In today's global economy, the risks to an investment are constantly changing, affected by changing commodity prices, government regulations, natural disasters, consumer sentiment, and countless other variables. Likewise, even if these variables don't affect a security directly, they can make an investment look cheap or rich relative to other securities that were affected.

The process for valuing a security is complicated, time consuming, and generally requires analyzing a lot of financial data. Much of the financial data is provided by the issuing company or a bank that is marketing a deal, and doesn't always paint the full, unbiased, picture. More important, most firms have access to a tremendous amount of financial data that would aid the valuation process, but few outside of technology groups know how to access it, or even know it exists.

This book will show you how to unlock the real potential of Bloomberg data, beyond simply using the Bloomberg Terminal. Using only Excel, without any programming experience, this book demonstrates how to access the data behind the Bloomberg screens, organize it the way you want, and connect it with your views and insights to make investment decisions. This book also discusses how to access data from IHS Markit, one of the best sources for corporate bond and loan data, especially pricing. Many banks, asset managers, and hedge funds already subscribe to Markit, but most of the data is used to support internal systems and rarely makes its way to the hands of analysts.

In addition to demonstrating how to access financial information, the second section of this book covers data analysis. This section describes how to use financial data to determine relative value, measure the risk of a portfolio of securities, calculate correlation between securities, and measure market trends by analyzing loan price movements, issuance, and refinancings.

Finally, we'll put all the pieces together by combining the data and analysis with your views to create custom reports laid out exactly the way you need. Instead of relying on canned reports, these reports will compare a company's performance using peer groups that you decide are appropriate, a corresponding benchmark index that makes sense to you, and financial fields and calculations that you find important.

Although these sections (data access, analysis, and reporting) are designed to be easily implemented, maintained, and updated automatically without an ounce of programming, this book also covers the same topics using C# (a programming language) for programmers or potential programmers. Data and information are valued in any industry, but none more so than finance, where a developer's ability to write code and query databases can make her more valuable as an analyst. This book will show examples of how to access financial information, perform different types of easy financial analysis on large datasets, and create financial reports using SQL Server Reporting Services (SSRS) without the need for a SQL server. If you are interested in an intermediate step between Excel and C#, we cover the same material using a Microsoft Access database.

This chapter dives deeper into each section of the book, highlighting key concepts and goals. It also breaks down how the book will benefit you depending on the asset class (equities, bonds, and loans) in which you're invested.

Overview

This book is broken down into three sections: Accessing Financial Data, Financial Data Analysis, and Creating Financial Reports. Each of these sections is meant to convey a practical set of goals detailed in this subsection.

Section I: Accessing Financial Data

Section I, comprising Chapters 2 through 4, covers how to access and store financial data on equities, indices, bonds, and bank loans using Bloomberg and Markit. By extracting this information from these systems, you will be able to do the following:

- Access additional data that isn't visible on Bloomberg screens
- Create tables containing corporate data that makes it possible to compare multiple companies, bonds, or loans, side by side
- Explore daily prices and facility information for most of the tradable corporate bond and loan markets
- Display only the fields that matter, arranged by your preference
- Override wrong or missing information using other sources
- Categorize companies to establish appropriate peer groups based on your views
- Combine Bloomberg and Markit data with your custom calculations and insights

At the end of the section, you will be able to slice and dice financial data that has been enhanced with your input, with far more flexibility than you could using a Bloomberg Terminal. Furthermore, the techniques in Chapter 3 will ensure that you store the data in a way that is easy to maintain and combine with other sets of data.

Section II: Financial Data Analysis

Section II, which includes Chapters 5 through 8, helps make sense of the financial data collected in Section I by putting it into context using financial analysis. Section II begins by comparing an individual security to its peers and expands to examining risk at a portfolio level and then, finally, incorporating broader market trends. By using the financial techniques in this section, you will be able to do the following:

- Determine the relationship between two securities (or indices) using correlation and regression
- Compare each security's performance to a cohort made up of securities with similar risk and return characteristics
- Rank securities by their relative performance using a weighted z-score
- Measure portfolio risk-adjusted return by calculating variance, standard deviation, and Sharpe ratio
- "Bucket" a portfolio into different groups to highlight unseen concentrations and trends

- Establish portfolio thresholds by using different metrics to highlight risks
- Use Markit data to identify meaningful trends in prices, new issue spreads, and refinancings

At the end of this section, you will be able to put the different datasets collected in Section I into perspective, highlight risks, and identify trends. Additionally, the methods described in Chapter 6 will show you how to maintain a history and identify any issues in the data from Section I.

Section III: Creating Financial Reports

Section III (Chapters 9 and 10) incorporates the lessons from Sections I and II and demonstrates how to build analytic reports for individual companies and portfolios. In this section, the data and analysis from earlier sections will be displayed and charted exactly the way you prefer. This section will demonstrate how to do the following:

- Build two-page analytic ("Tear Sheet") reports for individual companies that incorporate important historical financials, custom notes, relative value comparison of the company to its peers, and price trends with research analyst targets
- Calculate time-weighted (geometric) portfolio returns, annualized portfolio returns, annualized portfolio standard deviation, and Sharpe ratio using historical returns for a portfolio or an index
- Build a two-page portfolio summary report that contains a high-level view of the portfolio's performance, growth, risk-adjusted return, and composition

At the end of this section, you will be able to create a custom professional company report by simply choosing the company's name from a drop-down list without any programming. Additionally, you will be able to chart the portfolio's performance and compare risk and return to benchmarks.

Financial Markets

This book focuses on three main financial markets: equities, corporate bonds, and corporate loans. Nevertheless, you can apply many of the lessons in this book directly to other markets like structured products, municipal bonds, and so on.

Equities

This book has a lot of great content for analysts focused on the equities markets. The first section of the book demonstrates how to create a table of fundamental and technical data (converted into a single currency) from Bloomberg for a list of companies or constituents of an index. Because it is in Excel, you can easily supplement the Bloomberg data with your own input. For instance, by adding your own Category column, you can correctly group similar companies together instead of relying on industry classifications, which are typically misleading. Moreover, Bloomberg has an overwhelming amount of financial corporate data. This book shows you how to find the exact information you're looking for instead of paging through dozens of screens for every company. Following are just some of the fields:

- Sector, Industry, Sub-Industry
- Short Interest Percent of Equity Float
- S&P and Moody's Ratings
- Market Cap, Enterprise Value, EPS
- Total Debt, Net Debt, Total Debt/EBITDA
- Dividend Gross Yield, Twelve-Month Total Return
- Three-Month and Year-to-Date Price Change (%)
- Interest Coverage, Free Cash Flow (FCF), FCF/Total Debt
- CDS Spread
- Buy, Sell, Hold Recommendations
- Gross Profit, TTM EBITDA
- Historical Financials

The second section of the book demonstrates how to calculate the relationship (correlation and Beta) between two companies or a company and a benchmark index. It also adds median performance data to the Excel company table for each custom category. You can use this median performance data to compare each company's performance against its peer group.

Finally, the third section shows you how to design your own company report instead of relying on third-party reports. By customizing your own report, you can include the fields that you want and your own notes and calculations.

Corporate Loans (Bank Debt, Leveraged Loans)

Like equities, the first section of this book pulls a series of useful fields from Bloomberg into Excel (or Access), including these:

- Margin, Floor, Index
- Maturity
- Moody's and S&P Facility Rating
- YTD and Three-Month Price Change

- Discount Margin, Yield
- Next Call Date, Call Price

However, unlike equities, the first section of this book shows how to access loan data from IHS Markit, which has a treasure trove of loan information. Moreover, the Markit data is for most of the tradable loan universe instead of a subset. Daily loan prices on almost every loan combined with facility information on each loan makes it possible for you to identify different trends such as loans selling off in a sector. Here is some of the Markit loan facility data:

- Issuer, Industry, Facility Type
- Sponsor, Lead Agent, Admin Agent
- Size, Spread, Floor, OID
- CUSIP
- Lien Type (1st lien, 2nd lien, etc.)
- Cov-Lite Flag
- Moody's and S&P Ratings
- Launch Date, Close Date, Maturity Date

In the second section, loans are categorized by their parent company's category as well as their risk and return characteristics, such as "Short CCC" for shorter CCC rated loans. Loans are then lined up against the median values for their peer groups to put their metrics into context. In addition to facility-level information and prices, Markit provides information on refinancings that we use in the second section of this book to identify trends such as spread tightening or widening by sector.

Corporate Bonds

Like equities, there is a lot of corporate bond data in Bloomberg that you can extract into an Excel (or Access) table. Some of these fields include the following:

- Coupon
- Maturity
- Moody's and S&P's Facility Ratings
- YAS Spread and YAS Yield (Spread and Yield from the Bloomberg YAS Screen)
- YTD and Three-Month Price Change
- Callable Flag, Next Call Date, Next Call Price

Like loans, bonds will also be categorized in the second section. The resulting median values for each category are then used as a benchmark for each bond in that category.

The Three Paths

The concepts in this book are implemented three different ways (paths), ranging in technical difficulty from simplest to complex: Excel, Microsoft Access, and C#. As the concepts in the chapters build on one another, so do the implementations. Hence, the "paths" nomenclature was used because you will use the same implementation as you traverse the book.

Because most people have familiarity with Excel, most chapters use Excel as the primary method of covering concepts. The Microsoft Access path builds on the Excel path by linking the database to the Excel workbooks and then demonstrates how to query the data instead of using complicated Excel formulas. The C# path uses code to extract data from third-party systems (Bloomberg and Markit), stores the data and analysis in Microsoft Access, and uses SSRS to generate reports.

There are two reasons why each chapter is broken down into the three paths. First, this book targets different audiences. These concepts can be very useful to a financial analyst who has years of Excel experience but has never used a database or written a line of code. Alternatively, for a developer, there are more straightforward ways to access, manipulate, and store data than using Excel. The second reason is to encourage those who have never used a database or written a line of code to try it. Although this book does not teach you how to query databases or write programs, you can combine what you learn herein with books that do, such as *Head First C#*, by Jennifer Greene and Andrew Stellman (O'Reilly). Moreover, first-time developers can use the Excel examples to better understand the C# code. The subsections that follow outline the benefits and drawbacks of each path.

Path 1: Microsoft Excel

It doesn't matter whether you're an analyst, programmer, scientist, accountant, or practically any other professional, if you work with numbers, you probably use Excel. Excel is one of the most powerful, flexible, and well-loved analytic programs on the market. In addition to its impressive collection of useful functions and charting tools, Excel has an intuitive interface that anyone can use. However, it is worth noting a few of its drawbacks relative to Access and C#:

- Although Excel is great at doing computation on a couple thousand rows, it is still very inefficient at processing very large sets of data. Large numbers of rows or columns can result in poor performance or even crashes.

- Excel formulas can quickly become long, complicated, and very difficult to read. Performing anything but the most basic computation can result in multiple inner-functions and array functions.

- Even though Excel formulas are very dynamic, they can be difficult to maintain. Simply inserting a column could introduce errors into formulas that easily can go unnoticed.
- Dynamic and long formulas can be difficult to debug when issues arise.

Path 2: Microsoft Access

Although Microsoft Access is nothing more than a very watered-down version of Microsoft's enterprise database software, SQL Server, almost everyone can use Access without having to answer a lot of questions from your IT department. Access is a great no-frills database application that makes it simple to link Excel data, import comma-separated vales (CSV) files, or create your own tables that can contain millions of rows (up to around 2 GB). If you have never used a database before, it is a powerful skill that isn't more difficult than using Excel. Like Excel, data is stored in rows and columns in database tables that are very similar to Excel worksheets except the columns are well defined (dates, text, numbers, etc.). However, instead of long Excel formulas, Access slices and dices data using a very easy language called Structured Query Language (SQL) that is easy to use and read. You can use SQL to connect data from multiple tables, and it contains many of the same aggregation functions as Excel (average, max, min, standard deviation, etc.). A simple query to get the number of books published in 2017 might look like this:

```
SELECT COUNT(*) FROM Books WHERE Year(PublicationDate) = 2017
```

In this book, those following Path 2 will first get the data from Bloomberg using Excel and then link the Excel worksheets to Access for querying. It is the ability to simply query data that makes Access so useful. However, Access also has its drawbacks:

- Its built-in reporting functionality is inferior to Excel's in many ways. In addition to being nonintuitive, it lacks a lot of Excel's charting features.
- Access is less flexible than Excel. You cannot simply start typing a formula in a cell or drop a chart next to a table.
- Accessing a value from the previous row in a query can be more complicated than it should be.
- Query results aren't as easy to format as Excel.
- Although Access can easily connect to Excel sheets for Bloomberg data, it cannot connect directly to Bloomberg.
- Although they are readable, SQL queries can also become complicated and long.

Path 3: C#

C# (pronounced "C sharp") is a programming language that utilizes the Microsoft .NET Framework. Despite being very powerful, C# is simple and easy to use. Moreover, Microsoft's Visual Studio integrated development environment (IDE)—a tool for writing code—contains one of the best designers for creating beautiful applications. Unlike Access and Excel, C# is not constrained by tables, rows, and columns. It can pull data from Excel, Access, a website, an email, Bloomberg, a text file, or pretty much anything else. C# can also tap into an endless number of math, scientific, and financial functions. Data and calculations can be passed to SSRS to generate beautiful reports that can be converted into PDFs or Excel files with a tiny amount of code. Lastly, because C# generates applications, it can easily be scheduled to update data, generate reports, or send emails. Nevertheless, C# comes with its drawbacks:

- C# requires a lot more upfront work than Excel. It takes dozens of lines of code to pull data from Bloomberg instead of a simple Excel formula.
- SSRS, which you use as the reporting tool in conjunction with C#, is powerful and full of features; however, it still isn't as easy or dynamic as Excel.
- Not everyone can install C# (.NET) on their computer at work without involving the IT department and getting special permission.
- Even though C# is one of the easier programming languages to understand, there is a learning curve. Like any programming language, C# has its own grammar and nuances.

Although I encourage you to explore new technologies, the concepts are more important than the implementation; use what works best for you and your situation.

Online Files

It's likely that you will download all the completed Excel workbooks, Access databases, and C# solutions from O'Reilly's website and modify them to suit your needs instead of reproducing each step. However, it is still important that you understand the purpose of each step so that you don't introduce mistakes. Furthermore, I cannot distribute all the data (especially from Markit) because of licensing issues, so some data will be replaced with made-up information.

You can download the files from *http://bit.ly/unlockFD_examples*.

Summary

When making an investment decision, ultimately it is the analyst's conviction that matters most. Conviction cannot be taught; it comes from years of experience making (and sometimes losing) money. It is experience that informs you whether the numbers don't make sense or if the CFO didn't quite answer the questions on the earnings call. All the data and analysis in the world doesn't make up for conviction, but the goal of this book is to give you an edge by putting more information at your fingertips to help develop conviction and find new investment ideas.

CHAPTER 2

Organizing Financial Data

Data! Data! Data! I can't make bricks without clay.
—Sherlock Holmes

Even though it is tempting to dive right into retrieving financial data from Bloomberg and other sources, taking a moment to plan where we are going to store the data will save you a lot of grief down the road. Coming up with a layout, or *schema*, is an essential step because unorganized data can quickly become cumbersome to update and error-prone. Take, for example, a Microsoft Excel workbook or Access database for tracking students, teachers, and classes. If it kept track of the teacher for each class using the teacher's full name and then the teacher married and decided to change her name, each reference to that name would need to be updated. If one instance were missed, it could lead to big issues down the road. If the school were large enough, it is also possible that two teachers could have the same full name, which could cause scheduling and payroll mistakes.

To solve this problem, we need to store our data in what is known as "third normal form." Put simply, we will create one database or Excel table for each set of data (a table for students, a table for teachers, a table for classes, etc.). The columns in these worksheets or tables will contain only the attributes that *belong* to their respective entity. This is referred to as a *has-a* relationship. This way, no information or attribute will be repeated. For instance, a teacher's full name would appear only in the Teacher table because a teacher "has-a" name. The Class table, containing information about classes (Biology, Math, etc.), shouldn't contain a column with the teacher's name because that would cause the information to be repeated.

However, this causes an issue of how to assign a teacher to a class, after all a class "has-a" teacher. When you need one table to refer to an entity (teacher, student, etc.) in another table, we use a *Primary Key*. A Primary Key is simply a unique identifier that never changes, such as a Teacher ID or social security number, that identifies a unique row in the table. Because the unique identifier never changes we can use it as a reference (also called a *Foreign Key*) in the Class table to reference a teacher in the Teacher table. Because the Class table references the teacher by a Primary Key, we need to update only the Teacher if the teacher were to change her name. Although this might sound complicated, simply remember that you should not store the same data in multiple places.

This chapter demonstrates how to create these example tables in Excel and Access and walks you through how to properly store and retrieve information.

Path 1: Excel

Excel Range Versus Excel Table

Excel is an amazing and very flexible tool because you can put data and formulas anywhere in a worksheet. However, without adding some structure, formulas can become very difficult to read and mistakes can happen and go unnoticed. People have lost money and their jobs because of errors in their models (a fancy word for an Excel sheet). One way to help avoid these issues is by converting an Excel range into an Excel table.

On an Excel worksheet, any connected group of cells is an Excel range. Excel ranges have very few limitations; they can be a single cell or the entire worksheet. An Excel table, on the other hand, adds structure to an Excel range by adding column headers and providing named references. For instance, if a list of students were kept in an arbitrary location on an Excel sheet, a formula for counting the number of students would look like:

```
=COUNTA(A1:A14)
```

If columns were shifted or new rows were added, it is possible that formula wouldn't count the right number of rows. However, if you convert that Excel range to an Excel table labeled "Student," the formula would look like:

```
=COUNTA(Student[StudentID])
```

In this case, you can rest assured that it will always include all the students inside the table. To populate an Excel range and convert it to an Excel table, use the following steps:

1. In row 2, label cells in columns A through E: StudentID, FirstName, LastName, DateOfBirth, and Sex.

2. In rows 3 through 8, add student data corresponding to the column headers in row 1.

3. Select every cell in the Excel range created in steps 1 and 2.

4. On the Excel ribbon, on the Home tab, select "Format as Table" (or press Ctrl-T). Make sure that the check box labeled "My table has headers" is checked, and then click OK.

Figure 2-1 shows several Excel tables that we will use to discuss third normal form and the proper way to store data.

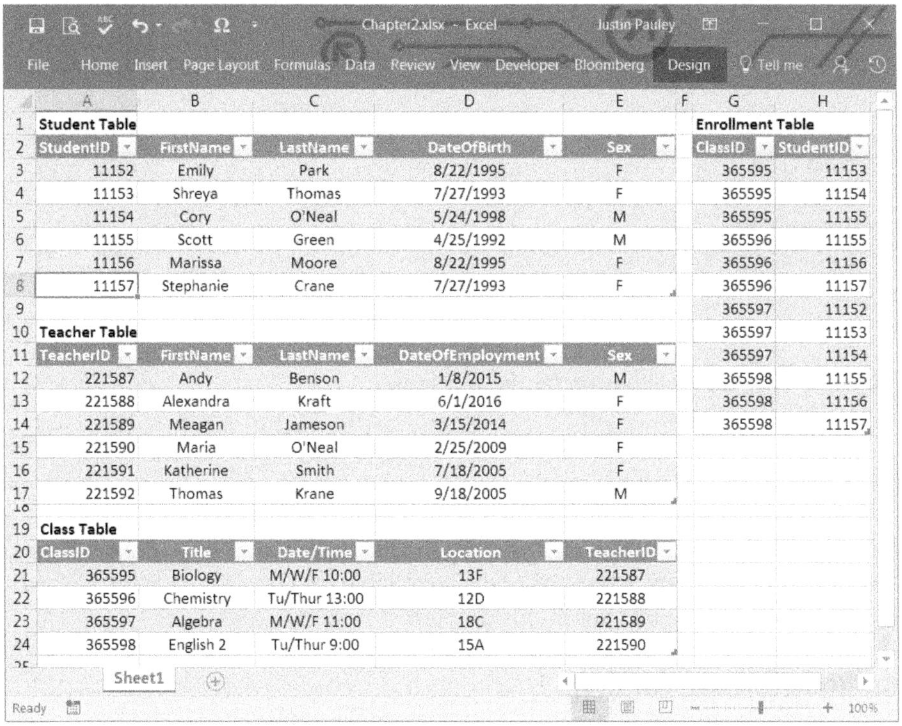

Student Table

StudentID	FirstName	LastName	DateOfBirth	Sex
11152	Emily	Park	8/22/1995	F
11153	Shreya	Thomas	7/27/1993	F
11154	Cory	O'Neal	5/24/1998	M
11155	Scott	Green	4/25/1992	M
11156	Marissa	Moore	8/22/1995	F
11157	Stephanie	Crane	7/27/1993	F

Teacher Table

TeacherID	FirstName	LastName	DateOfEmployment	Sex
221587	Andy	Benson	1/8/2015	M
221588	Alexandra	Kraft	6/1/2016	F
221589	Meagan	Jameson	3/15/2014	F
221590	Maria	O'Neal	2/25/2009	F
221591	Katherine	Smith	7/18/2005	F
221592	Thomas	Krane	9/18/2005	M

Class Table

ClassID	Title	Date/Time	Location	TeacherID
365595	Biology	M/W/F 10:00	13F	221587
365596	Chemistry	Tu/Thur 13:00	12D	221588
365597	Algebra	M/W/F 11:00	18C	221589
365598	English 2	Tu/Thur 9:00	15A	221590

Enrollment Table

ClassID	StudentID
365595	11153
365595	11154
365595	11155
365596	11155
365596	11156
365596	11157
365597	11152
365597	11153
365597	11154
365598	11155
365598	11156
365598	11157

Figure 2-1. An example of Excel tables

In addition to adding the colorful formats to your Excel range, converting to an Excel table enables the handy drop-down icon next to each column header that you can use to easily sort or filter. Furthermore, by right-clicking the Excel table and selecting Totals Row from the Table options, you can add a Total Row to the Excel table that will let you pick from multiple aggregate functions for each column (Figure 2-2).

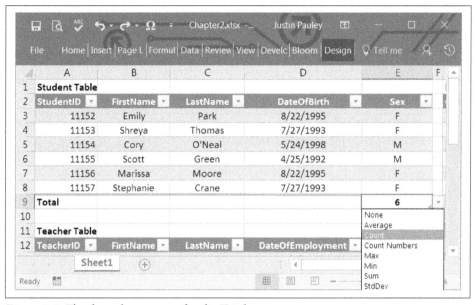

Figure 2-2. The drop-down menu for the Total row

It is important to label your tables. To do so, click any cell within the table, and then, on the ribbon, click the Design tab, and then type a name (like Student) in the text box labeled Table Name (in the upper-left corner). The tables in Figure 2-1 are labeled: Student, Teacher, Class, and Enrollment. Labeling is important because it makes the formulas that reference each Excel table much easier to read and write. This will become apparent later in this chapter.

Adding Reference Columns

Referring to Figure 2-1, the data in this example is separated into four tables: Student, Teacher, Class, and Enrollment. The Student table contains all of the attributes about each student, including a unique identifier (StudentID) that serves as a Primary Key. Likewise, the Teacher table contains all of the attributes about each teacher, including a unique identifier and Primary Key (TeacherID).

The Class table begins like the Student and Teacher table, with attributes for each class including a Primary Key (ClassID). However, because a class "has-a" teacher, it contains a column with the Primary Key from the Teacher table (TeacherID) to reference the teacher for the class. A column containing the Primary Key from another table is called a Foreign Key. The Enrollment table, which contains a list of students in each class, is actually made up of two Foreign Keys: the ClassID that identifies the class the student is enrolled in, and the StudentID that identifies the unique student in that class. Moreover, because each row in the Enrollment table is unique by definition (a student cannot be in the same class twice), we can use the combination of both ClassID and StudentID as the Primary Key to identify a unique row. When two or more columns are used together to form a Primary Key, it is called a *Composite Key* or *Composite Primary Key*.

However, because this is Excel, it would be annoying to have to reference multiple tables to identify the names of teachers, classes, and students. Instead, we can use the INDEX and MATCH functions to add columns from one table to another using the Primary and Foreign Keys. Importantly, we're not adding the attributes themselves to other tables and thus violating the rule about duplicate data; we are adding references or links. If the data in the originating table is updated, all references to that data will also be updated automatically.

Although many Excel users are familiar with the VLOOKUP function that is traditionally used to "look up" information in one set of data using identifiers in another set, VLOOKUP is inferior to the combination of the INDEX and MATCH functions. The key flaw in VLOOKUP is the reliance on column order and positioning. With VLOOKUP, the information you want to look up must be located to the right of the lookup value. In addition, if columns are added, removed, or moved, it could cause VLOOKUP to reference the wrong cell, resulting in a major issue. These problems don't exist when using INDEX and MATCH. The formula to add the teacher's name to the Class table where the TeacherID Foreign Key matches the TeacherID Primary Key in the Teacher column, would look like the following:

```
=INDEX(Teacher[FirstName],MATCH([TeacherID],Teacher[TeacherID],0))
```

Breaking the formula down, the INDEX function takes two parameters: a column name and a row number. The INDEX function returns the value of the cell from that column with that row number. The MATCH function takes three parameters: a lookup value, a column to search, and a match type (the match type should always be zero). The MATCH function returns the row number that contains the lookup value. Combined, the INDEX function returns the contents in the FirstName column from the Teacher table where the TeacherID column in the Class table matches the TeacherID column in the Teacher table. You can also combine it with the last name:

```
=INDEX(Teacher[FirstName],MATCH([TeacherID],Teacher[TeacherID],0))
 & " " &INDEX(Teacher[LastName],MATCH([TeacherID],Teacher[TeacherID],0))
```

This formula adds a column to the Enrollment table to display the Class Title from the Class table using the ClassID:

```
=INDEX(Class[Title],MATCH([ClassID],Class[ClassID],0))
```

This formula adds the student's full name to the Enrollment table:

```
=INDEX(Student[FirstName],MATCH([StudentID],Student[StudentID],0))
 &" "& INDEX(Student[LastName],MATCH([StudentID],Student[StudentID],0))
```

This formula adds the student's sex to the Enrollment table:

```
=INDEX(Student[Sex],MATCH([StudentID],Student[StudentID],0))
```

Note that if you change any of the source information (student or teacher name), the cells referenced using `INDEX` and `MATCH` will automatically update. Although this might seem a bit complicated, it will become natural the more you use it. Additionally, Excel has very nice autocomplete functionality with which you can choose from a list of fields as you type.

In addition to adding reference columns to Excel tables, sometimes it is helpful to add columns that contain summary information. This could include adding columns such as the number of students in each class to the Class table or adding the number of classes per teacher to the Teacher table. Using the named Excel tables and columns, adding a column to the Class table with the number of students is as easy as doing this:

```
=COUNTIF(Enrollment[ClassID],[@ClassID])
```

Or, taking it a step further, calculating the number of students per class who are female:

```
=COUNTIFS(Enrollment[ClassID],[ClassID],Enrollment[Student''s Sex],"F")
```

Note, copying and pasting formulas works differently in Excel tables. In an Excel range, copying and pasting will result in the formula being updated, referencing columns relative to the location of the copy. In an Excel table, copying and pasting a cell will result in the exact formula. To lock a cell in a formula for dragging (instead of using $s in the formula), you would reference cells like `Class[[ClassID]:[ClassID]]` instead of simply `[ClassID]`.

Data Validation

Making sure that the Primary and Foreign Keys are correct is very important. It would be a bad outcome if a Class had a TeacherID that did not exist in the Teacher table. Fortunately, Excel has a Data Validation tool that will help maintain these relationships. Excel's Data Validation tool enforces that a cell contains a value from a set list and can also highlight instances in which the set list changes and the Foreign Keys no longer match.

Unfortunately, however, the Data Validation tool works only with Named Ranges and not Excel table column names. Use the following steps to add a Named Range that links to the list of TeacherIDs in the Teacher table.

1. On the ribbon, click the Formulas tab. In the Defined Names group, click Define Name.

2. Next to Name, type **TeacherIDs**, and next to "Refers to," type **=Teacher[Teach erID]**, and then click OK.

   Next, add Data Validation to the TeacherID Foreign Key column in the Class table using the following steps:

3. In the Class Excel table, select the rows in the TeacherID column.

4. On the ribbon, click the Data tab. In the Data Tools group, click Data Validation, and then select Data Validation.

5. Select List under the Allow drop-down list. Uncheck Ignore blank. Set the Source to =TeacherIDs, and then click OK.

The result will be a drop-down box in each TeacherID cell in the Class table that will allow you to choose only a TeacherID that exists in the Teacher table. Additionally, by clicking Circle Invalid Data in the Data Validation drop-down list, Excel will draw a red circle around incorrect Foreign Keys. Figure 2-3 shows both the red circle and the drop-down data validation features.

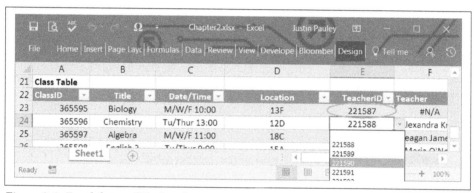

Figure 2-3. Excel data validation features

Paths 2 and 3: Tables in Access

Microsoft Access is a lot more rigid than Excel when it comes to data schemas and relationships between tables. This section demonstrates how to create tables in Access, establish relationships between them, and combine the data using queries. This section uses some of the same concepts as those used in the Excel examples, and it is recommended that you also read the Excel section.

The first step is to create the same tables as shown in Figure 2-1. In Design mode, add the columns for each table and set the Data Types of the Primary Key columns (StudentID, TeacherID, etc.) to Number. Right-click the Primary Key columns and then select Primary Key to establish that these columns are the Primary Keys for their respective tables. You do not need to do anything with Foreign Keys (TeacherID in the Class table).

Next, after populating the tables with data, on the ribbon, click Database Tools, and then click Relationships. Drag the Foreign Keys from one table to their respective Primary Keys in the other table (drag TeacherID in the Class table to TeacherID in the Teacher table). In the Edit Relationships dialog box (Figure 2-4), select Enforce Referential Integrity, which ensures that Foreign Keys match Primary Keys.

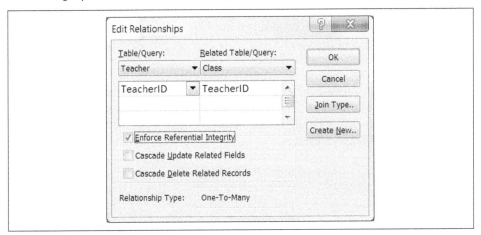

Figure 2-4. The Edit Relationships dialog box in Access

After all of the relationships are established, the Relationships tab should look like Figure 2-5. These relationships will cause an error if you try to add a row to the Class table with a TeacherID that doesn't exist in the Teacher table.

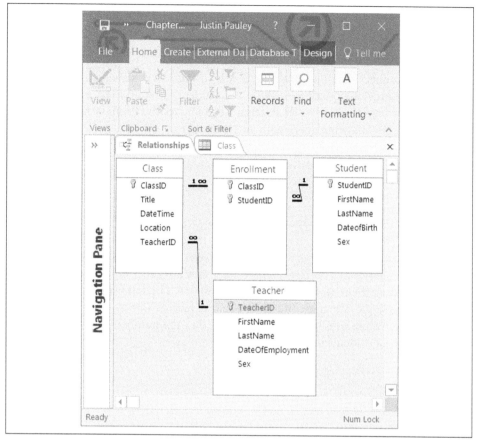

Figure 2-5. Table relationships in Access

Connecting the Data with Queries

Even though learning SQL might seem intimidating to those who are unfamiliar with it, it is a lot easier than it seems; arguably easier than some of the complicated Excel formulas found in this book. And although this book gives you a glimpse into how to use SQL, it is recommended that you read this in conjunction with *Getting Started with SQL*, by Thomas Nield (O'Reilly). Here's the basic syntax for a SQL query:

```
SELECT Column1, Column2, Column3 from TableName;
```

This query would display Column 1 through Column 3 for every row in table Table Name. You could also add a WHERE clause that would filter the results by some expression. For instance, the following would return all the StudentIDs from Enrollment table where the ClassId is 365595:

```
SELECT
StudentID
from Enrollment
WHERE ClassId=365595
```

You can also connect multiple tables together by using a JOIN statement. For instance, to modify the previous query to include the Student's first and last name from the Student table where the StudentID Foreign Key matches the Primary Key in the Student table, use the following query with an INNER JOIN:

```
SELECT
E.StudentID,
S.FirstName as [Student's First Name],
S.LastName as [Student's Last Name]
From Enrollment E
INNER JOIN Student S on S.StudentID=E.StudentID
WHERE  ClassId=365595
```

SQL queries can be very powerful tools for answering complicated questions. And although SQL queries can become complicated, they are generally easy to understand by simply reading them, unlike some Excel formulas. The following query connects the Class table to the Teacher table to display the teacher's name alongside the class information. Furthermore, it uses subqueries to pull the number of students and the number of female students in each class:

```
SELECT
C.ClassID,
C.Title,
C.DateTime,
C.Location,
T.FirstName as [Teacher's First Name],
T.Lastname as [Teacher's Last Name],
(Select count(*) from Enrollment E where E.ClassID=C.ClassID) as [# of Students],
(Select count(*) from Enrollment E
inner join Student S on S.StudentID=E.StudentID
where E.ClassID=C.ClassID and S.Sex='F' ) as [# of Female Students]
from Class C
INNER JOIN Teacher T on T.TeacherID=C.TeacherID
```

Summary

In this chapter, we covered the importance of planning your layout to keep your data organized and avoid headaches in the future. A good layout should use a unique identifier (Primary Key) to identify a security along with its attributes and reference the unique identifier instead of repeating the attributes ("third normal form"). It can be difficult to come up with unique identifiers for financial data; it is best to use the identifier that works most of the time and keep consistent. Regardless of which path you follow, Excel or Microsoft Access, the layout we will use is the same. In Chapter 3, we cover how to pull Bloomberg data into Excel and Access.

Bloomberg

Bloomberg Professional (aka Bloomberg Terminal) is one of the most useful tools a financial analyst can have. However, even though the Bloomberg Terminal itself has a lot of functionality, it cannot match the flexibility and analysis capabilities of Microsoft Excel or Access. In this chapter, we combine Bloomberg's financial data with the flexibility of Excel and Access to create a very powerful analytical tool. Moreover, Bloomberg's Excel Add-in and comprehensive .NET API makes accessing its financial data simple.

We will explore the common and useful features of the Excel Add-in and .NET API; for more information on other features, refer to the Bloomberg documentation available on DAPI <GO>.

 The data you extract from Bloomberg is for your own personal use. Distributing or providing access to the information you source from Bloomberg may violate the terms of your service. In addition, there are limits on the number of securities and fields that you can access in a day or month. For more information, refer to Bloomberg documentation (DAPI <GO> on Bloomberg) or ask your Bloomberg representative (BREP <GO>).

A word of caution before beginning: although Bloomberg scrubs and validates its data, it is possible that some Bloomberg information is incorrect. However, that is not an excuse for your analysis to be incorrect. Later in this book, we discuss techniques to identify and remove bad data from large datasets, but there is no substitute for reviewing data by hand to ensure its accuracy. If you think some Bloomberg data is incorrect, contact Bloomberg Help so that they can fix it for you and the rest of its users. Nevertheless, don't let the thought of incorrect data scare you, it is a rare occurrence, and when it comes to working with financial data, if you held out for perfect solutions you would never accomplish anything.

Identifying the Fields

The first step in retrieving data from Bloomberg through Excel or its API is identifying the correct fields that you want to retrieve. Fortunately, there are a few easy ways to find them.

The Mouse-Over

On many Bloomberg screens, you can simply hold your pointer over content to display a tool tip with the name of the corresponding Bloomberg Field. For example, pull up Apple's description screen by running: **AAPL US Equity DES <GO>**, and then move your pointer over "52 Wk H" (52-week High share price); a tool tip opens showing you Excel Field ID: HIGH_52WEEK, as shown in Figure 3-1.

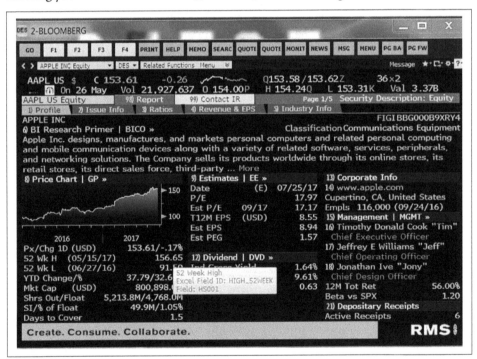

Figure 3-1. A tool tip showing the Excel Field ID

The labels can be ambiguous, so you should double-check the definition by using the FLDS <GO> command, discussed in the next section.

The FLDS Screen

Bloomberg allows users to search for fields using its FLDS screen. To access the FLDS screen, first pull up a security (such as Nokia FH Equity <GO>), and then use **FLDS <GO>**. After you open the FLDS screen, search for a field using the query text box (e.g., search for "market cap," as shown in Figure 3-2). This method is preferred to a mouse-over because, given the substantial number of fields, a search can pull up other, more useful fields than the one found on the tool tip. For instance, moving your pointer over Mkt Cap on the description screen (Excel Field ID: CUR_MKT_CAP) would not display the Currency Adjusted Market Cap field (Excel Field ID: CRNCY_ADJ_MKT_CAP) that pulls the market capitalization in a different currency (see Figure 3-2). Adjusting for currency is important if you're comparing two companies from different regions. In addition, the FLDS screen displays the current value for each field, making it is easier to identify the one you are looking for. Another great feature of the FLDS screen is the ability to drag fields from Bloomberg directly onto your Excel worksheet (you must turn on this feature under Options).

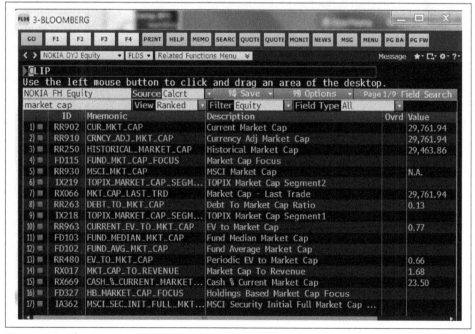

Figure 3-2. The FLDS screen

More important, using the FLDS screen, you can click a field to view a more detailed description and optional overrides (see Figure 3-3). Reading the description of each field is important before using it in your analysis. For example, you can use EQY_FUND_CRNCY, shown in Figure 3-3, to override the currency when requesting CRNCY_ADJ_MKT_CAP. Using overrides is discussed later in this chapter.

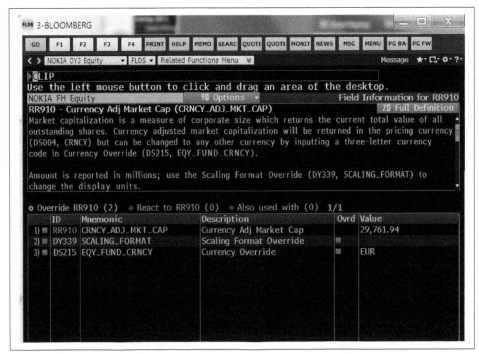

Figure 3-3. Bloomberg Field descriptions

Bloomberg Function Builder and Finding Fields in Excel

With Bloomberg Office Tools, you can access the functionality of the FLDS screen directly from Excel using intuitive menus. To do so, in Excel, on the ribbon, click the Bloomberg tab, and then, in the Create group, click Function Builder, as shown in Figure 3-4.

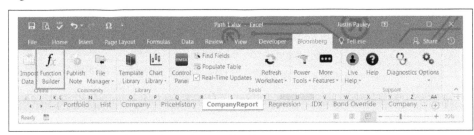

Figure 3-4. The Bloomberg tab on the Excel ribbon

Function Builder has many useful features, but here, we are going to focus on the Bloomberg Data Point (BDP) function. The BDP function, discussed in greater detail later in this chapter, retrieves a single data point from Bloomberg. After selecting BDP, you can use the Function Builder to search for a security and field, as demonstrated in Figure 3-5.

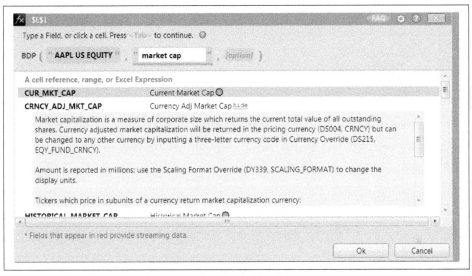

Figure 3-5. The Bloomberg Function Builder in Excel

Alternatively, to browse the library of fields using Bloomberg Field Search, again in Excel, on the Bloomberg tab, in the Tools group, select the Find Fields button (see Figure 3-6). Although it is useful to drill down by category, the FLDS screen is better for searching because it displays applicable fields with their values ranked by popularity.

Don't be tempted to skip the rest of the chapter after you discover how easy it is to use Field Search and the Function Builder. The next few sections demonstrate simple ways to pull data without hardcoding Bloomberg Fields into Excel formulas. This will ensure that your worksheets and database tables are easier to maintain and ready for Chapters 5 and 9.

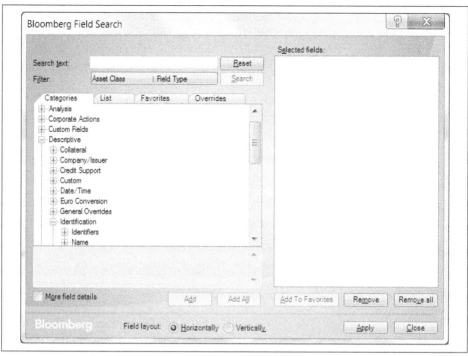

Figure 3-6. The Bloomberg Field Search dialog box in Excel

If All Else Fails...

If you still cannot find the field you are looking for, in Excel, on the Bloomberg tab, click Live Help and ask Bloomberg's Live Help for assistance. You also can click the Live Help button on the HELP <GO> screen in Bloomberg.

Excel Examples

Before we get to the worksheets and database tables, it is helpful to walk through the process of pulling data into Excel. Even if you are planning on exclusively using C# to access Bloomberg data, Excel is an efficient way to understand the different Bloomberg functions.

Pulling a Single Field (BDP)

As discussed earlier, you can use Bloomberg's BDP function to access a single data point, such as a price or rating, using a Bloomberg Field. The BDP function arguments are straightforward:

```
=BDP("Security","Field","Option 1", "Option 2",..."Option N")
```

You can use various identifiers for the *"Security"* argument. For instance, on a corporate bond, you can use its ISIN, CUSIP, or Bloomberg ID Number, such as: "US103186AA06 Corp," "103186AA0 Corp," or "EK1711978 Corp."

Using Open Text Corporation (`OTC CN Equity <GO>`) as an example, begin by pulling down the current market cap using the following Excel formula:

```
=BDP("OTC CN Equity", "CUR_MKT_CAP")
```

This Excel formula will return the same number labeled as Mkt Cap on the `DES <GO>` screen for OTC CN Equity (however, the DES Bloomberg screen displays the market cap in millions, whereas the Excel formula returns the full, unformatted number). As per the FLDS screen description of CUR_MKT_CAP, the value is stated in the company's pricing currency. You can pull that currency by using the following:

```
=BDP("OTC CN Equity","QUOTED_CRNCY")
```

This formula returns CAD, the Canadian Dollar exchange code. You can find a list of FX tickers on Bloomberg by using `FXTF <GO>`. You can pull Open Text's market cap in United States dollars either by providing an override field or by using the exchange rate. The appropriate override field to adjust the currency, as shown on the field description screen for CRNCY_ADJ_MKT_CAP (see Figure 3-3), is EQY_FUND_CRNCY. To use this override, you can either append two arguments to the `BDP` function (the first argument is the field we are overriding, and the second field is the value) or use the format OVERRIDE_FIELD=OVERRIDE_VALUE. For instance, to return Open Text Corporation's market cap in USD, in Excel, you would use either

```
=BDP("OTC CN Equity", "CRNCY_ADJ_MKT_CAP", "EQY_FUND_CRNCY", "USD")
```

or:

```
=BDP("OTC CN Equity", "CRNCY_ADJ_MKT_CAP", "EQY_FUND_CRNCY=USD")
```

As the field description screen for CRNCY_ADJ_MKT_CAP describes, the returned values are in millions. If you want to change the format of the returned market cap, use the other override field listed (also shown in Figure 3-3), SCALING_FORMAT. Clicking SCALING_FORMAT in the field description screen displays the available options. The following Excel formula changes the format to base units (UNT) instead of millions:

```
=BDP("OTC CN Equity", "CRNCY_ADJ_MKT_CAP", "EQY_FUND_CRNCY=USD",
"SCALING_FORMAT=UNT")
```

Alternatively, instead of using the override field, we could pull the "CAD to USD" exchange rate and adjust the market cap in Excel. To accomplish this, pull the

PX_LAST field for the CADUSD Spot Exchange Rate (which is just another security in Bloomberg, CADUSD Curncy <GO>) using the following formula:

```
=BDP("CADUSD Curncy","PX_LAST")
```

You might notice that our two results (one, the CRNCY_ADJ_MKT_CAP formula and, two, the product of CUR_MKT_CAP and the CADUSD exchange rate) do not match. This is likely because of different pricing sources.

 Bloomberg provides multiple pricing sources for securities. It is important that you understand which pricing source(s) you are using.

You can view your pricing source by going to PCS <GO> after loading a security or pulling the PRICING_SOURCE field using a BDP formula. In addition, QFX <GO> provides explanations for the various currency pricing sources and PCSS <GO> provides explanations for other pricing sources.

To override your default pricing source and pull the CADUSD exchange rate using the Bloomberg Composite Rate (CMP) for London's currency market (CMPL), use the following formula, which adds CMPL to the security argument:

```
=BDP("CADUSD CMPL Curncy","PX_LAST")
```

For other securities, such as a corporate bond, override the default pricing source by using an "@" symbol inside the security argument:

```
=BDP("US103186AA06@BVAL Corp","PX_BID")
```

Table 3-1 contains a basic summary of Bloomberg's PCSS screen.

Table 3-1. Pricing source summary

Pricing source	Description
BGN	A real-time composite based on quotes from multiple contributors
BVAL	Combines direct market observations with quantitative pricing models
MSG1	Bloomberg mines prices from your inbox
TRAC	TRACE is FINRA's Corporate and Agency Bond price Dissemination Service. Access to real-time bond price information requires permission and a subscription fee. Nonsubscribers view pricing information on a four-hour delay.

One last BDP optional argument worth mentioning is "Fill". A request for a field that is not applicable to a security will return "#N/A N/A" by default. The "Fill" argument changes the returned value for nonapplicable requests to one you provide. For instance, requesting CUR_MKT_CAP for a private company like Dell would result in "#N/A N/A", but you can change this to a simple dash ("-") by using the following formula:

```
=BDP("DELL US Equity","CUR_MKT_CAP","Fill=-")
```

To return an empty cell, set the Fill argument to B ("Fill=B").

Pulling Bulk Data (BDS)

You might have noticed that the FLDS screen sometimes displays Show Bulk Data in the Value column; this indicates that the field will return multiple values. For instance, the FLDS screen for Microsoft (MSFT US Equity <GO>) displays Show Bulk Data next to BLOOMBERG_PEERS. Clicking Show Bulk Data displays multiple company names that represent the "list of the security's peers, as evaluated by a Bloomberg proprietary algorithm." To pull this list into Excel, use the BDS function, which has similar syntax to the BDP function:

```
=BDS("Security","Field","Option 1", "Option 2",..."Option N")
```

Unlike the BDP function, the BDS function pulls data into multiple rows and/or columns and has several different options.

The list returned from BDS will overwrite existing data in the cells it populates, so ensure that you put the function in a blank range.

You can use the **DIRECTION** parameter to specify how the returned values are arranged, either horizontally across columns or vertically across rows (vertical is the default). To return BLOOMBERG_PEERS for Microsoft horizontally across columns, use the following formula:

```
=BDS("MSFT US Equity","BLOOMBERG_PEERS","DIRECTION=HORIZONTAL")
```

The **SORTASC** (sort ascending), **SORTDESC** (sort descending) parameters control the order of the returned data. You can set these parameters to either the column number or column name (which can be displayed by setting the **HEADERS** parameter to Y). For instance, to return the BLOOMBERG_PEERS data in alphabetical order use

```
=BDS("MSFT US Equity","BLOOMBERG_PEERS","SORTASC=1")
```

or:

```
=BDS("MSFT US Equity","BLOOMBERG_PEERS","SORTASC=Peer Ticker")
```

The **STARTROW**, **ENDROW**, **STARTCOL**, and **ENDCOL** parameters limit the data that is returned. If you set STARTROW to three, the first two rows would be excluded from the returned data. Likewise, by setting ENDROW to four, items after the fourth row would be excluded. Using a combination of these parameters, such as setting STARTROW to two and ENDROW to two, will retrieve only the second element in the list. You can use these parameters in combination with the SORTASC and SORTDESC parameters. For instance, to retrieve the first two BLOOMBERG_PEERS, sorted alphabetically, use the following:

```
=BDS("MSFT US Equity","BLOOMBERG_PEERS","SORTASC=1","ENDROW=2")
```

Throughout this paragraph, key parameters are emphasized with bold font. See also Table A-2 in the Appendix.

The **AGGREGATE** parameter combines the BDS results into a single cell. You can use it in combination with the **SEPARATOR** parameter that customizes the way the data is aggregated. Valid values for the **SEPARATOR** parameter include: B (blank), C (comma), or SC (semicolon). For instance, the following formula returns the first two BLOOMBERG_PEERS, in a single cell, separated by a semicolon:

```
=BDS("MSFT US Equity","BLOOMBERG_PEERS","ENDROW=2","AGGREGATE=Y","SEPARATOR=SC")
```

To pull the last three dividend payments for Microsoft into one cell, begin by using the following formula to display the dividend history for Microsoft:

```
=BDS("MSFT US Equity","DVD_HIST_ALL","HEADERS=Y")
```

Figure 3-7 shows the results.

Declared Date	Ex-Date	Record Date	Payable Date	Dividend Amount	Dividend Frequency	Dividend Type
6/14/2016	8/16/2016	8/18/2016	9/8/2016	0.36	Quarter	Regular Cash
9/15/2015	5/17/2016	5/19/2016	6/9/2016	0.36	Quarter	Regular Cash
12/2/2015	2/16/2016	2/18/2016	3/10/2016	0.36	Quarter	Regular Cash
9/15/2015	11/17/2015	11/19/2015	12/10/2015	0.36	Quarter	Regular Cash
6/9/2015	8/18/2015	8/20/2015	9/10/2015	0.31	Quarter	Regular Cash
3/10/2015	5/19/2015	5/21/2015	6/11/2015	0.31	Quarter	Regular Cash
12/3/2014	2/17/2015	2/19/2015	3/12/2015	0.31	Quarter	Regular Cash
9/16/2014	11/18/2014	11/20/2014	12/11/2014	0.31	Quarter	Regular Cash
6/10/2014	8/19/2014	8/21/2014	9/11/2014	0.28	Quarter	Regular Cash
3/11/2014	5/13/2014	5/15/2014	6/12/2014	0.28	Quarter	Regular Cash
11/19/2013	2/18/2014	2/20/2014	3/13/2014	0.28	Quarter	Regular Cash
9/17/2013	11/19/2013	11/21/2013	12/12/2013	0.28	Quarter	Regular Cash
6/12/2013	8/13/2013	8/15/2013	9/12/2013	0.23	Quarter	Regular Cash
3/11/2013	5/14/2013	5/16/2013	6/13/2013	0.23	Quarter	Regular Cash
11/28/2012	2/19/2013	2/21/2013	3/14/2013	0.23	Quarter	Regular Cash
9/18/2012	11/13/2012	11/15/2012	12/13/2012	0.23	Quarter	Regular Cash
6/13/2012	8/14/2012	8/16/2012	9/13/2012	0.20	Quarter	Regular Cash
3/13/2012	5/15/2012	5/17/2012	6/14/2012	0.20	Quarter	Regular Cash
12/14/2011	2/14/2012	2/16/2012	3/8/2012	0.20	Quarter	Regular Cash
9/20/2011	11/15/2011	11/17/2011	12/8/2011	0.20	Quarter	Regular Cash

Figure 3-7. Showing dividend history with BDS

Second, ensure that the results are sorted correctly by adding "SORTDESC=Record Date":

```
=BDS("MSFT US Equity","DVD_HIST_ALL","HEADERS=Y","SORTDESC=Record Date")
```

Third, to remove all but the top three rows, add "ENDROW=3". Also, remove the HEADERS parameter because that will be included in the row count:

```
=BDS("MSFT US Equity","DVD_HIST_ALL","SORTDESC=Record Date","ENDROW=3")
```

Fourth, isolate the Dividend Amount column (the fifth column) by using Startcol and Endcol:

```
=BDS("MSFT US Equity","DVD_HIST_ALL","SORTDESC=Record Date","ENDROW=3",
    "STARTCOL=5","ENDCOL=5")
```

Finally, use the AGGREGATE and SEPARATOR parameters to join the data into one cell by using a comma:

```
=BDS("MSFT US Equity","DVD_HIST_ALL","SORTDESC=Record Date","ENDROW=3",
    "STARTCOL=5","ENDCOL=5","AGGREGATE=Y","SEPARATOR=C")
```

To add these last three dividends together using the Excel SUM function, use the **ARRAY** parameter that converts the result to an Excel array that can be used in Excel aggregate functions such as AVERAGE or MEDIAN. Like any Excel array functions, you must press Ctrl-Shift-Enter in the formula bar after you type it in:

```
=SUM(BDS("MSFT US Equity","DVD_HIST_ALL","SORTDESC=Record Date","ENDROW=3",
    "STARTCOL=5","ENDCOL=5","ARRAY=TRUE"))
```

The final parameter to mention is **PCS**, which changes the pricing source. For example, to set the pricing source to BGN, append "PCS=BGN" to the BDS formula.

Pulling Historical Data (BDH)

In addition to extracting a security's most recent financial data, you can pull historical data for many fields by using the Excel BDH function. Historical values are available if indicated as such on the field description screen. As with the BDP and BDS functions, the first two arguments to BDH are SECURITY and FIELD. To pull a field's value for one specific date, the only additional argument allowed is the date of your request. For example, to pull Apple's equity price on July 1, 2015 use the following:

```
=BDH("AAPL US Equity","PX_LAST","7/1/2015")
```

However, to pull historical data for a period of time, supply a start and end date. For example, to pull Apple's equity price between June 2, 2014 and June 30, 2014 use this:

```
=BDH("AAPL US Equity","PX_LAST","6/2/2014","6/30/2014")
```

It is a good idea to clear any data below the BDH formula to ensure that nothing is accidently overwritten or mistakenly incorporated.

A specific date, such as in the previous example, should be supplied in a format consistent with your computer's defaults (typically MM/DD/YYYY in the United States or DD/MM/YYYY in Europe). Supplying an empty string ("") as an end date defaults to today's date.

The date arguments are flexible and, in addition to specific dates, the arguments allow for different date types and relative dates. There are three different date types: Fiscal (F), Calendar (C), or Actual (A), which you can see listed in Table 3-2. You can also use these date types to indicate relative dates to specific points in time, such as "-1AW" to indicate one week ago.

Table 3-2. Bloomberg date types

Type	Daily	Weekly	Monthly	Quarterly	Semi-Annual	Annual
Fiscal	—	—	—	FQ	FS	FY
Calendar	CD	CW	CM	CQ	CS	CY
Actual	AD	AW	AM	AQ	AS	AY

Fiscal refers to the specific company's fiscal calendar. For instance, using the following formula to pull Plantronics, Inc.'s (PLT US Equity <GO>) historical equity price for first quarter 2016 returns values starting on June 30, 2016, whereas many fiscal first quarters start in March:

```
=BDH("PLT US Equity","PX_LAST","FQ1 2016","")
```

Calendar and Actual date types are best described by how they are different. With Actual, "-1AW" is exactly seven days ago; "-1AY" is exactly one year ago; etc. Calendar, on the other hand, "-1CW" will round and return the last active day before the start of last week, and "-1CY" will return one day before the start of last year.

As an example, the following formula will start on June 13, 2016, exactly three months or one quarter from September 13, 2016.

```
=BDH("AAPL US Equity","PX_LAST","-1AQ","9/13/2016")
```

Whereas the following formula will start on March 31, 2016, the day before the prior quarter (September 13 is in the third quarter of the year, April is in the second quarter of the year).

```
=BDH("AAPL US Equity","PX_LAST","-1CQ","9/13/2016")
```

By default, BDH will return values only for trading days and, as such, will skip holidays where markets are closed. However, not all markets share the same holiday calendar and Bloomberg will use the calendar corresponding to the security's exchange. For instance, the historical prices for Apple (AAPL US Equity <GO>) from July 1 to July 10, 2016, will not include July 4, because it is not a trading day in the United States. However, Lloyds Banking Group (LLOY LN Equity <GO>) would display a value on July 4 because that date is not a holiday in London. To display Lloyds' historical prices using US trading days, include the **CDR** parameter as follows:

```
=BDH("LLOY LN Equity","PX_LAST","7/1/2016","7/10/2016","CDR=US")
```

For a full list of calendar codes, go to CDR <GO>. Alternatively, to specify which days to return, regardless of holidays, use the **DAYS** parameter. In addition to the default value for trading days (T), you can set the DAYS parameter to W for all weekdays or A for all calendar days. For instance, the following formula will display Apple's share price from July 1 through July 10, including weekends and holidays (July 4):

```
=BDH("AAPL US Equity","PX_LAST","7/1/2016","7/10/2016","DAYS=A")
```

Because the markets were closed on the weekends and holidays, the BDH will automatically use the last available date's value. To change this behavior, set the **Fill** parameter to one of the following:

C, P, *or* Previous
> Same as default, uses the last available date's value

N, E, *or* Error
> Displays an error message

F
> Uses the next available date's value

B *or* Blank
> Displays a blank cell

NA
> Returns an Excel N/A error

PNA
> Uses the previous date's value if available otherwise returns Excel N/A error

Or, specify text, such as "Market Closed" by using this:

```
=BDH("AAPL US Equity","PX_LAST","7/1/2016","7/10/2016","DAYS=A",
"FILL=Market Closed")
```

Throughout this section, key parameters are emphasized with bold font. See also Table A-4 in the Appendix.

To display the data at a frequency other than daily, supply the **PERIOD** parameter. You can set the **PERIOD** parameter to the same date types listed in Table 3-2. For instance, the following formula displays Apple's share close price on the 15th of every month from January 2016 through September 2016:

```
=BDH("AAPL US Equity","PX_LAST","1/15/2016","9/15/2016","PERIOD=AM")
```

You can combine the **PERIOD** parameter with relative dates to display Apple's share price every month end from the beginning of the year:

```
=BDH("AAPL US Equity","PX_LAST","-CY","","PERIOD=CM")
```

Additionally, when requesting price fields, use the **QUOTE** parameter to display the daily average for the given period instead of the close value, for example:

```
=BDH("AAPL US Equity","PX_LAST","-CY","","PERIOD=CM","QUOTE=A")
```

On Monday, June 9, 2014, Apple's share price went from $645.57 to $92.70 after a 7-for-1 stock split. However, Apple's share price history using BDH shows Apple's shares closing at $92.2243 on June 6, 2014. This is because Bloomberg automatically adjusts for spin-offs, stock splits/consolidations, stock dividend/bonus, and rights offerings/ entitlements. If you don't want this adjustment, reconfigure your settings by using the DPDF <GO> screen or set the **CAPCHG** parameter to N like so:

```
=BDH("AAPL US Equity","PX_LAST","6/1/2014","6/10/2014","CAPCHG=N")
```

In addition, the DPDF <GO> screen has options to adjust for Normal Cash Dividends and Abnormal Cash Dividends. To override these features in the BDH function, set **CSHADJNORMAL** or **CSHADJABNORMAL** to Y or N. Alternatively, simply ignore all the DPDF preferences by setting the USEDPDF parameter to N.

To adjust the currency of the returned values, set the **FX** parameter to a currency code, such as "FX=USD" or "FX=CAD".

Bloomberg also includes several parameters to change the way the values are displayed. **POINTS** controls the maximum number of dates to return, such as "POINTS=5" will return only five dates. To display the dates in descending order instead of the default ascending order, set the SORT parameter to D for descending. The BDH function can also take **DIRECTION, ARRAY**, and **PCS** parameters that work the same way as with the BDS function. However, when using the ARRAY parameter, you'll likely want to use it in combination with the **DATES** parameter. Setting "Dates=HIDE" will return only the values without the date column. Finally, some fixed income securities display yield instead of price when you request PX_LAST; to change it to PRICE set **QUOTETYPE** to P for price.

Comparable Securities

A security's performance cannot be measured in isolation; it must be put into context. In other words, to understand the performance of one bond or stock, you should compare it to its peers in different ways. Determining the list of appropriate peers is important and, although many have tried, it is too subjective to be done automatically. Depending on your analysis, it might make sense to compare Apple's stock performance to the performance of the NASDAQ index, the broader S&P 500 index, or a custom index of companies you categorize. Additionally, the number of securities in your sample set is also important. Including too few securities might yield insignificant results but including too many can give you misleading results.

This section discusses a variety of different indices and methods for finding comparable securities.

Indices

There is no shortage of well-known equity indices available on Bloomberg, such as the S&P 500 (SPX Index <GO>), the Dow Jones Industrial Average (INDU Index <GO>), NASDAQ Composite Index (CCMP Index <GO>), and the Russell 2000 Index (RTY Index <GO>). Each index is different and the number of included companies range from 30 to more than 5,000. For instance, the Wilshire 5000 index (W5000 Index <GO>) contains almost all publicly traded companies with headquarters in the United States. Furthermore, there are several "subindices," some of which are created by Bloomberg, that include a subset of companies from their broader parent. For example, the Russell 3000 Technology Index (RGUST Index <GO>) is a capitalization-weighted index of technology companies in the Russell 3000.

In addition to the common indices, on August 24, 2016, Bloomberg acquired Barclays Risk Analytics and Index Solutions Ltd., and, as a result, Bloomberg customers have access to a large set of indices, cobranded Bloomberg Barclays Indices. To browse through the different indices, use IN <GO>. The Bloomberg Barclays US Corporate High Yield Bond Index, for instance, contains 2,152 USD-denominated, high-yield, fixed-rate corporate bonds.

For a more targeted index, try searching. Simply searching for "Bloomberg HY Technology" will come up with Bloomberg USD High Yield Corporate Bond Index Technology (BUHYTE Index <GO>), a rules-based, market-value weighted index of publicly issued, high-yield, fixed-rate, USD, corporate bonds issued by technology companies.

Alternatively, several large banks and financial institutions provide their clients custom indices on Bloomberg. Bank of America Merrill Lynch customers can access the bank's US High Yield Technology Index (H0TY Index <GO>) as well as many others.

There are two easy methods to pull an index's constituent list into Excel. Either use MEMB <GO> and select Excel under the Output option or use the BDS formula to pull the INDX_MEMBERS field:

```
=BDS("BUHYTE Index","INDX_MEMBERS")
```

Sometimes the Excel export or BDS function will return a different type of security identifier than the one in your analysis. For instance, the previous formula example used to pull the index members returned a list of Bloomberg Unique Identifiers (such as "COLW3497804") instead of ISINs. To remain consistent, use the BDP function to pull you preferred identifier. Although not often the case, sometimes the returned identifiers have a prefix that must be stripped off before being passed to the BDP function. In this case, we must strip off the "CO" from each identifier using the Excel SUBSTITUTE function and append the "Corp" to make it a valid identifier. The following formula passes the corrected Security field to the BDP function to retrieve an ISIN (ID_ISIN):

```
=BDP(SUBSTITUTE(N4,"CO","",1) & " Corp","ID_ISIN")
Note: Cell N4 contains the ID COLW3497804
```

Peers

We have discussed previously how to use the BDS function to retrieve a list of the security's peers, as evaluated by a Bloomberg proprietary algorithm using this formula:

```
=BDS("MSFT US Equity","BLOOMBERG_PEERS")
```

Algorithms are far from perfect when it comes to identifying comparable securities. Fortunately, Bloomberg provides a screen to show us the correlation between securities. Figure 3-8 shows the Peer Correlation (PC) screen (PC <GO>) for Microsoft (MSFT US Equity <GO>). The PC screen is a useful way of finding relevant securities and indices.

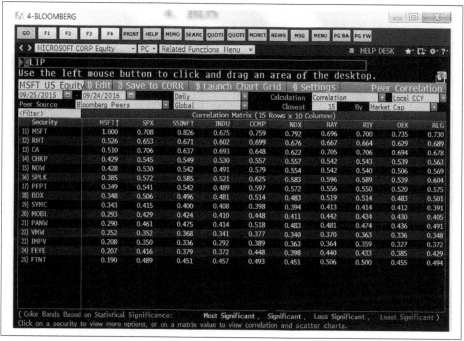

Figure 3-8. The Peer Correlation screen for Microsoft

Related Securities

The Related Securities (RELS <GO>) screen provides a comprehensive overview of the selected security's issuer. As the Related Securities screen for First Data Corp shows in Figure 3-9, it has several debt securities.

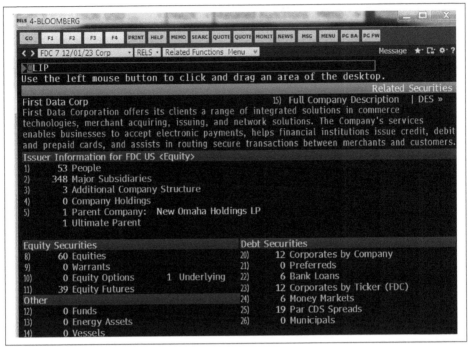

Figure 3-9. The Related Securities screen for First Data Corp

Simply clicking the "Corporates by Company" link brings up a list of securities issued by First Data Corp, split into multiple tabs by security type. Take note: as Figure 3-10 shows, the results are listed in order of highest relevance (as indicated by the Relevance Indicator icon in the first column). The Relevance Indicator, based on Bloomberg's proprietary algorithm, is a very useful way to ensure that the most relevant security is included in your analysis.

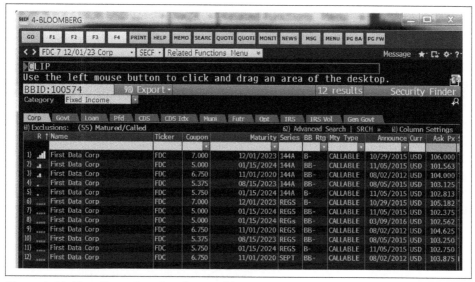

Figure 3-10. First Data Corp bonds sorted by relevance

Paths 1 and 2: Excel and Access

This section goes over the steps to create a new workbook with worksheets for corporations, corporate bonds, loans, and indices. By pulling the data from Bloomberg into these worksheets, it places a lot of information at your fingertips. Additionally, these worksheets are used in the analysis chapters in the second part of the book. If you're following Path 2, the worksheets created in this section are linked to Microsoft Access in Chapter 5.

The fields/columns in the tables that follow were chosen to demonstrate some of the basic types of financial data. They represent a very small subset of those that are available on Bloomberg.

Corporate Bonds, Loans, and Indices

Let's begin by creating a new workbook and naming the first worksheet **Bond**. Then, use Table 3-3 to populate the first two rows of the new worksheet. Table 3-3 contains four columns: the Excel column letter; the Bloomberg Field (aka Mnemonic) to be stored in row 1; the human readable description of the data to be stored in row 2; and the description of the Bloomberg Field for reference. For instance, cell C1 should contain BOND_TO_EQY_TICKER and cell C2 should contain CompanyID. Likewise, cell D1 should contain SECURITY_DES, and cell D2 should contain "Security Description." Note that Bloomberg Fields are not case-sensitive. After populating the

Excel range (A1 through T2), convert the Excel range containing just the used cells in row 2 (A2 through T2) to an Excel table called **Bond**.

Table 3-3. Bond worksheet columns and Bloomberg map

Column	Input into row 1	Input into row 2	Description
A	[Intentionally blank]	BondID	
B	[Intentionally blank]	BBID	
C	BOND_TO_EQY_TICKER	CompanyID	Bond issuer's equity ticker
D	SECURITY_DES	Security Description	Bloomberg description of security
E	CPN_TYP	Coupon Type	Type of interest (Fixed, Floating)
F	CPN	Fixed Coupon	Current interest rate
G	MATURITY	Maturity	Maturity date of bond
H	RTG_MOODY	Moody's Rating	Moody's rating
I	RTG_SP	S&P Rating	S&P rating
J	QUOTED_CRNCY	Currency	Quoted currency
K	PAYMENT_RANK	Rank	Payment rank (Senior Unsecured, Secured, etc.)
L	PX_LAST	Price	Last price
M	CHG_PCT_YTD	YTD Px Chg	Year-to-date price change (percent)
N	CHG_PCT_3M	3M Px Chg	Three-month price change (percent)
O	YAS_YLD_SPREAD	YAS Spread	At current price, the difference in basis points (bps) between the bond's yield and its default benchmark yield. Default settings controlled by YASD <GO> screen.
P	YAS_BOND_YLD	YAS Yield	At current price, the bond's yield. Default settings controlled by YASD <GO> screen
Q	CALLABLE	Callable?	Can the bond be called/redeemed?
R	NXT_CALL_DT	Next Call Date	Next date bond can be redeemed by issuer
S	NXT_CALL_PX	Next Call Price	The price the bond can be redeemed at on next call date
T	[Intentionally blank]	Bond Comments	

The resulting Bond table should look like Figure 3-11.

To link all the information together, we need to come up with a unique identifier for each bond, loan, company, and so on. After all, this book would be useless if you couldn't sort bonds by their company's industry simply because that information was on another worksheet. Unfortunately, coming up with a unique identifier for each security can be challenging. For instance, a corporate bond might be issued under both Regulation S (Reg S) and Rule 144a and, as such, can have two sets of identifiers (a 144a International Securities Identification Number [ISIN] and Committee on Uniform Security Identification Procedures [CUSIP] as well as a Reg S ISIN and CUSIP).

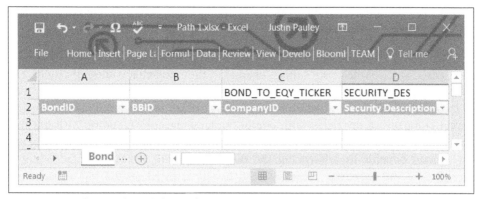

Figure 3-11. The Bond worksheet after initial layout

Complicating matters more, even though all of the identifiers reference the same bond, different funds can have different rules for investing in the 144a series than the Reg S series. As such, it is possible that prices and liquidity can vary between 144a and Reg S. Furthermore, similar issues exist for equities because private companies don't have stock tickers and public companies can have different tickers depending on the exchange. Although there is no perfect solution, you should be fine if you remain consistent. For the purposes of this book, as unique identifiers we will use 144a ISINs for corporate bonds, stock tickers with exchange codes for companies, and Bloomberg identifiers for loans. I will also note that CUSIP is a licensed product from CUSIP Global Services, and it might require you to obtain a license before storing and using CUSIPs in a database.

Using the layout from Table 3-3, list 144a ISINs of corporate bonds in column A of the Bond worksheet under the BondID header. Multiple bonds issued by the same company can be included, but it is important not to list duplicate ISINs. Next, add a formula in the second column, BBID, that converts the ISINs into a security recognized by Bloomberg. As we discussed earlier in this chapter, simply add " Corp" after a bond's ISIN to make it a valid Bloomberg identifier, like so:

```
=[@BondID]&" Corp"
```

Notice the space before "Corp." This is important, and the result should look something like: "US004498AA90 Corp." After we have a list of Bloomberg identifiers in the BBID column, we are ready to pull Bloomberg data into our worksheet. Type the following formula into cell C3, which should be the cell directly under the CompanyID column header:

```
=BDP(Bond[@[BBID]:[BBID]], C$1, "Fill=-")
```

By specifying the name of the table and column in the formula like Bond[@[BBID]:[BBID]] instead of just [@BBID], the cell reference is locked and can be copied or dragged to fill in the rest of the worksheet. For clarity, without cell references the formula would look something like this:

```
=BDP("US004498AA90 Corp","BOND_TO_EQY_TICKER","Fill=-")
```

As described earlier in this chapter, the formula should pull the BOND_TO_EQY_TICKER field from Bloomberg for each bond. The BOND_TO_EQY_TICKER will return the equity ticker for the bond's issuer (or first parent company equity ticker with equity fundamental information). We'll use this data later to come up with a list of companies for our Company worksheet. There are three main benefits to referencing the Bloomberg Field instead of hardcoding it directly into the Excel BDP formula. First, having it listed on the top of each row makes it easier to quickly look up the current field and change it to another field by changing one cell. Second, by using a reference, it is simple to add another field by inserting a column and putting the Bloomberg Field on the first row. Third, using the same formula reduces chances for error.

Figure 3-12 shows what the Bond worksheet should look like (cell D3 is being edited to show the formula).

Figure 3-12. The Bond worksheet with Bloomberg data

You can add conditional formatting to highlight the duplicate cells by selecting column A in Excel, and then, on the ribbon, on the Home tab, click Conditional Formatting, point to Highlight Cell Rules, and then select Duplicate Values.

The Loan worksheet is going to be set up almost exactly like the Bond worksheet with one exception: use Bloomberg ID Numbers (such as "BL2015081" for Zebra Technology Term Loan B) instead of ISINs. You can use a different identifier as the Primary Key for the Loan table if you are consistent and set the values in the BBID column to a valid berg identifier. Use the first two columns in Table 3-4 to populate the first two rows of the Loan worksheet. Convert the second row into an Excel table called **Loan**. Use the same formulas as the Bond table to populate the remaining cells.

Table 3-4. Loan worksheet columns and Bloomberg map

Input into row 1	Input into row 2	Description
[Intentionally blank]	LoanID	Contains the unique identifier for each loan
[Intentionally blank]	BBID	Contains the full Bloomberg Identifier
ISSUER_PARENT_EQY_TICKER	CompanyID	Loan issuer's equity ticker
SECURITY_DES	Security Description	Bloomberg description of security
LN_CURRENT_MARGIN	Margin	Margin or spread above benchmark in coupon
INDEX_FLOOR	Floor	Floor on index if applicable
RESET_IDX	Index	Benchmark index for coupon
MATURITY	Maturity	Maturity date
RTG_MOODY	Moody's Rating	Moody's rating
RTG_SP	S&P Rating	S&P rating
PX_LAST	Price	Last price
CHG_PCT_YTD	YTD Px Chg	Year-to-date price change (percent)
DISC_MRGN_ASK	DM	Discount margin (DM) based on current ask price
YLD_YTM_ASK	Yield	Yield to maturity based on ask price
CALLABLE	Callable?	Can the bond be called/redeemed?
NXT_CALL_DT	Next Call Date	Next date bond can be redeemed by issuer
NXT_CALL_PX	Next Call Price	The price the bond can be redeemed at on next call date
[Intentionally blank]	Loan Comments	

Create an Index worksheet called **IDX** (not "Index," because that word is a reserved word in Microsoft Access). The Index worksheet is set up like the Loan worksheet with one exception: instead of the BBID using "Corp" in the BBID column, as in "BL2015081 Corp," use "Index" as in "SPX Index." Use the first two columns in Table 3-5 to populate the first two rows of the IDX worksheet. Convert the second row into an Excel table called "IDX." Use the same formulas as the Bond table to populate the remaining cells.

Table 3-5. IDX worksheet columns and Bloomberg map

Input into row 1	Input into row 2	Description
[Intentionally blank]	IndexID	Contains the unique identifier for each loan
[Intentionally blank]	BBID	Contains the full Bloomberg Identifier
NAME	Name	Name of the index
PX_LAST	Price	Last price
CHG_PCT_HIGH_52WEEK	52 Week High	Percent difference between current price and highest price in last 52 weeks
CHG_PCT_LOW_52WEEK	52 Week Low	Percent difference between current price and lowest price in last 52 weeks
CHG_PCT_YTD	YTD Px Change	Percent price change year to date
CHG_PCT_3M	3M Px Change	Percent price change over last three months
CURRENT_TRR_1YR	12M Total Return	One-year total return; dividends are reinvested

Company Worksheet

The Company worksheet is different from the Bond, Loan, and IDX worksheets in a few ways. First, because many of the metrics are notional amounts, a currency override is needed in several columns. Second, although most of the Bloomberg columns will contain the same formula, the five-year CDS Spread requires a slight tweak that will be addressed later. Finally, the Company worksheet includes a Category column that will be manual input (not automated from Bloomberg) and a Net Debt/EBITDA column that is derived from other Bloomberg columns.

Create a new worksheet called **Company** and begin by putting the word **Currency** in cell A1 and **USD** in cell B1. We will reference the B1 cell later in our Bloomberg formulas to make sure that all the dollar amounts are in United States dollars (USD).

Then, use the fields in Table 3-6 to fill in the columns in rows two and three. For instance, cell C2 should contain the word "NAME" and cell C3 should contain the word "CompanyName." Likewise, cell E2 should contain the word "GICS_SEC-TOR_NAME" and cell E3 should contain the word "Sector." Cells A2 and B2 should remain blank. Convert the cells in row 3 into an Excel table called "Company." The columns marked with an asterisk (*) use the currency override as described later in this section.

Table 3-6. Company worksheet columns and Bloomberg map

Input into row 2	Input into row 3	Description
[Intentionally blank]	CompanyID	Contains the unique identifier for each Company
[Intentionally blank]	BBID	Contains the full Bloomberg Identifier
NAME	CompanyName	The name of the company
COMPANY_IS_PRIVATE	Private	Indicates if the company is private
GICS_SECTOR_NAME	Sector	Global Industry Classification Standard (GICS) sector classification
GICS_INDUSTRY_NAME	Industry	Global Industry Classification Standard (GICS) industry classification
GICS_SUB_INDUSTRY_NAME	Sub-Industry	Global Industry Classification Standard (GICS) subindustry classification
RTG_SP_LT_LC_ISSUER_CREDIT	S&P Rating	S&P long-term obligation issuer rating
RTG_MDY_LT_CORP_FAMILY	Moody's Rating	Moody's long-term corporate family rating
CRNCY_ADJ_MKT_CAP*	Market Cap	Currency adjusted market capitalization
SHORT_AND_LONG_TERM_DEBT*	Total Debt	Sum of short-term and long-term debt (in millions)
NET_DEBT*	Net Debt	Net debt of the company
CRNCY_ADJ_CURR_EV*	Enterprise Value	Currency adjusted enterprise value
TRAIL_12M_EBITDA*	TTM EBITDA	Trailing 12-month EBITDA
PE_RATIO	PE Ratio	P/E Ratio, ratio of the stock price and the company's earnings per share

Input into row 2	Input into row 3	Description
EQY_DVD_YLD_IND	Dividend Gross Yield	The most recently announced gross dividend, annualized, divided by the current price
CURRENT_TRR_1YR	12M Total Return	One-year total return. Dividends are reinvested.
CHG_PCT_YTD	YTD Px Change	Percent price change year to date
CHG_PCT_3M	3M Px Change	Percent price change over last three months
SALES_REV_TURN*	Total Revenue	Company's total operating revenues less various adjustments to Gross Sales
TOT_DEBT_TO_EBITDA	Total Debt/EBITDA	Total Debt divided by Trailing twelve-month EBITDA
INTEREST_COVERAGE_RATIO	Interest Coverage	Earnings before interest and taxes (EBIT) divided by total interest incurred
TRAIL_12M_FREE_CASH_FLOW*	FCF	Trailing twelve-month free cash flow
FCF_TO_TOTAL_DEBT	FCF/Total Debt	Trailing twelve-month free cash flow divided by Total Debt
CRNCY_ADJ_PX_LAST*	Price	Currency adjusted last price
CHG_PCT_HIGH_52WEEK	52 Week High Change	Percent difference between current price and highest price in last 52 weeks
CHG_PCT_LOW_52WEEK	52 Week Low Change	Percent difference between current price and lowest price in last 52 weeks
CDS_SPREAD_TICKER_5Y	5yr CDS Spread Ticker	Bloomberg ticker for five-year credit default swap par spread
TOT_BUY_REC	Buy Recommendations	Total number of research analyst buy recommendations
TOT_SELL_REC	Sell Recommendations	Total number of research analyst sell recommendations
TOT_HOLD_REC	Hold Recommendations	Total number of research analyst hold recommendations
[Intentionally blank]	Net Debt/EBITDA	
[Intentionally blank]	5yr CDS Spread	
[Intentionally blank]	Category	
[Intentionally blank]	Company Comments	

You might have noticed that some columns, such as Moody's Rating and Price, exist in multiple tables, and this appears to contradict what I said earlier about storing the same information in multiple places. However, in these instances, the Moody's Rating column in the Company table refers to the Moody's Corporate Family Rating (the company's rating) and the "Moody's Rating" in the Bond table refers to Moody's issue rating (the bond's rating). Similarly, the Price column in the Company table refers to the company's share price, whereas in the Loan table it corresponds to the price of the loan. If this causes you confusion, you can always use more precise column names, such as "Loan Price" and "Bond Price."

Next, place your list of company tickers in column A under the CompanyID column header. This list should at least include all the tickers in the CompanyID columns from the Bond and Loan worksheets. Next, append " Equity" to the end of the CompanyID columns to create a valid Bloomberg identifier using the following formula in the BBID column:

```
=[@CompanyID]&" Equity"
```

Again, it is important to note the space before the word "Equity" such that your cells should look like "SVR US Equity." Next, construct a similar BDP function to the one used in the Bond and Loan worksheets except add a currency override, as discussed earlier in this chapter. Every cell, starting with the first row under the CompanyName header and excluding the four columns (Net Debt/EBITDA, 5yr CDS Spread, Category, and Company Comments), should contain the following:

```
=BDP(Company[@[BBID]:[BBID]], C$2,"EQY_FUND_CRNCY",$B$1,"Fill=-")
```

For clarity, without using references, this formula would look like this:

```
=BDP("SVR US Equity", "NAME","EQY_FUND_CRNCY","USD","Fill=-")
```

Although the NAME Bloomberg Field doesn't take, or need, a currency override, it does not cause problems and allows for a consistent formula across most columns. The Net Debt/EBITDA column is included at the end to demonstrate how to include a column that doesn't pull from Bloomberg. The formula for that column divides the Net Debt column by the TTM EBITDA column when the EBITDA column isn't blank:

```
=IF([@[TTM EBITDA]]<>"-",[@[Net Debt]]/[@[TTM EBITDA]],"-")
```

A Credit Default Swap (CDS) is a complicated credit derivative that is outside the scope of this book. Suffice it to say, a CDS is essentially an insurance contract on a bond (or other security) that investors can either buy (e.g., receive protection) or sell (e.g., sell protection). Understanding the cost of that protection, or spread, is an important market indicator of a company's performance. All else equal, the wider the CDS spread, the more implied risk. Use the CDS_SPREAD_TICKER_5Y Bloomberg Field in the 5yr CDS Spread Ticker column to find the ticker for the five-year CDS and, if it exists, get the CDS spread by placing the following formula in the 5yr CDS Spread column:

```
=IF([@[5yr CDS Spread Ticker]]="-","",
BDP([@[5yr CDS Spread Ticker]]& " Corp", "PX_LAST","Fill=-"))
```

Like the Bond and Loan worksheets, it is important that the Primary Key (CompanyID) is unique. You can highlight duplicates the same way as we discussed for the Bond worksheet. Furthermore, fill the Category column with the proper categorization for each company.

Although most of the columns are fields from Bloomberg, the *most important information will come from you*. For instance, Bloomberg will tell you that, per Global Industry Classification Standard (GICS), Apple is a "Technology Hardware, Storage, and Peripherals" company. However, Bloomberg will also tell you that Western Digital is a "Technology Hardware, Storage, and Peripherals" company, despite the stark differences between the two businesses. As an analyst, you must use your best judgment to come up with a category for different companies to compare their performance. In addition to providing your own category, enhancing your data with your subjective views will make your analysis a lot more powerful. For instance, Bloomberg cannot tell you how forthcoming the CFO was on the last earnings call or whether you believe the company's projections.

References and Overrides

The following subsections walk through referencing related information from other worksheets as well as overriding missing or incorrect Bloomberg information.

References

Next, we will modify the worksheets to include columns from other worksheets, such as including the full name of a company (CompanyName) in the Bond worksheet. Although the most common solution uses the Excel VLOOKUP function, there are a couple of issues with VLOOKUP as described in Chapter 2. A better, but slightly more complex, solution is combining the Excel INDEX and MATCH functions.

The MATCH function searches a range for a value and returns its position, and the INDEX function returns the value of a cell in a particular position. Add a column to the Bonds table called "Company Name" by using the following formula:

```
=INDEX(Company[CompanyName],MATCH([@CompanyID],Company[CompanyID],0))
```

You can add as many references to other worksheets as you would like, but you should indicate (using color, or bold) that this data is being sourced from another worksheet. Also, either use Data Validation (mentioned in Chapter 2) or include a column on the Bond and Loan worksheets that indicate whether the CompanyID exists on the Company worksheet. The following formula returns TRUE if the company is found on the Company worksheet; otherwise it returns FALSE:

```
=NOT(ISERROR(VLOOKUP([@CompanyID],Company[CompanyID],1,FALSE)))
```

Overrides

If you find missing or incorrect data, updating the worksheet directly and replacing the Bloomberg formula will create a mess to maintain. Instead, you can modify data returned by Bloomberg (or add missing data) by creating override worksheets (Bond Override, Loan Override, Company Override). These override worksheets will contain the information you want to change.

To create an override for the Bond worksheet, begin by creating a new worksheet called **Bond Override**. Then, in row one, add the column headers **BondID** and **Over ride Date** in columns A and B, respectively. Next, add the other column headers to row one from the Bond table to enable them to be overridden. After that, select the cells with the column headers (including BondID and Override Date) and convert it into an Excel table (as described in Chapter 2) named **BondOverride**.

To accommodate for an override table, alter the formula in the Bond worksheet containing the `BDP` function. Constructing a formula that is not dependent on column orders can become a bit complex.

Our existing `BDP` formula for CompanyID

```
=BDP(Bond[@[BBID]:[BBID]], C$1, "Fill=-")
```

will become:

```
=IF(IFERROR(VLOOKUP(Bond[@[BondID]:[BondID]],BondOverride,
    MATCH(Bond[[#Headers],[CompanyID]],BondOverride[#Headers],0),
    FALSE),"")="",BDP(Bond[@[BBID]:[BBID]], C$1, "Fill=-"),
    VLOOKUP(Bond[@[BondID]:[BondID]],BondOverride,
    MATCH(Bond[[#Headers],[CompanyID]],BondOverride[#Headers],0),
    FALSE))
```

That might look complicated, but it is rather simple after we break it down. Essentially, the formula will display the results of our original `BDP` function if the BondID does not exist on the BondOverride table or if the corresponding CompanyID (or whatever column the cell is in) cell on the BondOverride table is blank.

In the first part, the formula searches the BondOverride table for the BondID (using `VLOOKUP` because we will always know the location of the column) and returns the data in the column that has the same name as the CompanyID column in the Bond table (found using the `MATCH` function we discussed earlier). If this results in an error (because the column doesn't exist or the BondID could not be found), it will return a blank cell.

Then, if the first part returns a blank cell, the `IF` function will return the results of the original `BDP` function; otherwise, it will return the results of the `VLOOKUP`. After this adjustment, data from rows added to the BondOverride table will appear on the Bonds worksheet. The process of adding an override worksheet is the same for loans and companies.

Path 3: Bloomberg C# API

Bloomberg provides a powerful API with which you can access in C# the same information as we've explored in Excel.

Setting Up Microsoft Access for Use with C#

First, let's begin by creating a new database in Access. In this database, we are going to create four tables: Company, Bond, Loan, and IDX. These tables will contain the information from Bloomberg. A fifth table will be needed to store the map of Bloomberg Fields to database table and column.

Second, create the Company table by using the schema described in Table 3-7. Set the columns in the tables below denoted by an asterisk (*) as a Primary Key.

 In Microsoft Access, when you set a data type to Number, you need to change the Field Size to Double in the property window.

Table 3-7. Company table design

Field name	Data type
CompanyID*	Short Text
BBID	Short Text
CompanyName	Short Text
IsPrivate	Short Text
Sector	Short Text
Industry	Short Text
SubIndustry	Short Text
SPRating	Short Text
MoodyRating	Short Text
MarketCap	Number
TotalDebt	Number
NetDebt	Number
EV	Number
EBITDA	Number
TotalRevenue	Number
TotalDebtToEBITDA	Number
InterestCoverage	Number
FCF	Number
FCFToTotalDebt	Number
Price	Number
YrHi	Number
YrLow	Number
CDS5YrTicker	Short Text
NetDebtToEBITDA	Number
CDSSpread5Yr	Number
Category	Short Text
CompanyComments	Long Text
PERatio	Number
DVDYield	Number
TotalReturn12M	Number
PxChgYTD	Number

Field name	Data type
PxChg3M	Number
RecBuy	Number
RecSell	Number
RecHold	Number

Third, create the Bond table using the schema described in Table 3-8.

Table 3-8. Bond table design

Field name	Data type
BondID*	Short Text
BBID	Short Text
CompanyID	Short Text
SecurityDes	Short Text
CpnType	Short Text
FixedCpn	Number
Maturity	Date/Time
MoodyRating	Short Text
SPRating	Short Text
Currency	Short Text
Rank	Short Text
Price	Number
PxChgYTD	Number
PxChg3M	Number
YASSpread	Number
YASYield	Number
IsCallable	Short Text
NextCallDate	Date/Time
NextCallPrice	Number
BondComments	Long Text

Fourth, create the Loan table using the schema described in Table 3-9.

Table 3-9. Loan table design

Field name	Data type
LoanID*	Short Text
BBID	Short Text
CompanyID	Short Text
SecurityDesc	Short Text
CpnType	Short Text
Margin	Number

Field name	Data type
Floor	Number
Index	Short Text
Maturity	Date/Time
MoodyRating	Short Text
SPRating	Short Text
Currency	Short Text
Rank	Short Text
Price	Number
PxChgYTD	Number
PxChg3M	Number
DM	Number
Yield	Number
IsCallable	Short Text
NextCallDate	Date/Time
NextCallPrice	Number
LoanComments	Long Text

Fifth, we will create the Index table using the schema described in Table 3-10.

Table 3-10. Index table design

Field name	Data Type
IndexID*	Short Text
BBID	Short Text
IndexName	Short Text
Price	Number
YrHi	Number
YrLow	Number
PxChgYTD	Number
PxChg3M	Number
TotalReturn12M	Number

Sixth, create a table called Map that will contain the mapping between Bloomberg Fields and our database table structure by using Table 3-11. Both DestTable and Dest-Col should be designated as a Primary Key (thus creating a Composite Primary Key).

Table 3-11. Map table design

Field name	Data type
DestTable*	Short Text
DestCol*	Short Text
BloombergFLD	Short Text

Finally, insert the rows from Table 3-12 into the Map table. Later in this section we discuss how this mapping will be used dynamically to load Bloomberg data into your Access database.

Table 3-12. Map table data

DestTable	DestCol	BloombergFLD
Company	CompanyName	NAME
Company	IsPrivate	COMPANY_IS_PRIVATE
Company	Sector	GICS_SECTOR_NAME
Company	Industry	GICS_INDUSTRY_NAME
Company	SubIndustry	GICS_SUB_INDUSTRY_NAME
Company	SPRating	RTG_SP_LT_LC_ISSUER_CREDIT
Company	MoodyRating	RTG_MDY_LT_CORP_FAMILY
Company	MarketCap	CRNCY_ADJ_MKT_CAP
Company	TotalDebt	SHORT_AND_LONG_TERM_DEBT
Company	NetDebt	NET_DEBT
Company	EV	CRNCY_ADJ_CURR_EV
Company	EBITDA	TRAIL_12M_EBITDA
Company	TotalRevenue	SALES_REV_TURN
Company	TotalDebtToEBITDA	TOT_DEBT_TO_EBITDA
Company	InterestCoverage	INTEREST_COVERAGE_RATIO
Company	FCF	TRAIL_12M_FREE_CASH_FLOW
Company	FCFToTotalDebt	FCF_TO_TOTAL_DEBT
Company	Price	CRNCY_ADJ_PX_LAST
Company	YrHi	CHG_PCT_HIGH_52WEEK
Company	YrLow	CHG_PCT_LOW_52WEEK
Company	CDS5YrTicker	CDS_SPREAD_TICKER_5Y
Company	PERatio	PE_RATIO
Company	DVDYield	EQY_DVD_YLD_IND
Company	TotalReturn12M	CURRENT_TRR_1YR
Company	PxChgYTD	CHG_PCT_YTD
Company	PxChg3M	CHG_PCT_3M
Company	RecBuy	TOT_BUY_REC
Company	RecSell	TOT_SELL_REC
Company	RecHold	TOT_HOLD_REC
Bond	CompanyID	BOND_TO_EQY_TICKER
Bond	SecurityDes	SECURITY_DES
Bond	CpnType	CPN_TYP
Bond	FixedCpn	CPN
Bond	Maturity	MATURITY
Bond	MoodyRating	RTG_MOODY

DestTable	DestCol	BloombergFLD
Bond	SPRating	RTG_SP
Bond	Currency	QUOTED_CRNCY
Bond	Rank	PAYMENT_RANK
Bond	Price	PX_LAST
Bond	PxChgYTD	CHG_PCT_YTD
Bond	PxChg3M	CHG_PCT_3M
Bond	YASSpread	YAS_YLD_SPREAD
Bond	YASYield	YAS_BOND_YLD
Bond	IsCallable	CALLABLE
Bond	NextCallDate	NXT_CALL_DT
Bond	NextCallPrice	NXT_CALL_PX
Loan	CompanyID	ISSUER_PARENT_EQY_TICKER
Loan	SecurityDesc	SECURITY_DES
Loan	CpnType	CPN_TYP
Loan	Margin	LN_CURRENT_MARGIN
Loan	Floor	INDEX_FLOOR
Loan	Index	RESET_IDX
Loan	Maturity	MATURITY
Loan	MoodyRating	RTG_MOODY
Loan	SPRating	RTG_SP
Loan	Currency	QUOTED_CRNCY
Loan	Rank	PAYMENT_RANK
Loan	Price	PX_LAST
Loan	PxChgYTD	CHG_PCT_YTD
Loan	PxChg3M	CHG_PCT_3M
Loan	DM	DISC_MRGN_ASK
Loan	Yield	YLD_YTM_ASK
Loan	IsCallable	CALLABLE
Loan	NextCallDate	NXT_CALL_DT
Loan	NextCallPrice	NXT_CALL_PX
Index	IndexName	NAME
Index	Price	PX_LAST
Index	YrHi	CHG_PCT_HIGH_52WEEK
Index	YrLow	CHG_PCT_LOW_52WEEK
Index	PxChgYTD	CHG_PCT_YTD
Index	PxChg3M	CHG_PCT_3M
Index	TotalReturn12M	CURRENT_TRR_1YR

Bloomberg C# API

In this section, we discuss using Bloomberg's Desktop API with C#. This section covers accessing reference data (like using BDP in Excel) and historical data (like BDH in Excel). Finally, it will demonstrate how to populate the Access database. For more advanced topics, Bloomberg has plenty of documentation on other useful API features on its WAPI <GO> screen. Much of the content in this section is derived from the examples and documentation Bloomberg provided.

 As a reminder, you are subject to data limits, and I recommend that you do not make repeated requests for static data.

Before coding, download the API libraries by visiting the WAPI <GO> screen on Bloomberg and selecting API Download Center. Click the Download button next to Desktop API and save and unzip the resulting zip file into your local *blp* directory (typically *C:\blp*).

Next, in Visual Studio, create a new C# console application by right-clicking your project and selecting Add Reference. Browse to *C:\blp\DAPI\APIv3\DotnetAPI \v3.10.1.2\lib* (you might need to adjust for a different version or local *blp* folder), and then add a reference to *Bloomberglp.Blpapi.dll*.

Next, in your *Program.cs* file, add the appropriate using directives for the Bloomberg classes referenced in our code:

```
using Event = Bloomberglp.Blpapi.Event;
using Element = Bloomberglp.Blpapi.Element;
using Message = Bloomberglp.Blpapi.Message;
using Name = Bloomberglp.Blpapi.Name;
using Request = Bloomberglp.Blpapi.Request;
using Service = Bloomberglp.Blpapi.Service;
using Session = Bloomberglp.Blpapi.Session;
using SessionOptions = Bloomberglp.Blpapi.SessionOptions;
using InvalidRequestException =
        Bloomberglp.Blpapi.InvalidRequestException;
using Datetime = Bloomberglp.Blpapi.Datetime;
```

Bloomberg recommends precomputing the hash values used by their GetElement and GetValue methods, so include the following statements in the body of the Program class:

```
class Program
{
    private static readonly Name SECURITY_DATA = new Name("securityData");
    private static readonly Name SECURITY = new Name("security");
    private static readonly Name FIELD_DATA = new Name("fieldData");
```

```
private static readonly Name RESPONSE_ERROR = new Name("responseError");
private static readonly Name SECURITY_ERROR = new Name("securityError");
private static readonly Name FIELD_EXCEPTIONS =
new Name("fieldExceptions");
private static readonly Name FIELD_ID = new Name("fieldId");
private static readonly Name ERROR_INFO = new Name("errorInfo");
private static readonly Name CATEGORY = new Name("category");
private static readonly Name MESSAGE = new Name("message");
```

Finally, to run our code within an instance of our `Program` class instead of the static `Main` function, create a method called `BasicExample` in the `Program` class and call it from the `Main` method:

```
static void Main(string[] args)
{
  Program p = new Program();
  p.BasicExample();
}
```

Basic Reference Example

The `BasicExample` method establishes a connection to Bloomberg and sends a request for data to Bloomberg's reference data service. The response from Bloomberg's reference data service is handled in the next method, `ProcessResponse`. There are two parts to establishing a connection to Bloomberg using its API. First, as shown in the `BasicExample` method code example that follows, the program must establish a session that connects to your Bloomberg Terminal. Then, that session object is used to access one of Bloomberg's services.

All Bloomberg data must be accessed through one of its "services." In the case of reference data, use its `refdata` service. The `BasicExample` method tries to open the `refdata` service using the `OpenService` method, and, if that is successful, it uses the `GetService` method to obtain a `Service` object.

Next, the code creates a `Request` object using the `Service` object's `CreateRequest` method that will contain the list of securities and fields to retrieve. Bloomberg recommends bundling multiple security and field requests together instead of sending multiple requests.

The code then adds a list of securities to the request by appending them to the `Request` object's "securities" element. The security can be specified in multiple ways; the code example that follows demonstrates how to reference a bond by its CUSIP and a company by its ticker. Similar to "/cusip" and "/ticker," "/isin" or "/bbgid" are acceptable to identify bonds by their ISIN or Bloomberg Global Identifier, respectively.

Next, the fields are also added to the request by appending them to the `Request` object's `fields` element. The API uses the same field names as the Excel BDP function.

As shown in this example, to provide an override for a field, such as override the currency to EUR for CRNCY_ADJ_MKT_CAP, append elements to the `Request` object's `overrides` element and set their `fieldId` and `value` before sending the request.

Then, the code sends the request to Bloomberg and catches any invalid request exceptions.

After a request is sent, the code polls the `Session` object for a response using its `NextEvent` method. It is possible for larger requests that the API will return partial responses, in which case, you should continue polling the `Session` object. However, after the API sends back a nonpartial response (or the session status comes back as terminated), stop polling and stop the session. After any response is received, pass the event to the `ProcessResponse` method (defined later).

Let's see how this all plays out in code:

```
private void BasicExample()
{
    //Establish a Bloomberg Session,
    //otherwise display error and exit
    SessionOptions sessionOptions = new SessionOptions();
    Session session = new Session();
    bool sessionStarted = session.Start();
    if (!sessionStarted)
    {
        System.Console.Error.WriteLine("Failed to start session.");
        return;
    }
    //Open RefData Bloomberg Service
    if (!session.OpenService("//blp/refdata"))
    {
        System.Console.Error.WriteLine("Failed to open //blp/refdata");
        return;
    }
    Service refDataService = session.GetService("//blp/refdata");

    // Create new request
    Request request = refDataService.CreateRequest("ReferenceDataRequest");

    //Add securities to request
    Element securities = request.GetElement("securities");
    securities.AppendValue("/ticker/AAPL US Equity");
    securities.AppendValue("/cusip/319963BP8");

    //Add Bloomberg Fields to request
    Element fields = request.GetElement("fields");
    fields.AppendValue("CRNCY_ADJ_MKT_CAP");
    fields.AppendValue("PX_LAST");

    //Adding override to request
    //following 4 statements set EQY_FUND_CRNCY=EUR
```

```csharp
Element overrides = request["overrides"];
Element override1 = overrides.AppendElement();
override1.SetElement("fieldId", "EQY_FUND_CRNCY");
override1.SetElement("value", "EUR");

//Send Request
try
{
    session.SendRequest(request, null);
}
catch (InvalidRequestException e)
{
    System.Console.WriteLine(e.ToString());
}

//While we haven't errored
//or retrieved entire response
bool done = false;
while (!done)
{
    Event eventObj = session.NextEvent();
    //A partial response will be followed by
    // more partial responses or completed response
    if (eventObj.Type == Event.EventType.PARTIAL_RESPONSE)
    {
        ProcessResponse(eventObj);
    }
    //Most of the time, you just get a completed response
    else if (eventObj.Type == Event.EventType.RESPONSE)
    {
        ProcessResponse(eventObj);
        done = true;
    }
    else
    {
        foreach (Message msg in eventObj)
        {
            System.Console.WriteLine(msg.AsElement);
            if (eventObj.Type == Event.EventType.SESSION_STATUS)
            {
                if (msg.MessageType.Equals("SessionTerminated"))
                {
                    done = true;
                }
            }
        }
    }
}
session.Stop();
}
```

The next method is the `ProcessResponse` method. This method handles the data returned by Bloomberg in the preceding `BasicExample` method. Within the `Event` object passed to the `ProcessResponse` method, there is a collection of `Message` objects. Each of these `Message` objects can contain either an error, indicating that the request failed, or a collection of security elements. Each security element contains either an error, indicating that there was an issue with that security, or a collection of fields and possibly a collection of field errors. The `ProcessResponse` function should iterate through these various collections to get the returned values.

If there wasn't an error in the message, the code will iterate through each security element, pull out the list of returned fields, and iterate through those. Even though the following code retrieves the field's value as a string, there are methods to retrieve it as different datatypes (discussed later in this chapter).

Finally, for each security element, check to see if there is a collection of field exceptions and display them.

Here's what the code looks like:

```
private void ProcessResponse(Event eventObj)
{
    //Responses can contain multiple messages
    foreach (Message msg in eventObj)
    {
        // if the message is an error, display and continue
        if (msg.HasElement(RESPONSE_ERROR))
        {
            Element error = msg.GetElement(RESPONSE_ERROR);
            Console.WriteLine("Request failed: "
            + error.GetElementAsString(CATEGORY) +
            " (" + error.GetElementAsString(MESSAGE) + ")");
            continue;
        }
        // For each of the requested securities in the response
        Element securities = msg.GetElement(SECURITY_DATA);
        for (int i = 0; i < securities.NumValues; ++i)
        {
            //Create references for security object and ticker
            Element security = securities.GetValueAsElement(i);
            string ticker = security.GetElementAsString(SECURITY);

            //If security has error, display and continue
            if (security.HasElement("securityError"))
            {
                Element error = security.GetElement(SECURITY_ERROR);
                Console.WriteLine("Security Error: "
                + error.GetElementAsString(CATEGORY) +
                " (" + error.GetElementAsString(MESSAGE) + ")");
                continue;
            }
```

```
//For each field in request
// Display data from Bloomberg
Element fields = security.GetElement(FIELD_DATA);
if (fields.NumElements > 0)
{
    for (int j = 0; j < fields.NumElements; ++j)
    {
        Element field = fields.GetElement(j);
        System.Console.WriteLine(field.Name + "\t\t" +
            field.GetValueAsString());
    }
}

//If there were exceptions with particular fields
//Display them
Element fieldExceptions = security.GetElement(FIELD_EXCEPTIONS);
if (fieldExceptions.NumValues > 0)
{
    for (int k = 0; k < fieldExceptions.NumValues; ++k)
    {
        Element fieldException =
            fieldExceptions.GetValueAsElement(k);

        Element error = fieldException.GetElement(ERROR_INFO);
        Console.WriteLine("Field Exception: "
        + fieldException.GetElementAsString(FIELD_ID) + " "
        + error.GetElementAsString(CATEGORY) +
        " (" + error.GetElementAsString(MESSAGE) + ")");

    }
}
                }
            }
        }
    }
}
```

Basic Historical Example

To emulate the Excel BDH function and pull a history of information for a Bloomberg Field requires a few tweaks. First, add the precomputed hash value for "date" inside the body of our Program class:

```
private static readonly Name DATE = new Name("date");
```

Next, change the request declaration to the following:

```
Request request = refDataService.CreateRequest("HistoricalDataRequest");
```

Next, set the additional arguments for a historical request. Earlier in this chapter, we discussed the various arguments to the BDH function. Refer to Table 3-13 for the equivalent API arguments.

Table 3-13. API arguments for historical request

Argument	BDH equivalent	Comments
startDate	—	Start date in YYYYMMDD format
endDate	—	End date in YYYYMMDD format
periodicityAdjustment	—	ACTUAL, CALENDAR, or FISCAL
periodicitySelection	—	DAILY, WEEKLY, MONTHLY, QUARTERLY, SEMI_ANNUALLY, YEARLY
currency	FX	Three letter ISO code; for example, USD, GBP
overrideOption	Quote	Set to OVERRIDE_OPTION_GPA to use average price in quote calculation instead of closing price
pricingOption	QuoteType	PRICING_OPTION_PRICE for price, PRICING_OPTION_YIELD for yield
nonTradingDayFillOption	Days	NON_TRADING_WEEKDAYS, ALL_CALENDAR_DAYS, ACTIVE_DAYS_ONLY
nonTradingDayFillMethod	Fill	PREVIOUS_VALUE or NIL_VALUE for blank
adjustmentNormal	CshAdjNormal	Set to true or false
adjustmentAbnormal	CshAdjAbnormal	Set to true or false
adjustmentSplit	CapChg	Set to true or false
adjustmentFollowDPDF	UseDPDF	Set to true or false
calendarCodeOverride	CDR	For example, "US" or "JN"

In the BasicExample function, set the startDate and endDate fields of the Request object to the dates using a "YYYYMMDD" date format before sending the request:

```
request.Set("startDate", "20140601");
request.Set("endDate", "20140625");
```

Like Excel, you can also set the period selection to DAILY, WEEKLY, MONTHLY, QUAR
TERLY, or YEARLY by setting the periodicitySelection fields in the Request object:

```
request.Set("periodicitySelection", "DAILY");
```

The full method looks as follows:

```
private void HistoryExample()
{
    SessionOptions sessionOptions = new SessionOptions();
    Session session = new Session();
    bool sessionStarted = session.Start();
    if (!sessionStarted)
    {
        System.Console.Error.WriteLine("Failed to start session.");
        return;
    }
    if (!session.OpenService("//blp/refdata"))
    {
        System.Console.Error.WriteLine("Failed to open //blp/refdata");
        return;
```

```
                }

        Service refDataService = session.GetService("//blp/refdata");

        //Use HistoricalDataRequest
        Request request = refDataService.CreateRequest("HistoricalDataRequest");

        Element securities = request.GetElement("securities");
        securities.AppendValue("/ticker/MSFT US Equity");
        securities.AppendValue("/ticker/AAPL US Equity");

        Element fields = request.GetElement("fields");
        fields.AppendValue("PX_LAST");
        fields.AppendValue("PX_OPEN");

        // Set Dates and period
        request.Set("startDate", "20140601");
        request.Set("endDate", "20140612");
        request.Set("periodicitySelection", "DAILY");

        try
        {
            session.SendRequest(request, null);
        }
        catch (InvalidRequestException e)
        {
            System.Console.WriteLine(e.ToString());
        }


        bool done = false;
        while (!done)
        {
            Event eventObj = session.NextEvent();
            if (eventObj.Type == Event.EventType.PARTIAL_RESPONSE)
            {
                ProcessHistoryResponse(eventObj);
            }
            else if (eventObj.Type == Event.EventType.RESPONSE)
            {
                ProcessHistoryResponse(eventObj);
                done = true;
            }
            else
            {
                foreach (Message msg in eventObj)
                {
                    System.Console.WriteLine(msg.AsElement);
                    if (eventObj.Type == Event.EventType.SESSION_STATUS)
                    {
                        if (msg.MessageType.Equals("SessionTerminated"))
                        {
```

```
                            done = true;
                        }
                    }
                }
            }
        }
        session.Stop();
    }
```

Because the response to a historical data request isn't identical to the response from a reference data request, you need to change the function call in the `while` loop from `ProcessResponse` to `ProcessHistoryResponse`.

The `ProcessHistoryResponse` method will look similar to the `ProcessResponse` method with a couple of exceptions. First, unlike a reference response, the `SECURITY_DATA` element in a historical data response is not an array: it contains one security. Second, the `FIELD_DATA` contains a date in addition to a value.

The code will loop through the `FIELD_DATA` collection, which will contain one element for each day. Within each of those elements will be another `Element` collection for each requested field, including the date itself. Because the date is part of the collection, it is pulled out by name and ignored while looping through the rest of the collection for the other fields.

Here's the complete code:

```
private void ProcessHistoryResponse(Event eventObj)
{
    foreach (Message msg in eventObj)
    {
        if (msg.HasElement(RESPONSE_ERROR))
        {
            Element error = msg.GetElement(RESPONSE_ERROR);
            Console.WriteLine("Request failed: "
            + error.GetElementAsString(CATEGORY) +
            " (" + error.GetElementAsString(MESSAGE) + ")");
            continue;
        }


        Element securityData = msg.GetElement(SECURITY_DATA);
        string security = securityData.GetElement(SECURITY).GetValueAsString();
        Console.WriteLine(security);

        Element fieldData = securityData.GetElement(FIELD_DATA);
        if (fieldData.NumElements > 0)
        {
            for (int i = 0; i < fieldData.NumElements; i++)
            {
                Element element = fieldData.GetValueAsElement(i);
                //Pull the date from the returned field and display
```

```
Datetime date = element.GetElementAsDatetime(DATE);
Console.WriteLine(date.ToSystemDateTime().ToShortDateString());

//For the remaining fields (not DATE), display.
for (int f = 0; f < element.NumElements; f++)
{
    Element field = element.GetElement(f);
    if (!field.Name.Equals(DATE))
    {
        Console.WriteLine(field.Name + " = "
        + field.GetValueAsString());
    }
}
}
}
}
}
}
```

Populating Access Database

In this section, we populate the database tables using the Bloomberg API. The code in this section iterates through the bonds, loans, and companies in their respective tables and requests from the Bloomberg API the Bloomberg Fields listed in the Map table. The Map table also includes the corresponding column to store the resulting information from Bloomberg.

Before we begin

Before beginning, there are a few items to address. First, to connect C# to Microsoft Access, you need to install the appropriate version of OleDb drivers that works with your version of Microsoft Access. For instance, use Microsoft.ACE.OLEDB.12.0 to connect to Microsoft Access 2016.

Next, create a new C# solution for a console application in Visual Studio and place a copy of your Access database in the project's directory. Then, using the database file in the project's directory, populate the Bond, Loan, Index, and Company tables with the appropriate identifiers. For each of those tables, populate the Primary Key column and the BBID column either by manually inputting the identifiers or paste them in from Excel (hint: to paste multiple rows from Excel, in Access, on the Home tab, click Paste, and then click Paste Append). Leave the rest of the columns in each table blank; they will be filled using the API.

Creating a typed dataset

There are numerous ways to connect your C# code to a database, but I prefer using typed datasets because they are simple, it separates the database queries from the code, and it makes the code simpler to read. In Visual Studio, right-click your project, select Add, select New Item, and then choose DataSet. Name the new dataset **ADS.xsd**. Next, in the Server Explorer pane, right-click Data Connections and select Add Connection. Choose Microsoft Access Database File as your Data source, click the Browse button adjacent to "Database file name" and then, in the project's directory, choose the Access database file and then click OK. Next, in the Server Explorer pane, navigate to and select the tables in the Tables folder and drag them onto your new dataset. Your dataset should look like Figure 3-13.

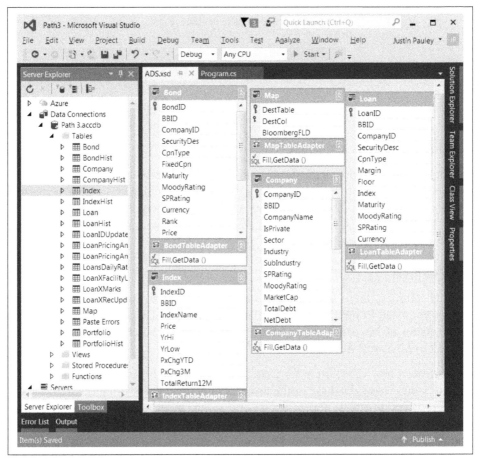

Figure 3-13. ADS dataset

The code

This project will be like the one we used for retrieving reference data. Begin by including the same reference to the Bloomberg *.dll* in the */blp* directory, adding the same using directives, and adding the same precomputed Name objects. As shown in the following code, the Run method is called, which populates our dataset from Access, pulls data for bonds, loans, and companies, and then updates the database:

```
using Event = Bloomberglp.Blpapi.Event;
using Element = Bloomberglp.Blpapi.Element;
using Message = Bloomberglp.Blpapi.Message;
using Name = Bloomberglp.Blpapi.Name;
using Request = Bloomberglp.Blpapi.Request;
using Service = Bloomberglp.Blpapi.Service;
using Session = Bloomberglp.Blpapi.Session;
using DataType = Bloomberglp.Blpapi.Schema.Datatype;
using SessionOptions = Bloomberglp.Blpapi.SessionOptions;
using InvalidRequestException =
        Bloomberglp.Blpapi.InvalidRequestException;
using System.Data;

namespace Path3_Load
{
    class Program
    {
        private ADS DS = new ADS();
        private static readonly Name SECURITY_DATA = new Name("securityData");
        private static readonly Name SECURITY = new Name("security");
        private static readonly Name FIELD_DATA = new Name("fieldData");
        private static readonly Name RESPONSE_ERROR = new Name("responseError");
        private static readonly Name SECURITY_ERROR = new Name("securityError");
        private static readonly Name FIELD_EXCEPTIONS =
        new Name("fieldExceptions");
        private static readonly Name FIELD_ID = new Name("fieldId");
        private static readonly Name ERROR_INFO = new Name("errorInfo");
        private static readonly Name CATEGORY = new Name("category");
        private static readonly Name MESSAGE = new Name("message");

        static void Main(string[] args)
        {
            Program p = new Program();
            p.Run();
        }
        private void Run()
        {

            FillDataSet();
            RunBonds();
            RunLoans();
            RunCompanies();
            RunIndex();
            int rowc= UpdateDataSet();
        }
```

The FillDataSet method is rather simple; it uses a TableAdapterManager to populate the dataset from Access:

```
private void FillDataSet()
{
    using (ADSTableAdapters.TableAdapterManager tm =
    new ADSTableAdapters.TableAdapterManager())
    {
        tm.BondTableAdapter = new ADSTableAdapters.BondTableAdapter();
        tm.LoanTableAdapter = new ADSTableAdapters.LoanTableAdapter();
        tm.CompanyTableAdapter = new ADSTableAdapters.CompanyTableAdapter();
        tm.IndexTableAdapter = new ADSTableAdapters.IndexTableAdapter();
        tm.MapTableAdapter = new ADSTableAdapters.MapTableAdapter();
        tm.BondTableAdapter.Fill(DS.Bond);
        tm.LoanTableAdapter.Fill(DS.Loan);
        tm.CompanyTableAdapter.Fill(DS.Company);
        tm.IndexTableAdapter.Fill(DS.Index);
        tm.MapTableAdapter.Fill(DS.Map);
        tm.Connection.Close();
    }
}
```

In the RunBonds method, iterate through the list of bonds in the database and populate a Dictionary object (secIds) with the security identifiers used to reference each
bond and the corresponding bond DataRow. Then, using the Map table, populate
another Dictionary object (fields) with the Bloomberg Field and corresponding
destination column to store the requested data. Finally, pass the two Dictionary
objects to a generic function, FetchData, that will perform the actual request:

```
private void RunBonds()
{
    Dictionary<string,DataRow> secIds = new Dictionary<string, DataRow>();
    Dictionary<string, string> fields = new Dictionary<string, string>();

    foreach (ADS.BondRow bond in DS.Bond)
    {
        secIds.Add("/isin/" + bond.BondID,bond);

    }
    foreach (ADS.MapRow map in DS.Map.Where(x => x.DestTable == "Bond"))
    {
        fields.Add(map.BloombergFLD, map.DestCol);
    }
    FetchData(secIds, fields, "Bond");
}
```

The FetchData method creates a Bloomberg session, gets an instance of the reference
data service, adds the list of security identifiers and fields from the two Dictionary
objects (secIds, and fields) to a Bloomberg request and sends the request. The
method also accepts an optional array of KeyValuePair to add overrides (used later to
access company data). Finally, the FetchData method polls the Session object for
responses and, on a response or partial response, passes the Event object to a Process
Response method along with the Dictionary objects and the name of the table:

```csharp
private void FetchData(
    Dictionary<string, DataRow> secIds,
    Dictionary<string, string> fields,
    string table,
    params KeyValuePair<string, string>[] overrides)
{
    // Open session and service
    Session session = new Session();
    bool sessionStarted = session.Start();
    if (!sessionStarted)
    {
        System.Console.Error.WriteLine("Failed to start session.");
        return;
    }
    if (!session.OpenService("//blp/refdata"))
    {
        System.Console.Error.WriteLine("Failed to open //blp/refdata");
        return;
    }

    Service refDataService = session.GetService("//blp/refdata");

    // Create request
    Request request = refDataService.CreateRequest("ReferenceDataRequest");

    // add each security to the request
    Element securities = request.GetElement("securities");
    foreach (string id in secIds.Keys)
    {
        securities.AppendValue(id);
    }
    // add each field to the request
    Element requestedFields = request.GetElement("fields");
    foreach (string field in fields.Keys)
    {
        requestedFields.AppendValue(field);
    }

    //Optionally, if there are overrides, add them to request
    if (overrides != null)
    {
        Element overrideElement = request["overrides"];

        foreach (KeyValuePair<string, string> or in overrides)
        {
            Element o = overrideElement.AppendElement();
            o.SetElement("fieldId", or.Key);
            o.SetElement("value", or.Value);
        }
    }
    // send the request
    try
```

```
    {
        session.SendRequest(request, null);
    }
    catch (InvalidRequestException e)
    {
        System.Console.WriteLine(e.ToString());
    }

    // Process the response
    bool done = false;
    while (!done)
    {
        Event eventObj = session.NextEvent();
        if (eventObj.Type == Event.EventType.PARTIAL_RESPONSE)
        {
            ProcessResponse(eventObj, fields, table, secIds);
        }
        else if (eventObj.Type == Event.EventType.RESPONSE)
        {
            ProcessResponse(eventObj, fields, table, secIds);
            done = true;
        }
        else
        {
            foreach (Message msg in eventObj)
            {
                System.Console.WriteLine(msg.AsElement);
                if (eventObj.Type == Event.EventType.SESSION_STATUS)
                {
                    if (msg.MessageType.Equals("SessionTerminated"))
                    {
                        done = true;
                    }
                }
            }
        }
    }
    session.Stop();
}
```

The ProcessResponse method uses the data from the Bloomberg response to populate the Dictionary object secIds. As ProcessResponse loops through the requested
data, it uses the requested ticker to look up the DataRow in the secIds Dictionary
created in our RunBonds method.

Next, the code pulls the list of returned fields, uses the field's Dictionary to get the
corresponding DataTable column, and then clears the contents from the DataRow
object by setting it to null. Then the code inspects the "Datatype" property of the field
Bloomberg returned to determine the appropriate method for accessing the returned
value. For instance, if field.Datatype is set to DataType.FLOAT64 then it uses the

field.GetValueAsFloat64() method, whereas if field.Datatype is set to Data
Type.DATETIME, it uses the Field.GetValueAsDatetime() method. Also, check that
the DataColumn in the ADS dataset will accept values of the returned datatype before
setting the column in the DataRow to the returned value:

```
private void ProcessResponse(
    Event eventObj,
    Dictionary<string, string> fields,
    string table,
    Dictionary<string, DataRow> secIds
    )
{
    foreach (Message msg in eventObj)
    {
        if (msg.HasElement(RESPONSE_ERROR))
        {
            Element error = msg.GetElement(RESPONSE_ERROR);
            Console.WriteLine("Request failed: "
            + error.GetElementAsString(CATEGORY) +
            " (" + error.GetElementAsString(MESSAGE) + ")");
            continue;
        }

        Element securities = msg.GetElement(SECURITY_DATA);
        for (int i = 0; i < securities.NumValues; ++i)
        {
            Element security = securities.GetValueAsElement(i);

            if (security.HasElement("securityError"))
            {
                Element error = security.GetElement(SECURITY_ERROR);
                Console.WriteLine("Security Error: "
                + error.GetElementAsString(CATEGORY) +
                " (" + error.GetElementAsString(MESSAGE) + ")");

                continue;
            }

            Element fieldExceptions = security.GetElement(FIELD_EXCEPTIONS);
            if (fieldExceptions.NumValues > 0)
            {
                for (int k = 0; k < fieldExceptions.NumValues; ++k)
                {
                    Element fieldException =
                        fieldExceptions.GetValueAsElement(k);

                    Element error = fieldException.GetElement(ERROR_INFO);
                    Console.WriteLine("Field Exception: "
                    + fieldException.GetElementAsString(FIELD_ID) + " "
                    + error.GetElementAsString(CATEGORY) +
                    " (" + error.GetElementAsString(MESSAGE) + ")");
```

```
        }
}

// pulls the ticker that we used in our request, like /ISIN/123123434
string ticker = security.GetElementAsString(SECURITY);

// the row from our dataset with this id.
DataRow row = secIds[ticker];


Element fieldElements = security.GetElement(FIELD_DATA);
if (fieldElements.NumElements > 0)
{

    for (int j = 0; j < fieldElements.NumElements; ++j)
    {
        Element field = fieldElements.GetElement(j);

        //Using the Map table to find the destination column.
        DataColumn dc =
        row.Table.Columns[fields[field.Name.ToString()]];
        row[dc] = DBNull.Value;
        switch (field.Datatype)
        {
            case DataType.BOOL:
                if (dc.DataType == typeof(bool))
                {
                    row[dc] = field.GetValueAsBool();
                }
                break;
            case DataType.DATE:
                if (dc.DataType == typeof(DateTime))
                {
                    row[dc] =
                    field.GetValueAsDate().ToSystemDateTime();
                }
                break;
            case DataType.DATETIME:
                if (dc.DataType == typeof(DateTime))
                {
                    row[dc] =
                    field.GetValueAsDatetime().ToSystemDateTime();
                }
                break;
            case DataType.FLOAT32:
                if (dc.DataType == typeof(double))
                {
                    row[dc] =
                    Convert.ToDouble(field.GetValueAsFloat32());
                }
                break;
```

```csharp
        case DataType.FLOAT64:
            if (dc.DataType == typeof(double))
            {
                row[dc] = field.GetValueAsFloat64();
            }
            break;
        case DataType.INT32:
            if (dc.DataType == typeof(int))
            {
                row[dc] = field.GetValueAsInt32();
            }
            break;
        case DataType.INT64:
            if (dc.DataType == typeof(long))
            {
                row[dc] = field.GetValueAsInt64();
            }
            break;
        case DataType.STRING:
            if (dc.DataType == typeof(string))
            {
                row[dc] = field.GetValueAsString();
            }
            break;
        case DataType.CHAR:
            if (dc.DataType == typeof(char))
            {
                row[dc] = field.GetValueAsChar();
            }
            else if (dc.DataType == typeof(string))
            {
                row[dc] =
                Convert.ToString(field.GetValueAsChar());
            }
            else if (dc.DataType == typeof(bool))
            {
                char c = field.GetValueAsChar();
                if (c == 'Y')
                    row[dc] = true;
                else if (c == 'N')
                    row[dc] = false;
            }
            break;
        default:
            Console.WriteLine("Missing Column Type");
            break;
    }

    System.Console.WriteLine(field.Name + "\t\t" +
        field.GetValueAsString());
    }
}
```

```
        }
    }
}
```

The `RunLoans` method is very similar to the `RunBonds` method except instead of using ISINs, it uses tickers to identify loans:

```
private void RunLoans()
{
    Dictionary<string, DataRow> secIds = new Dictionary<string, DataRow>();
    Dictionary<string, string> fields = new Dictionary<string, string>();

    foreach (ADS.LoanRow loan in DS.Loan)
    {
        secIds.Add("/ticker/" + loan.LoanID + " Corp", loan);

    }
    foreach (ADS.MapRow map in DS.Map.Where(x => x.DestTable == "Loan"))
    {
        fields.Add(map.BloombergFLD, map.DestCol);
    }
    FetchData(secIds, fields, "Loan");
}
```

The `RunCompanies` method is very similar to the `RunLoans` method except a `KeyValue Pair` is passed to the `FetchData` method to override EQY_FUND_CRNCY. In addition, a post-fetching section of code is included that sets the NetDebtToEBITDA column in the database and also creates a new request for five-year CDS spread using the five-year CDS ticker, if it exists. The following demonstrates how to extend the other functions to add different custom calculations.

```
private void RunCompanies()
{
    Dictionary<string, DataRow> secIds = new Dictionary<string, DataRow>();
    Dictionary<string, string> fields = new Dictionary<string, string>();

    foreach (ADS.CompanyRow company in DS.Company)
    {
        secIds.Add("/ticker/" + company.CompanyID + " Equity", company);

    }
    foreach (ADS.MapRow map in DS.Map.Where(x => x.DestTable == "Company"))
    {
        fields.Add(map.BloombergFLD, map.DestCol);
    }
    FetchData(secIds, fields, "Company", new KeyValuePair<string, string>(
    "EQY_FUND_CRNCY", "USD"));

    // Post-fetching tasks
    secIds.Clear();
```

```
    fields.Clear();
    foreach (ADS.CompanyRow company in DS.Company)
    {
        //Set Net Debt/EBITDA
        if (company.IsNetDebtNull() == false
            && company.IsEBITDANull() == false
            && company.EBITDA > 0)
        {
            company.NetDebtToEBITDA = company.NetDebt / company.EBITDA;
        }
        // 5yr cds
        if(company.IsCDS5YrTickerNull() == false)
        {
            secIds.Add("/ticker/" + company.CDS5YrTicker + " Corp", company);
        }
    }
    if(secIds.Count >0)
    {
        fields.Add("PX_LAST", DS.Company.CDSSpread5YrColumn.ColumnName);
        FetchData(secIds, fields, "Company");
    }
}
```

The RunIndex method is very similar to the RunLoans method except we reference the Index by appending "Index" after the IndexID instead of "Corp":

```
private void RunIndex()
{
    Dictionary<string, DataRow> secIds = new Dictionary<string, DataRow>();
    Dictionary<string, string> fields = new Dictionary<string, string>();

    foreach (ADS.IndexRow index in DS.Index)
    {
        secIds.Add("/ticker/" + index.IndexID +" Index", index);

    }
    foreach (ADS.MapRow map in DS.Map.Where(x => x.DestTable == "Index"))
    {
        fields.Add(map.BloombergFLD, map.DestCol);
    }
    FetchData(secIds, fields, "Index");
}
```

The final method, UpdateDataSet, saves the updated dataset back to Access and returns the number of rows updated:

```
private int UpdateDataSet()
{
    int rowc = 0;
    using (ADSTableAdapters.TableAdapterManager tm =
    new ADSTableAdapters.TableAdapterManager())
    {
        tm.BondTableAdapter = new ADSTableAdapters.BondTableAdapter();
```

```
        tm.LoanTableAdapter = new ADSTableAdapters.LoanTableAdapter();
        tm.CompanyTableAdapter = new ADSTableAdapters.CompanyTableAdapter();
        tm.IndexTableAdapter = new ADSTableAdapters.IndexTableAdapter();
        rowc = tm.UpdateAll(DS);
        tm.Connection.Close();
    }
    return rowc;
}
```

 When you run your code from within Visual Studio, it creates a local copy of databases in the */bin/Debug* folder of your project and saves all updated changes to that copy instead of updating the version in your project's directory.

Summary

This chapter introduced techniques that you can use to create an Excel workbook or Access database that not only pulls data automatically from Bloomberg, but stores it in a consistent and easily maintainable layout. Although this is already useful for financial analysis, upcoming chapters cover data analysis and reporting techniques for enhancing your Excel workbook or Access database.

CHAPTER 4

IHS Markit: Big Corporate Data

This chapter covers how to retrieve financial information from IHS Markit, one of the best sources for financial data covering the universe of corporate bonds, loans, and a range of different products. Unlike Bloomberg, Markit offers its clients access to retrieve pricing and reference data on almost the entire spectrum of tradable bonds and loans, without restrictions. Working with very large sets of financial data opens the door to different types of useful analysis, such as looking for trends in daily price changes for thousands of syndicated loans based on spread, rating, or other characteristics. Many banks, asset managers, and hedge funds already subscribe to Markit data; however, most of the data is used to support internal systems and rarely makes its way to the hands of analysts.

Chapter 8 discusses the different types of analysis on large datasets, whereas this chapter focuses on the different types of data available, how to retrieve the data, and techniques for storing the data with Excel and Microsoft Access based on the path you are following.

This chapter does not cover all of the products IHS Markit offers. To learn more about Markit and its complete range of products, visit *https://www.markit.com*. Most of the field descriptions used in this chapter are from Markit's documentation.

Corporate Loans

Corporate loans (also referred to as bank loans, leveraged loans, or syndicated loans), are loans issued by corporations that are typically rated noninvestment grade. Markit provides reference data (facility information, ratings, identifiers, etc.) and performance information (pricing, financials, analytics, etc.) on most of the investable global market.

Data Request

Fortunately, Markit makes it very simple to request data using their Markit Loans Automated Data Exchange. Each type of data Markit provides is referred to as a "channel," which you can access in either comma-separated value (CSV) or Extensible Markup Language (XML) format using a customized web request. The web request is simply a URL (website) containing parameters, such as firm, username, password, and other options. For instance, accessing loan prices (LoanXMarks channel) in CSV is as simple as visiting the following URL in a web browser:

```
https://loans.markit.com/loanx/LoanXMarks.csv?LEGALENTITY=firmname
    &USERNAME=user1&PASSWORD=password1
```

This URL downloads a CSV file that you can open in Microsoft Excel. Switching the *.csv* extension to *.xml* in the URL will return an XML document that is both human-readable and machine-readable (designed to be read by applications). If the parameters, like your username, contain special characters, you must encode them to avoid problems; for example, instead of "/", you need to use "%2F". A quick search on the internet for "URL encoder" will return multiple websites that can assist you with the encoding.

 You can download most of the information discussed in this section manually from Markit's website at *http://www.markit.com*.

Facility Information

The *Facility Update* channel will return reference data on every loan facility that was updated since your last request; contact *support@markit.com* to receive the initial file of facility data. As such, if you sent two consecutive requests with no interval between them, the second request would return an empty result. Use the following URL syntax to access facility data in CSV format:

```
https://loans.markit.com/loanx/LoanXFacilityUpdates.csv?LEGALENTITY=
mylegalentity&USERNAME=user1&PASSWORD=mypassword
```

The file returned will have columns defined in Table 4-1. Because Markit has a partnership with S&P, some of the columns (denoted by an asterisk [*]) are accessible only to clients that also have an agreement with S&P. In addition, some columns (denoted by **) must be specifically requested from Markit (you can contact *support@markit.com*) before they will appear in the results. Columns denoted with *** require both an agreement with S&P and a specific request to Markit.

Table 4-1. Facility update columns

Column	Description
LoanX ID	Unique Identifier for each loan.
PMD ID	Unique identifier associated with a particular issuer/tranche combination. This can be a positive or negative number.
PMD Trans ID*	Unique ID by which PMD/LCD identifies a Transaction, or loan package.
Issuer Name	Name of borrower or issuer.
Issuer ID*	A generated unique identifier associated with a particular issuer.
Deal Name	Name of borrower. This is usually the same as preceding cell but can include date and type of deal.
Facility Type	Specific loan type; TLB, bridge loan, etc.
LoanX Facility Type	Markit consolidates the PMD Facility Type into one of currently 16 standardized values.
Facility Status*	Specific instrument type: bridge, 364-day, subord, Term Loan Amortizing.
LoanX Facility Type Code*	Code representation of LoanX Facility Type + LoanX Facility Category.
LoanX Facility Category*	Markit simplifies the PMD Facility type to one of the following: Institutional, RC, TLA, Other.
Industry	Industry classification based on SIC code
Initial Amount	Facility amount in MM.
Initial Spread	Original LIBOR spread.
Maturity Date	Final maturity date.
Ticker***	The issuer's ticker symbol.
Currency***	Currency of the loan.
LoanX Currency Code*	Standardized currency abbreviation.
SP Org ID***	S&P's assigned Org ID.
Commitment Fee*	Commitment Fee.
Sponsor*	Sponsor of the loan.
LoanX Sponsor Code*	Sponsor name as a numeric code.
Launch Date*	Launch date of the loan.
Close Date*	Close date of the loan.
State*	State of issuer.
Country*	Country of issuer.
LoanX Country Code*	Standardized Country abbreviation.
Pro Rata Assignment*	Pro Rata Assignment Minimum.
Institutional Assignment*	Institutional Assignment Minimum.
Pro Rata Fee*	Pro Rata Fee.
Institutional Fee*	Institutional Fee.
Facility Fee*	Annual fee paid on the full amount of a facility.
Consent*	Agent, company, both.
Security*	Assets securing the loan.
LoanX Security Code*	Standardized Security abbreviation.
Lead Agent*	Lead agent.
LoanX Lead Agent Code*	A generated unique identifier associated with an agent name.
Admin Agent*	Administrative agent.

Column	Description
LoanX Admin Agent Code*	A generated unique identifier associated with an agent name.
Document Agent*	Documentation agent.
LoanX Doc Agent Code*	A generated unique identifier associated with an agent name.
Syndicate Agent*	Syndication agent.
LoanX Synd Agent Code*	A generated unique identifier associated with an agent name.
Initial SP Rating*	Initial S&P rating.
Industry Code*	Industry code.
SIC Code*	SIC code.
SIC Description*	SIC description.
Industry Segment ID*	Industry segment ID.
Industry Segment Description*	Industry segment description.
Status Code*	Code for internal status.
Status	Description of internal status.
Cancelled*	Flag to indicate the deal was cancelled.
Created Time	Date a facility record was created.
Modified Time	Date a facility record was modified.
Term*	Term of the loan, in years.
RC Term*	Term of the RC loan, in years.
TLA Term*	Term of the TLA loan, in years
TLB Term*	Term of the TLB loan, in years.
TLD Term*	Term of the TLD loan, in years.
OID*	Original offering price of the loan at issuance.
Libor Floor*	The minimum base rate paid in the event Libor is below the specified floor level.
Lien Type***	Seniority of the debt within the levels of borrower's capital structure.
Cov-Lite***	Flag to indicate the tranche is cov-lite.

Table 4-1 shows that the Facility Update data contains a lot of useful information, especially for S&P clients. You can use this data in many interesting ways; for instance, you could use it to determine global issuance trends (spreads and original issue discounts [OIDs] by rating or industry) or total upcoming maturities by industry. The LoanX ID column is the Primary Key and corresponds to exactly one loan.

The *Recommended Updates* channel provides information on refinancing and other reasons a loan might become inactive. The Recommended Updates channel, similar to the Facility Update channel, will return new records only since your last request. You can retrieve the Recommended Updates by using the following URL syntax:

```
https://loans.markit.com/loanx/LoanXRecUpdates.csv?LEGALENTITY=myfirm&USERNAME=
user1&PASSWORD=mypassword
```

Table 4-2 lists and describes the columns returned by the Recommended Updates request.

Table 4-2. Recommended Update columns

Column	Description
LoanX ID	Unique Identifier for each loan.
LCD ID	Identifier for S&P LCD Data.
Issuer Name	Name of borrower or issuer.
Dealname	Name of borrower. This is usually the same as preceding cell but can include date and type of deal.
Facility Type	Specific loan type; TLB, bridge loan, etc.
Industry	Industry classification based on SIC code
Initial Amount	Facility Amount in MM.
Final Maturity	Final maturity date.
Initial Spread	Original LIBOR spread.
Facility Status	Active/ inactive status (A or I).
Inactive Date	Date of status change, always in the past.
Inactive Reason	Reason for status change.
Replacement LoanX ID	The LoanX ID for the replacement loan.
Replacement PMD ID	Replacement Unique identifier associated with a particular issuer/tranche combination. This can be a positive or negative number.
Replacement Issuer Name	Replacement Name of borrower or issuer.
Replacement Deal Name	Replacement Name of borrower; usually same as preceding cell, but can include date and type of deal.
Replacement Facility Type	Replacement Specific loan type; TLB, bridge loan, etc.
Replacement Industry	Replacement Industry classification based on SIC code
Replacement Initial Amount	Replacement Facility Amount in MM.
Replacement Final Maturity	Replacement Final maturity date.
Replacement Initial Spread	Replacement Original LIBOR spread.
Replacement Status	Replacement Facility Status.

The first set of columns in the Recommended Update dataset (LoanX ID through Facility Status) contain details on the original loan before it became inactive. The Inactive Date and Inactive Reason indicate the date and cause for the original loan to become inactive. The remaining columns (prefaced with "Replacement") are details on the loan that replaced the original loan, if applicable. For instance, if a loan with the LoanX ID of LX123456 was refinanced with the proceeds of another loan, LoanX ID LX98765, there would be one row with LX123456 in the LoanX ID column, and LX98765 in the Replacement LoanX ID column. If the replacement columns are blank, there isn't a corresponding new loan. Both the original LoanX ID and Replacement LoanX ID will correspond to rows in the Facility Update data. It is also possible that the replacement loan was subsequently refinanced and might appear in another row in the Recommend Update data as a LoanX ID.

Even though the purpose of the table is to update a portfolio with the latest information in the event of a refinancing or termination, this data has a lot of other uses. For instance, you can use this data to track refinancing trends such as the percentage and average spread tightening of loans originally rated B+ in the past three months, by industry. You can also use it to determine the average number of months before final maturity a typical loan will refinance.

The *Daily Ratings* channel provides the most recent rating information from Moody's and S&P for each actively priced loan. Use the following URL syntax to request the latest Daily Ratings data (CSV only):

```
https://loans.markit.com/loanx/LoansDailyRatings.csv?LEGALENTITY=firmname
&USERNAME=user1&PASSWORD=pw239876
```

Alternatively, provide an optional DATE argument to specify the date of ratings to send using the format MM-DD-YY. Historical ratings data is available for the most recent 10 business days and the most recent three month-ends. For example, to request daily ratings for May 14, 2016, use the following:

```
https://loans.markit.com/loanx/LoansDailyRatings.csv?LEGALENTITY=firmname
&USERNAME=user1&PASSWORD=pw239876&DATE=05-14-16
```

Table 4-3 contains the columns returned from a Daily Ratings request.

Table 4-3. Daily Rating columns

Column	Description
As of Date	Date the file was created
LoanX ID	Unique Identifier for each loan
Price Date	Date of the Bid and Offer provided
Moody's Rating	Rating provided by Moody's
Moody's Rating Date	Date the rating was last updated by Moody's
Moody's Watch	Watch list description from Moody's
Moody's Watch Date	Date the watch list was last updated
Moody's Outlook	Outlook provided by Moody's
Moody's Outlook Date	Date the outlook was last updated by Moody's
S&P Rating	Rating provided by S&P
S&P Rating Date	Date the rating was last updated by S&P
S&P Watch	Watch list description from S&P
S&P Watch Date	Date the watch list was last updated
S&P Outlook	S&P's outlook value
S&P Outlook Date	Date the outlook was last updated by S&P

Because Markit provides the dates of the rating updates, you can use this data to construct a history for an individual loan or, thinking bigger, to track rating changes across an industry, a set of companies, or determine the correlation between falling loan prices and downgrades.

The *LoanID Updates* channel provides a mapping from Markit's LoanX IDs to CUSIPs or other identifiers. The LoanID Updates channel, similar to the Facility Update channel, will return new records only since your last request. Use the following URL syntax to request LoanID Updates:

```
https://loans.markit.com/loanx/LoanIDUpdates.csv?LEGALENTITY=mylegalentity
&USERNAME=user1&PASSWORD=mypassword
```

Table 4-4 contains the columns returned from the LoanID Updates request.

Table 4-4. LoanID Updates columns

Column	Description
Identifier	An industry-standard unique identifier associated with a particular issuer/tranche combination (typically stores the CUSIP)
Identifier Type	Specifies the source of the Identifier (e.g., "CUSIP")
LoanX ID	Unique identifier for each loan
Valid From	Date the Identifier was mapped to the LoanX ID
Valid To	Date the Identifier was unmapped from the LoanX ID
Modified Time	Date the Identifier Mapping was edited

The Identifier column in the returned dataset will contain a CUSIP when the Identifier Type column contains the word "CUSIP." The mapping between LoanX ID and CUSIP is important because LoanX ID is unique to Markit, whereas CUSIP is used by multiple systems (including Bloomberg). As a reminder, CUSIP is a licensed product from CUSIP Global Services, and it might require you to obtain a license before storing and using CUSIPs in a database.

Loan Pricing, Financials, and Analytics

You use the *Marks* channel to get daily loan prices for thousands of US and European loans. Here's the basic URL syntax:

```
https://loans.markit.com/loanx/LoanXMarks.xml?LEGALENTITY=firmname
&USERNAME=user1&PASSWORD=password
```

The URL can also handle two additional parameters. You can include the RELATIVE VERSION parameter to request data up to 10 business days in the past. For instance, providing a RELATIVEVERSION of -1 returns marks as of two business days prior to today ("0" is the default and will return marks as of previous business day):

```
https://loans.markit.com/loanx/LoanXMarks.xml?LEGALENTITY=firmname
&USERNAME=user1&PASSWORD=password&RELATIVEVERSION=-1
```

North American buy-side clients can also set the EOD parameter to Y after 4 PM EST to request today's closing prices:

```
https://loans.markit.com/loanx/LoanXMarks.xml?LEGALENTITY=firmname
&USERNAME=user1&PASSWORD=password&EOD=Y
```

European clients requesting end of day pricing for European securities can use a different URL after 4 PM GMT:

```
https://loans.markit.com/loanx/LoanXMarksUK.csv?LEGALENTITY=firmname
&USERNAME=eurouser&PASSWORD=password&EOD=Y
```

Table 4-5 contains the descriptions of the columns returned by the Marks channel.

Table 4-5. Marks column descriptions

Column	Description
LoanXID	Unique identifier for each loan.
Mark Date	Date of price.
Evaluated Price	Midpoint of close bid/close offer.
Bid	Average bid for facility on mark date subject to change through the trading day.
Offer	Average offer for facility on mark date subject to change through the trading day.
Depth	Depth is generally the count of the contributing dealers.
Close Bid	Closing bid captured at 4 PM Eastern time. This will not change.
Close Offer	Closing offer captured at 4 PM Eastern time. This will not change.
Close Date	Date of Close bid and offer.
Contributed	Returns "Yes" if your company contributed to the average mark.

Many firms across Wall Street use Markit loan prices to mark their positions nightly but there is a lot more for which you can use this data. You can use it to answer questions such as these:

- How many loans currently trading above $90 have ever traded below $70?
- Are there any loans we sold that have since fallen in price by more than 10%?
- Are there any industries or rating groups that are under/over performing the market?
- Which loans were the biggest movers this day, week, month, quarter, year?
- Is there a strong correlation between a ratings downgrade and a change in price?
- Which loans are trading above par and are currently callable?

Taking it even further, Markit provides a plethora of daily analytics on each loan using its *Loan Performance* channel. Use the following URL syntax to request loan performance (CSV only):

```
https://loans.markit.com/loanx/LoanPricingAndAnalytics.csv?LEGALENTITY=firmname
&USERNAME=user1&PASSWORD=password
```

The returned loan performance dataset has more than 200 columns containing most of the useful columns from other channels (facility, pricing, ratings) as well as the following:

- Daily, monthly, and yearly returns
- Spread; duration; modified duration; PV01; remaining weighted average life; yield to maturity; and yield to a one-, two-, three-, four-, and five-year call
- Current yield
- Thirty-, 60-, and 90-day average bid
- Daily, monthly, and yearly price change in percentage and point terms

Finally, Markit also provides access to S&P's Capital IQ financial data for Capital IQ clients using its *Financial Statement* channel. Use the following URL syntax to request all financial statement data since January 2007 (CSV only):

```
https://loans.markit.com/loanx/FinancialStatement.csv?LEGALENTITY=firmname
&USERNAME=user&PASSWORD=password
```

The URL syntax also accepts an optional parameter, `TIMEFRAME`, which you can set to `LatestAvailable` to return only the latest available financial statement data:

```
https://loans.markit.com/loanx/FinancialStatement.csv?LEGALENTITY=firmname
&USERNAME=user&PASSWORD=password&TIMEFRAME=LatestAvailable
```

Table 4-6 contains the column descriptions for the Financial Statement data.

Table 4-6. Financial Statement columns

Column	Description
SP_COMPANY_ID	S&P Capital IQ identifier
Currency	Currency of the financial data
Year	Year of the financial statement
Quarter	Quarter of the financial statement
Is_Annual	Indicator of annual data
Is_Latest	Indicator of the most recent information available
Total_Sr_Secured_EBITDA	Total senior secured debt/EBITDA
Sr_Debt_EBITDA	Senior debt/EBITDA
Sr_Sub_Debt_EBITDA	Senior subordinated debt/EBITDA
Jr_Sub_Debt_EBITDA	Junior subordinated debt/EBITDA

Column	Description
Sub_Debt_EBITDA	Subordinated debt/EBITDA
Total_Debt_EBITDA	Total debt/EBITDA
Net_Debt_EBITDA	(Total debt − cash and ST investments)/EBITDA
Total_Assets	Total assets
Revenue	Revenue
EBITDA	Earnings before interest, tax depreciation, and amortization
Retained_Earnings	Retained earnings
EBITDA_INT	EBITDA/interest expense
Quick_Ratio	(Total cash and short-term investments + accounts receivables)/total current liabilities
Current_Ratio	Total current assets/total current liabilities
Total_Debt_Capital	Total debt/total capital
Total_Debt_Equity	Total debt/total equity

Although Chapter 3 discussed how to pull a lot of this information from Bloomberg, this feature in Markit can pull the complete history for a large set of companies. Unfortunately, to connect this information to a LoanX ID, you need to make a separate request to the *Financial Statement Map* channel using the following syntax (CSV only):

```
https://loans.markit.com/loanx/FinancialStatementMap.csv?LEGALENTITY=firmname
&USERNAME=user&PASSWORD=xxxxx
```

This URL request will return data containing an LXID (LoanX ID) column as well as an SP_COMPANY_ID column that you can use to connect other Markit datasets with the S&P Capital IQ financial statements data.

Corporate and Sovereign Bonds

In addition to providing pricing for corporate loans, Markit provides a daily pricing and analytics CSV file for corporate and sovereign bonds. Unlike loan pricing, bond prices are delivered over SSH File Transfer Protocol (SFTP). The server and credentials for the SFTP server is provided by Markit. To price thousands of bonds, Markit "builds an issuer curve using data that is cleaned and corroborated with multiple observable sources." Bonds without observable sources are priced by using interpolation or limited extrapolation of observable data.

Markit's bond pricing data contains more than 90 columns, including the following:

- Static bond reference data (CUSIP, Maturity, Currency, etc.)
- Market data sources for pricing the bond
- Clean and dirty bid, ask, and mid prices
- Yield-to-worst (YTW) using bid, ask, and mid prices

- Asset Swap Spread using bid, ask, and mid prices
- Z-spread based on bid, ask, and mid prices
- G-spread based on bid, ask, and mid prices
- PV01
- Effective, modified, and Macaulay duration based on bid, ask, and mid prices
- Convexity based on bid, ask, and mid prices
- Option Adjusted Spread (OAS) based on bid, ask, and mid prices.
- Depth and liquidity statistics

Path 1: Storing Markit Information in Excel

Fortunately, Markit delivers all of its content in CSV files that Excel can open. Unfortunately, Excel was not designed to handle very large datasets, although it has become better in newer versions. Furthermore, Excel requires a few extra steps to ensure that duplicate rows are removed. Nevertheless, this section walks through recommended techniques for storing Markit data from CSV files in Excel. Even though you can keep the Markit data in the same workbook as the Bloomberg data, I recommend that that you store Markit data in a separate workbook because large datasets are slow to deal with in Excel.

Begin by creating a new worksheet for each desired dataset (channel). For the Facility Update and Loan ID Updates worksheet, contact *support@markit.com* and request the full CSV file that contains all the facility information for each loan and the entire mapping from LoanX ID to CUSIP. Optionally, request historical information on the other channels, as well. For the other tables, use the URL syntax provided earlier in this chapter to download a CSV file for each channel.

Next, copy and paste the contents of the CSV files into their corresponding worksheet (e.g., Marks CSV data into a Marks worksheet). Add a column to the end in row 1 with the header labeled "Duplicate Check." As described in Chapter 2, convert each range in each worksheet to an Excel table by selecting all the cells (including the "Duplicate Check" header), and then, on the ribbon, on the Home tab, click the "Format as Table" button (or press Ctrl-T), and select any table style you prefer. When prompted, check the box marked "My table has headers." Choose a name for each Excel table, such as "LoanFacilities," "LoanUpdates," and "LoanPrices."

Some tables (Facility Update, Recommended Update, and LoanID Updates) can use LoanX ID as their Primary Key because only the latest data is important and it would not make sense to keep a history of these tables. If a row is added to these tables with the same LoanX ID, the existing row should be removed. To accomplish this, add this formula in the Duplicate Check column that counts the number of rows with the same LoanX ID (or Identifier for LoanID Updates) and a newer Modified Time (or Inactive Date for RecUpdates):

```
=SUMPRODUCT(N([LoanX ID]=[@[LoanX ID]]),N([Modified Time]>[@[Modified Time]]))
```

This formula demonstrates how to use a combination of the Excel SUMPRODUCT and N functions to return a count based on multiple columns. The N function returns 1 when the conditional statement argument is true (there is a LoanX ID in the LoanX ID column that matches the current row's LoanX ID and that same row's Modified Time is greater than the current row's Modified Time), otherwise it returns zero. SUM PRODUCT returns the sum of the products of the N functions. The formula works because when both N statements are true, it will add 1 to the result (1 multiplied by 1 equals 1), but if either are false, it will add zero to the result (1 multiplied by 0 equals 0). You can safely remove any row for which the resulting formula is greater than zero because there is another row with the same LoanX ID and a more recent Modified Time.

Going forward, to add data to these sheets after using the URLs to request an updated CSV file from Markit, copy all of the rows and columns from the CSV (exclude the header) and, in the destination worksheet, right-click any row header (the box to the very left containing the row numbers) and select "Insert Copied Cells" to insert the rows from the CSV file into the worksheet. Then, ensure that the formula in the Duplicate Check column is copied into these new rows. Remove any duplicate entries.

For tables that could contain a history, such as Marks, Daily Ratings, and Financial Statements, either keep only the latest data by clearing the entire sheet every time you retrieve data from Markit (or, using the same formula as the other tables to ensure only one LoanX ID exists) or use the following formula in the Duplicate Check column that returns the count of rows with the same LoanX ID and Mark Date (or As of Date):

```
=SUMPRODUCT(N([@[LoanX ID]]=[LoanX ID]),N([@[Mark Date]]=[Mark Date]))
```

Path 2: Importing Markit Data into Microsoft Access

This section covers how to import Markit CSV files into Access and maintain the data going forward. First, contact *support@markit.com* and request the full Facility Update and LoanID CSV files that contain all of the facility information for each loan and the entire mapping from LoanX ID to CUSIP. Then, perform the following steps:

1. In Access, on the ribbon, click External Data, and then select Text File.

2. Click the browse button and select one of the CSV files retrieved from Markit, such as *LoanXFacilityUpdates.csv*.

3. Select the option "Import the source data into a new table in the current database."

   This creates a new table using the data from the CSV file.

4. Click Okay. Choose the Delimited option, and then click Next.

5. On the next screen, choose "Comma" delimiter, set the Text Qualifier drop-down box to the double quote symbol ("), and then check the box labeled First Row Contains Field Names.

6. On the next screen, simply click Next.

   The data types will be changed later.

7. On the next screen, select "No primary key."

   The Primary Keys will be set later.

8. Click the Finish button to complete the import.

9. Repeat steps 1 through 8 to import all of the CSV files for each channel.

10. Right-click one of the tables, and then select Design View.

11. Select the columns indicated in Table 4-7, and then click the Primary Key button.

    This step sets the appropriate columns as Primary Keys for the table.

12. Adjust the Data Type for columns containing dates to Date/Time, and then set the Data Type for numbers to Double.

For a complete list of data types for each table, read the Markit documentation.

Table 4-7. Primary Keys for Markit tables

Table name	Primary Key(s)
LoanIDUpdates	Identifier, Modified Time
LoanPricingAndAnalytics	PricingAsOf, LoanX ID
LoansDailyRatings	Date, LoanX ID
LoanXFacilityUpdates	LoanX ID, Modified Time
LoanXMarks	LoanX ID, Mark Date
LoanXRecUpdates	LoanX ID, Inactivation Date
FinancialStatement	SP_COMPANY_ID, Year, Quarter
FinancialStatementMap	LXID

The date columns were included in the Primary Key list in Table 4-7 to prevent Access from excluding updated rows from future imports. To delete rows that have the same LoanX ID but an earlier Modified Date, use the following query (adjust table and column names as necessary):

```
Delete
FROM LoanXFacilityUpdates r
```

```
where r.[Modified Time] < (select max(r2.[Modified Time])
from LoanXFacilityUpdates r2 where r2.[LoanX ID]=r.[LoanX ID])
```

Going forward, to update these tables with new CSV files, use the same Text File but-ton on the External Data tab on the ribbon, but select "Append a copy of the records to the table" option and choose the appropriate table for the file you selected. Follow the same directions used on the first import. On the final screen, select "Save import steps" to create a quick way to repeat these steps. To rerun the import, choose the name of the saved import after selecting Saved Imports on the External Data menu, and then click Run.

Path 3: Importing Markit Data Using C#

This section describes how to import data from Markit into Microsoft Access using C#. First, follow the steps presented in Path 2 to create the initial tables by importing them from the CSV files and setting the appropriate Primary Keys and data types. Next, in Visual Studio, create a new console application project. Add a reference to Micorosft.VisualBasic by right-clicking on References and selecting the Add Refer-ence check box adjacent to Mirosoft.VisualBasic under Assemblies/Framework.

In *Program.cs*, begin by adding the following using directives:

```
using System.Data;
using System.Data.OleDb;
using System.Net;
using Microsoft.VisualBasic.FileIO;
```

Within the body of the Program class, add the following properties, making changes to the database location, and Markit credentials:

```
private string ConnStr =
"Provider=Microsoft.ACE.OLEDB.12.0;Data Source=..\\..\\Path 3.accdb";
private string FIRM = "MyCompanyName";
private string USERNAME = "MyMarkitUserName";
private string PASS = "MyMarkitPassword";
```

As discussed earlier, install and use the appropriate OleDB driver for the appropriate version of Microsoft Access. Next, in the Main method, create an instance of the Pro gram class and call the Run method that will be created next:

```
static void Main(string[] args)
{
    Program p = new Program();
    p.Run();
}
```

In the Run method, call a ProcessURL method (created later) with the URL syntax of the Markit request, the name of the table in the Access database, and the name of the

Primary Key for tables that should be searched and updated instead of appended. For tables that build a history, pass null for the primary key argument:

```csharp
public void Run()
{

    ProcessURL(
        "https://loans.markit.com/loanx/LoanXFacilityUpdates.csv?LEGALENTITY="
        + FIRM + "&USERNAME=" + USERNAME + "&PASSWORD=" + PASS,
        "LoanXFacilityUpdates",
        "LoanX ID");

    ProcessURL(
        "https://loans.markit.com/loanx/LoanXRecUpdates.csv?LEGALENTITY="
        + FIRM + "&USERNAME=" + USERNAME + "&PASSWORD=" + PASS,
        "LoanXRecUpdates",
        "LoanX ID");

    ProcessURL(
        "https://loans.markit.com/loanx/LoanIDUpdates.csv?LEGALENTITY="
        + FIRM + "&USERNAME=" + USERNAME + "&PASSWORD=" + PASS,
        "LoanIDUpdates",
        "Identifier");

    ProcessURL(
        "https://loans.markit.com/loanx/LoanXMarks.csv?LEGALENTITY="
        + FIRM + "&USERNAME=" + USERNAME + "&PASSWORD=" + PASS,
        "LoanXMarks",
        null);
    ProcessURL(
        "https://loans.markit.com/loanx/LoansDailyRatings.csv?LEGALENTITY="
        + FIRM + "&USERNAME=" + USERNAME + "&PASSWORD=" + PASS,
        "LoansDailyRatings",
        null);

    ProcessURL(
        "https://loans.markit.com/loanx/LoanPricingAndAnalytics.csv?LEGALENTITY="
        + FIRM + "&USERNAME=" + USERNAME + "&PASSWORD=" + PASS,
        "LoanPricingAndAnalytics",
        null);
}
```

The ProcessURL method uses WebClient to download the CSV file from Markit using the url parameter. Then, as it loops through the CSV file, it checks to see if it should update or insert a new row based on the Primary Key. The data is updated or inserted where the column names match the column headers in the CSV file.

The ProcessURL method starts by populating a dataset with the current rows from the database (using the FillDataSet method defined later). Next, it uses the Web Client class to download the CSV file from Markit into a temporary file location.

Next, the method instantiates a `TextFieldParser` class and sets the properties for parsing a CSV file and starts a `while` loop until the end of file is reached. On the first line, it populates the header `List` instance with the column array from the parser. This will contain the column names from the CSV file. On the following lines, it populates the `col` string array with the column array from the parser; this will contain a row of data to populate the database.

The method then checks whether the `primaryKey` argument was passed; if so, it finds the associated row in the database. If the `primaryKey` argument was not passed or the corresponding row in the database does not exist, a new `DataRow` is created.

Next, the columns of the database table are populated if the CSV file contains a column with the same name and the data can be converted to the column's datatype.

If the `DataRow` instance was created instead of found, it needs to be added to the `DataTable`. Then, the `DataSet` is updated (using the `UpdateDataSet` method defined later).

Here's what the code looks like:

```
private void ProcessURL(string url, string table, string primaryKey)
{
    DataSet ds = FillDataSet(table);
    WebClient client = new WebClient();

    string tmpfile =
    System.Environment.GetFolderPath(Environment.SpecialFolder.InternetCache) +
    "\\" + Guid.NewGuid().ToString() + ".csv";
    client.DownloadFile(url, tmpfile);

    using (TextFieldParser parser = new TextFieldParser(tmpfile))
    {
        parser.Delimiters = new string[] { "," };
        parser.TextFieldType = FieldType.Delimited;
        parser.SetDelimiters(",");
        parser.TrimWhiteSpace = true;

        List<string> header = null;
        while (!parser.EndOfData)
        {
            if (header == null)
            {
                header = new List<string>(parser.ReadFields());
                continue;
            }
            string[] col = parser.ReadFields();

            DataRow row = null;
            if (primaryKey != null)
            {
```

```csharp
            var rows = ds.Tables[table].Select("[" + primaryKey + "]='"
                + col[header.IndexOf(primaryKey)] + "'");
            if (rows.Count() > 0)
            {
                row = rows[0];
            }
        }
        if (row == null)
        {
            row = ds.Tables[table].NewRow();
        }
        foreach (DataColumn dc in ds.Tables[table].Columns)
        {
            if (header.Contains(dc.ColumnName))
            {
                string val = col[header.IndexOf(dc.ColumnName)];
                if (dc.DataType == typeof(string))
                {
                    row[dc] = val;
                }
                else if (dc.DataType == typeof(DateTime))
                {
                    DateTime foo;
                    if (DateTime.TryParse(val, out foo))
                        row[dc] = foo;
                }
                else if (dc.DataType == typeof(double))
                {
                    double foo;
                    if (Double.TryParse(val, out foo))
                        row[dc] = foo;
                }
                else if (dc.DataType == typeof(Int32))
                {
                    int foo;
                    if (Int32.TryParse(val, out foo))
                        row[dc] = foo;
                }
                else
                    Console.WriteLine("Unhandled Column Type");
            }
        }
        if (row.RowState == DataRowState.Detached)
            ds.Tables[table].Rows.Add(row);

    }
    parser.Close();
}
int rowc = UpdateDataSet(ds, table);
Console.WriteLine("Updated " + rowc + " in table " + table);
}
```

The only remaining methods to create are the `FillDataSet` method that populates a `DataSet` instance with contents from the Access database file, and the `UpdateDataSet` method that updates the Access database file:

```
private DataSet FillDataSet(string table)
{
    DataSet ds = new DataSet();
    using (OleDbConnection conn = new OleDbConnection(ConnStr))
    {
        string cmdStr = "SELECT * FROM " + table;

        OleDbCommand cmd = new OleDbCommand(cmdStr, conn);
        OleDbDataAdapter da = new OleDbDataAdapter(cmd);
        conn.Open();
        da.Fill(ds, table);
        conn.Close();
    }
    return ds;
}
private int UpdateDataSet(DataSet ds, string table)
{
    int rowc = 0;
    using (OleDbConnection conn = new OleDbConnection(ConnStr))
    {
        string cmdStr = "SELECT * FROM " + table;

        OleDbCommand cmd = new OleDbCommand(cmdStr, conn);
        OleDbDataAdapter da = new OleDbDataAdapter();
        da.SelectCommand = cmd;
        OleDbCommandBuilder cb = new OleDbCommandBuilder(da);
        cb.QuotePrefix = "[";
        cb.QuoteSuffix = "]";
        conn.Open();
        da.UpdateCommand = cb.GetUpdateCommand();
        da.InsertCommand = cb.GetInsertCommand();
        rowc = da.Update(ds, table);

        conn.Close();
    }
    return rowc;
}
```

Summary

Almost every firm that participates in the corporate markets as either investors or dealers will require access to pricing services such as those offered by Markit. However, this data is often captured and used by back-office systems for accounting or risk purposes and, all too often, never makes its way into the hands of those who could also benefit: the analysts. Although Markit is one of many providers of reference and pricing data, its simple API that can retrieve a wealth of information as demonstrated in this chapter makes the company ideal for analysts with limited technology resources. Of course, simply accessing this information is useful, but there is a lot of value in the different types of analysis that can be done only on large sets of financial data such as this. The topic of analysis on large financial datasets is covered in Chapter 8.

CHAPTER 5

Financial Data Analysis

It is a capital mistake to theorize before one has data.
—Sherlock Holmes

The data we collected in earlier chapters can help determine a security's intrinsic or absolute value, but it doesn't tell the entire story; we need context. For instance, knowing that a company's stock price is up 5 percent in the last six months does not inform you whether the company outperformed or underperformed the overall market or its peers. The goal of financial analysis, and the purpose of this section, is to make sense of financial data and put it into context to support investment decisions.

The following chapters split financial analysis into three categories:

Relative value analysis

Chapter 6 explores techniques to compare an individual security to its peers and the broader market. Relative value is more than simply comparing past performance of two securities: it is determining whether one security is rich or cheap relative to another. This is much easier said than done because quantifying the upside and downside of each investment is subjective and ultimately at the heart of what makes a successful analyst. For example, if two bonds are trading at a discount to par and have similar credit risk but one of them matures a year earlier than the other, how much additional yield should the longer bond have to make them equivalent investments? The answer depends on a lot of different factors including your market outlook. Chapter 6 goes over how to weigh these different factors and rank securities by a custom "score."

Risk analysis

Chapter 7 explores techniques to identify potential risks at both the security and portfolio level. For individual securities, metrics (such as price, Credit Default Swap [CDS] spread, and rating) can be used to identify outliers. For instance, risky outliers might be securities that are currently below $70 or securities that have had a 10 percent price drop in the last month. At the portfolio level, security metrics (such as maturities, ratings, industry, countries, etc.) are aggregated to identify risks such as high sector concentration.

Market analysis

Chapter 8 focuses on gaining insight from aggregating and summarizing large sets of market data. For example, breaking down the thousands of daily prices from Markit by sector, rating, or other attributes can identify trends. These trends can then be used to make assumptions about individual securities. For example, if 85 percent of healthcare loans trading above par with margins wider than 450 bps have refinanced in the last two months, there is a good chance loans in your portfolio with similar characteristics might also be refinanced. Market analysis is important to understanding the broader story and empirical evidence can be more advantageous than pure anecdotal evidence.

Before we jump into financial analysis, there are a few concepts and tasks that we should cover. This chapter looks at how to ensure that you are analyzing correct and sufficient sets of data in subsequent chapters. In addition, this chapter also covers how to set up the Portfolio worksheet or database table used in later chapters. Finally, because you might want to track your portfolio and other data over time, we explore methods for keeping a history.

Data Integrity

The first and one of the most important steps in any financial analysis is ensuring that the data you are using is accurate. However, there are many cases for which the data you are using in your analysis isn't perfect. For those times, you must understand how your results can be affected by starting with less-than-perfect information.

Checking the Data

Most financial information provided by sources such as Markit or Bloomberg is correct, but, we can be certain of one thing: there can be mistakes. Before making investment decisions, it is critical that the information on which you're basing it is reviewed and verified. Moreover, even if the information from these sources is correct, it can be misleading or misused. Here are examples of things to check:

- When performing mathematical operations (add, subtract, multiply, etc.) on financial data, make sure that all amounts are in the same currency.

- Some financial data might be stored in different units (thousands, millions, full amounts, etc.), so ensure that the units are consistent.

- Financial data is not always reported at the same frequency for each entity. Thus, when comparing different sets of financial information, it is important to take into consideration the "as of" date.

Sample Size

The number of securities in the analysis is important. Including too few securities can make your analysis unreliable, but including too many might give you misleading results. Without getting into too much math, to determine the minimum sample size, use the formula shown in Figure 5-1.

$$n = \frac{N \times Z^2 \times p \times (1-p)}{(N-1) \times e^2 + Z^2 \times p \times (1-p)}$$

Figure 5-1. A sample size formula

Here's what the variables represent:

n

   The minimum required sample size

N

   Size of the universe (population)

Z

   This is the z-score based on confidence level: 90% = 1.65, 95% = 1.96, 99% = 2.58. For instance, to say the outcome is correct in 95 percent of cases, use 1.96 as the value for *Z*. Additional z-score values for confidence levels are easily found online.

p

   If you expect a specific proportion, you can use it to reduce the required sample size. If the proportion isn't known, use a normal distribution (set *p* = 50%).

e

   Maximum margin of error. For instance, if you're comfortable with the results being off by 5 percent to reduce the required sample size, set *e* = 5%.

One example would be, to use a sample of the 4,226 loans in Markit's database with a confidence level of 95 percent and a 5 percent margin of error, the analysis should include 352 loans.

Outliers

Examining the number of standard deviations between a value and the median is a good method for checking data for outliers that might or might not be data issues. The more standard deviations from the median a value is, the more likely it is an outlier and therefore a potential data issue. To accomplish this, simply take the absolute difference between a value and the median (middle value) for the entire series and divide it by the standard deviation of the same series. In Microsoft Excel, use the MEDIAN and STDEV functions. Thus, the formula to display the number of standard deviations the "3M Px Chg" values are from the median would be as follows:

```
=ABS([@[3M Px Chg]]-MEDIAN([3M Px Chg]))/STDEV([3M Px Chg])
```

To calculate the median for rows based on the values in another column, use the IF function within the MEDIAN function. For example, the following array formula calculates the median Market Cap where the S&P Rating is BB+ (requires Ctrl-Shift-Enter):

```
=MEDIAN(IF(Company[S&P Rating]="BB+",Company[Market Cap]))
```

As you just saw, there are Excel functions for median and standard deviation. In C#, you need to write the functions as such:

```
public static double GetMedian(List<double> list)
{
    double median = 0;
    if (list.Count != 0)
    {
        // create new instance of list
        // so source list isnt modified
        // List should be ordered.
        List<double> sortedList = list.OrderBy(x => x).ToList();
        int size = sortedList.Count;
        int mid = size / 2;
        if (size % 2 != 0)
            median = sortedList[mid];
        else
            median = (sortedList[mid] + sortedList[mid - 1]) / 2;
    }
    return median;
}
public static double GetStandardDev(List<double> list)
{
    double stdev = 0;
    if (list.Count != 0)
    {
        double average = list.Average();
        stdev =
        Math.Sqrt((list.Sum(x => Math.Pow(x - average, 2))) / (list.Count() - 1));
    }
```

```
    return stdev;
}
```

It would not make sense to use this method to compare data that is not meant to be similar across securities, such as total debt or enterprise value.

In addition, when calculating the average values for large datasets, using median instead of average might help avoid issues with large outliers. For instance, a straight average of the maturity date column in a portfolio of bonds can be misleading if one bond matures tomorrow.

Portfolio

At this point in the book, the Bond, Loan, IDX, and Company worksheets (or database tables) should be populated with content from Bloomberg or manual input. This section covers creating a Portfolio worksheet (if you're following Path 1) and Portfolio database table (if you're following Paths 2 and 3). Although the portfolio table is designed to hold a set of securities that were purchased on a date with a size and price, you could use it for any subset of securities. We'll use the Portfolio worksheet/ table in later chapters to compare holdings to other sets of securities and the entire market.

Each row in the Portfolio worksheet or table will contain a PositionID to identify the unique position as well as other attributes:

PositionID
> This is the unique identifier (Primary Key) for the Portfolio table. We can simply use incrementing numbers as identifiers (1, 2, 3, etc.).

Type
> This refers to the type of investment (Bond, Loan, Equity, etc.).

SecurityID
> This is the Foreign Key that can point to the investment's Primary Key. For instance, this can be a CompanyID, a LoanID, or a BondID, depending on whether the investment is an equity, a loan, or a bond. It is one of the few times when the column name for the Foreign Key is different from the Primary Key.

Size
> Size can be either the number of shares for equity or the notional amount of a security. Keep in mind that you should never add the number of shares to a notional amount of a security.

PurchasePx
> The dollar amount used to purchase the security. This book assumes investments will be made in the same currency, but we could extend this table to handle multiple currencies.

PurchaseDate
> The date when the security was purchased

Position Comments
> We can use this field to store any thoughts you have on the position, such as your investment thesis or concerns.

Portfolio Worksheet

If you are using Excel, create a table with the columns described earlier and populate them with different positions. After entering data into the Portfolio worksheet, it should look like Figure 5-2 (we discuss the Price later in this section).

Figure 5-2. Portfolio worksheet example

To pull information from the other worksheets, enhancing the Portfolio worksheet, use the MATCH and INDEX functions. This will pull columns based on the Type and matching SecurityID. For instance, to bring the Company Name or Security Description based on the Type and SecurityID columns, use the following:

```
=IF([@Type]="Equity",INDEX(Company[CompanyName],MATCH([@SecurityID],
Company[CompanyID],0)),IF([@Type]="Loan",INDEX(Loan[Security Description],
MATCH([@SecurityID],Loan[LoanID],0)),IF([@Type]="Bond",
INDEX(Bond[Security Description],MATCH([@SecurityID],Bond[BondID],0)))))
```

This formula first checks whether Type is Equity; if so, it pulls the cell from the Company worksheet's Company Name column where the CompanyID matches the Portfolio worksheet's SecurityID column. If not, it checks whether Type is Bond (and subsequently Loan) and pulls the appropriate Security Description column. You can use the same technique to pull the current price (store it in a new column called Price):

```
=IF([@Type]="Equity",INDEX(Company[Price],MATCH([@SecurityID],
Company[CompanyID],0)),IF([@Type]="Loan",INDEX(Loan[Price],MATCH([@SecurityID],
Loan[LoanID],0)),IF([@Type]="Bond",INDEX(Bond[Price],
MATCH([@SecurityID],Bond[BondID],0)))))
```

After adding those two columns, we can calculate the market value for each position. Create a new column called "MarketValue" and use the following formula:

```
=IF([@Type]="equity",[@Price]*[@Size],[@Size]*[@Price]/100)
```

This formula divides bond and loan prices by 100 because those prices represent percentages, whereas equity prices do not.

Add another column called "BBID" that will contain the Bloomberg ID for each security. Use the following formula in this column:

```
=IF([@Type]="Equity",INDEX(Company[BBID],MATCH([@SecurityID],
Company[CompanyID],0)),IF([@Type]="Loan",INDEX(Loan[BBID],MATCH([@SecurityID],
Loan[LoanID],0)),IF([@Type]="Bond",INDEX(Bond[BBID],
MATCH([@SecurityID],Bond[BondID],0)))))
```

Finally, add a "% of Portfolio" column that will contain each position's market value–based weighting for the portfolio.

Use this formula in the new column:

```
=[@MarketValue]/SUM([MarketValue])
```

Add a Total row (a row at the bottom that aggregates values in each column) by right-clicking the table, and then, on the shortcut menu that opens, click Table, and then select Totals Row.

A Total row allows you to choose an aggregate function (such as sum, min, max, or even standard deviation) that is applied to the values in each column. Sum the MarketValue column by clicking the cell in the Total Row in the MarketValue column and then select Sum from the drop-down list. For the "% of Portfolio" column, select Max in the Total row drop-down list to display the largest single exposure in the portfolio.

Portfolio Database Table

Use the schema in Table 5-1 to create a Portfolio table with PositionID as the Primary Key.

Table 5-1. Portfolio table design

Field name	Data type
PositionID*	Number
Type	Short Text
SecurityID	Short Text

Field name	Data type
Size	Number
PurchasePx	Number
PurchaseDate	Date/Time
Position Comments	Short Text

After manually entering the data into the data table, pull in additional columns from other tables to enhance the Portfolio view by using the following query:

```
SELECT
p.*,
a.Price,
a.SecurityDes,
iif(p.type='equity',Price,Price/100) * p.size as MarketValue,
iif(p.type='equity',Price,Price/100) * p.size/(
   select
   sum(iif(p2.type='equity',a2.Price,a2.Price/100) * p2.size)
   from portfolio p2
   inner join
   (
     select BondID as SecurityID,Price,SecurityDes from Bond
     UNION
     select LoanID as SecurityID,Price,SecurityDesc from Loan
     UNION
     select CompanyID as SecurityID,Price,CompanyName as SecurityDes from Company
   ) a2 on a2.SecurityID=p2.SecurityID;
) as PctOfPortfolio
FROM Portfolio p
inner join
(
    select BondID as SecurityID,Price,SecurityDes from Bond
    UNION
    select LoanID as SecurityID,Price,SecurityDesc from Loan
    UNION
    select CompanyID as SecurityID,Price,CompanyName as SecurityDes from Company
) a on a.SecurityID=p.SecurityID;
```

This query joins the Portfolio table with an inner query that results in the relevant columns from the Bond, Loan, and Company tables. The inner join is also duplicated in the subquery to divide the market value of the current row by the total market value for the portfolio. The IIF function will divide the price column by 100 if it is a bond or loan price, because these are percentages.

Linking Excel Worksheets to Microsoft Access

If you are following Path 2, you must link the Excel worksheets created in Chapter 3 to Access. First, for each worksheet with Bloomberg Fields in the first row (Loan,

Bond, IDX, and Company), you need to create a named range to properly link the data to Access. Here's how to do that:

1. In the Excel workbook, on the ribbon, on the Formulas tab, in the Defined Names group, click Name Manager.

2. At the top of the dialog box that opens, click the New button and then, in the Name text box, enter **BondTable**, set the Scope list box to Workbook, and then, in the "Refers to" text box, enter **=Bond!$A$2:$AZ$9999**. Click OK.

   This creates a named range called BondTable that includes all of the cells in the Bond worksheet below the Bloomberg Fields row.

3. Repeat steps 1 and 2 to create LoanTable, IDXTable, and CompanyTable, adding **=Loan!$A$2:$AZ$9999**, **=IDX!$A$2:$AZ$9999**, and **='Company'!$A$3:$AZ$9999**, respectively. CompanyTable starts on row three because it has an extra row for the currency field.

   If you aren't using columns out to "AZ," you can specify a tighter range. Because the Portfolio worksheet begins on row one, a named range is not required.

4. After saving the Excel workbook, switch to Access, and then, on the ribbon, on the External Data tab, click the Import Excel Spreadsheet.

5. On the first page of the dialog box that opens, use the Browse button to select your Excel workbook, choose "Link to the data source by creating a linked table," and then click OK.

6. On the next screen, click Show Named Ranges, select BondTable, and then click Next.

7. On the next screen, select First Row Contains Column Headings, and then click Next.

8. On the next screen, change the Linked Table Name to Bond, and then click Finish.

   You should be able to open the Bond table and see all the data from Excel.

9. Repeat this process to link the Loan, IDX, and Company worksheets.

10. Link the Portfolio table following the same steps, but instead of selecting Show Named Ranges in the second screen, select Portfolio from the list of tables.

Keeping a History

Maintaining a history of values, such as the size of your portfolio or results of an analysis, can be very useful down the road and, if not maintained from the start, is difficult or impossible to re-create. Even though its usefulness might not be obvious at the outset, when you need it, you will be very glad you set it up. This section covers different techniques for maintaining a history of data based on the Path you are following.

As a rule of thumb, data storage (disk space on your hard drive) is very cheap and it is better to store too much information than too little.

Path 1: Excel

Unfortunately, Excel isn't a great tool for keeping a history because it does not handle very large sets of data well. This section covers how to compensate for this issue by maintaining a history of specific values in a single, easy-to-maintain, worksheet and keeping an entire history in separate workbooks using a simple batch file.

History worksheet

First, in the workbook that you created in Chapter 3, decide on a cell that you want to track and give it a defined name by using the Name Box located in the upper-left corner. For instance, to track the market value of your portfolio, select the cell in the Total row on your Portfolio worksheet in the MarketValue column. Then, in the Name Box, type **PortfolioMV**, as shown in Figure 5-3.

	F	G	H	I	J	K
	PurchasePx	PurchaseDate	Price	MarketValue	% Of Portfolio	Position Comments
2	12.25	3/15/2015	14.60	4,380,000	9.2%	
3	32.05	6/1/2014	24.00	4,800,000	10.1%	
4	99.5	7/27/2016	100.63	5,031,250	10.6%	
5	99.5	8/22/2013	100.44	3,515,313	7.4%	
6	100	5/24/2009	115.25	9,219,944	19.5%	
7	100	11/18/2015	103.73	7,520,063	15.9%	
8	80	8/16/2012	91.17	5,926,148	12.5%	
9	85	9/1/2015	106.93	2,138,598	4.5%	
10	81	11/18/2015	85.28	4,860,762	10.3%	
11				47,392,076	19.5%	

Figure 5-3. Naming a cell in Excel

Repeat this process with the cell containing the largest single exposure in the portfolio (the cell in the "% of Portfolio" column); give that cell the name **MaxPortfolioPct**.

Next, create a new worksheet called "Hist" that you will use to track these cells over time. This worksheet will contain one column that corresponds to the date of the historical data and one column per named cell from the first step. After this worksheet is completed, you can track additional named cells simply by adding a column header and copying a formula across. However, because these cells will be linked to current values in your other worksheets, you will need to manually copy and paste values every day you want to save the current values in the Hist worksheet. This step is explained in more detail later in this section.

In the Hist worksheet, begin by entering **Date** in the first cell (A1) and then, in columns B and C, enter the two named cells you just created, such that the first row should read Date, PortfolioMV, and MaxPortfolioPct.

Place this formula in the Date column (starting in cell A2):

```
=IF(ISFORMULA(A1),"-",TODAY())
```

This formula, when dragged down, will check if the cell above it contains a formula; if the above cell does not contain a formula, it displays today's date. Because, in a future step, each historical row will contain values instead of formulas, this will display today's date after the last historical value (or, in the case of the first day, the header) and a dash ("-") for each row beneath it.

In the PortfolioMV column (cell B2), place the following formula:

```
=IF(ISFORMULA(B1),"-",INDIRECT(B$1))
```

Like the Date column formula, this formula uses the INDIRECT function if the cell above it is a historical value (or, in the case of the first time, the column header cell); otherwise, it displays a dash. The INDIRECT function takes a named cell and displays its value. In other words, the formula will return the current value of PortfolioMV in the last row without a historical; otherwise, it displays a dash. Copy this formula into the MaxPortfolioPct column (cell C1) so that it reads as follows:

```
=IF(ISFORMULA(C1),"-",INDIRECT(C$1))
```

Then, drag the formulas in the first row down several rows. The first row should contain today's date, the current value of PortfolioMV, and the current value of MaxPortfolioPct. Every other row should contain a series of dashes.

To add additional columns, simply name the cell, add that name as a column header, and copy the formula from one of the other named cell columns.

Finally, because these formulas link to other cells and would change if the values of PortfolioMV or MaxPortfolioPct changed, we must convert the formulas in the row with today's date into values. To convert the formulas, right-click the row number next to the cell containing today's date and then, on the shortcut menu, select Copy. Next, right-click again on the row number next to the cell containing today's date and select "Values (V)" in the paste options. This should result in the formulas in that row converting to values and, as such, the row beneath the converted row should now display today's date and current information.

If you opened this worksheet tomorrow, the last row before the dashes would now contain that date and, if you changed the values of PortfolioMV or MaxPortfolioPct, those values would be changed only in the last row. Again, and on every day for which you want a record, you must copy and paste values for the last row. The resulting worksheet should look like Figure 5-4.

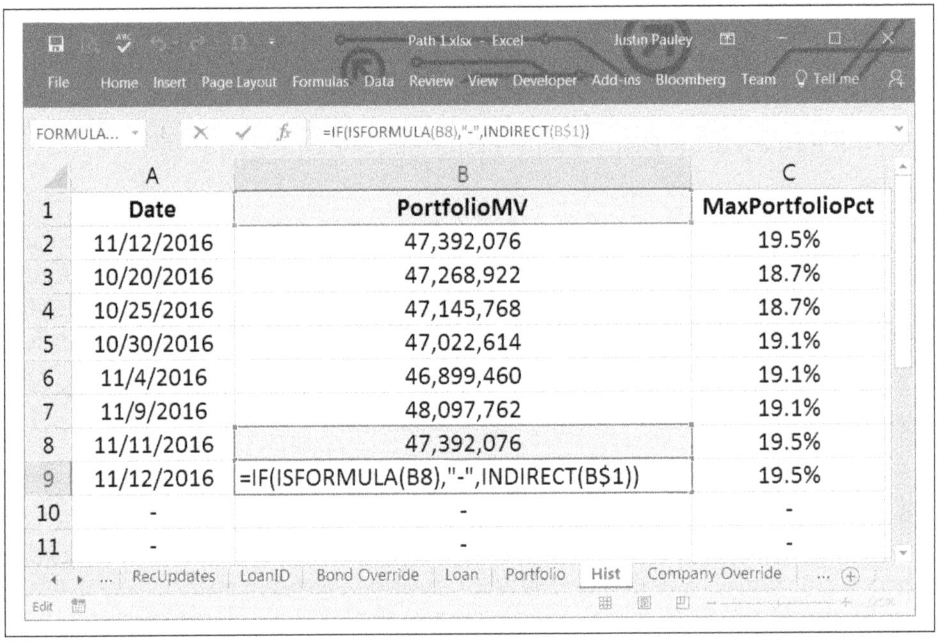

Figure 5-4. The Hist worksheet displaying a formula

Backup.bat

This section covers how to create an automated script to automatically back up your workbook daily. Let's begin by running the Notepad application. In the new text document paste the following (replace `"C:\drive\Path 1.xlsx"` with the full file path to your Excel workbook in both spots, keep the `"_%date..."` syntax before the period of the second instance):

```
copy "C:\drive\Path 1.xlsx"
"C:\drive\Path 1_%date:~10,4%%date:~4,2%%date:~7,2%.xlsx"
```

This command creates a copy of your Excel file (in this case *Path 1.xlsx*) and adds the current date (yyyyMMdd) to the filename (*Path 1_20161112.xlsx*).

Save the file and name it **backup.bat**. Files ending in ".bat" are batch files, meaning that Microsoft Windows will execute the commands within it if the file is launched.

Next, to automatically run this batch file daily, run the Task Scheduler application and select Create Basic Task. In the first screen of the dialog box that opens, type the

---

name **Excel Analysis Backup**, and then click Next. On the next screen, select Daily (or the frequency you prefer), and then click Next. On the next screen, choose the time of day you want to create the backup file, and then click Next. On the next screen, choose "Start a program," and then click Next. On the next screen, click the Browse button, choose the *backup.bat* file you just created, and then click Next. Click Finish to complete the scheduled task.

 To avoid historical worksheets from refreshing data from Bloomberg or recalculating other cells when you open them, first open a blank workbook, and then, on the Formulas tab on the ribbon, select Calculation Options, choose Manual, and then open the historical workbook.

Optionally, to pull values out of historical Excel files into one worksheet, create a new workbook file and reference cells in files like so (where PortfolioMVVal is a named cell in the file created on 11/12/2016):

```
='C:\drive\Path 1_20161112.xlsx'!PortfolioMVVal
```

You cannot reference cells that are part of an Excel table directly unless that workbook is open. To reference the PortfolioMV cell, you must create a cell (name it **PortfolioMVVal**) outside of the Excel table that references the PortfolioMV cell inside the table simply by using the following:

```
=PortfolioMV
```

You also cannot reference external cells using the INDIRECT function: each reference must be spelled out on the formula bar.

Path 2: Microsoft Access

To maintain a history in Access, begin by creating a table to store the historical information by copying an existing table. Here's how to do that:

1. To maintain a history of the Portfolio table, right-click the table in Access, and then, on the shortcut menu, select Copy, right-click again, and then select Paste.

2. Name the new table **PortfolioHist**, and then, under Paste Options, choose Structure Only (Local Table).

3. Repeat steps 1 and 2 to create history tables for the other tables.

4. Right-click the PortfoloHist table and select Design View.

5. In the Design View for the PortfolioHist table, add a row at the top of the table's schema and call the new field **HistDate**, set the Data Type to Date/Time, and then click Save.

6. Repeat steps 4 and 5 for the other tables.

7. Create the following queries that will insert the rows from the linked tables into the new history tables with today's date in the HistDate column:

BondHistQuery

```
INSERT INTO BondHist
SELECT now() AS HistDate, *
FROM Bond
WHERE BondID is not null;
```

PortfolioHistQuery

```
INSERT INTO PortfolioHist
SELECT now() AS HistDate, *
FROM Portfolio
WHERE SecurityID is not null;
```

CompanyHistQuery

```
INSERT INTO CompanyHist
SELECT now() AS HistDate, *
FROM Company
WHERE CompanyID is not null;
```

LoanHistQuery

```
INSERT INTO LoanHist
SELECT now() AS HistDate, *
FROM Loan
WHERE LoanID is not null;
```

IndexHistQuery

```
INSERT INTO IndexHist
SELECT now() AS HistDate, *
FROM Index
WHERE IndexID is not null;
```

 If the underlying table (Index, Loan, Company, Portfolio, Bond) schema changes, and the History table (IndexHist, LoanHist, etc.) schemas aren't changed to match, these queries will fail to run.

8. On the Create tab, click Macro.

9. Add a SetWarnings action to the macro and set Warnings On to No.

10. For each query that you created (PortfolioHistQuery, CompanyHistQuery, LoanHistQuery, BondHistQuery, and IndexHistQuery) add an OpenQuery action to the Macro and select the appropriate query.

11. Save the new macro as **HistMacro**.

    This new macro will execute all the queries and copy all of the data from each table into the appropriate historical database table.

To automate this macro:

12. Add a QuitAccess action at the end of HistMacro.

    This instructs Access to close when the macro is completed.

13. Run the Task Scheduler application and then select Create Basic Task.

14. Give the scheduled task a name, and then click Next.

15. Select your preferred frequency, and then click Next.

16. Designate the time the macro should run, and then click Next.

17. Select "Start a program," and then click Next. Browse to your *msaccess.exe*

    This is typically *C:\Program Files (x86)\Microsoft Office\root\Office16\MSAC-CESS.EXE*.

18. Add the optional argument: `"c:\path\to\access.accdb" /x HistMacro`, and then click Next and Finish.

    The `/x` argument instructs Access to launch the macro upon startup.

Path 3: C#

Writing code to populate the history tables is optional, the macro solution presented for Path 2 will work. However, if you prefer to keep everything in code, use the following solution.

Like Path 2, begin by creating a table in Access to store the historical information by copying the structure from an existing table. For instance, to maintain a history of the Portfolio table, in Access, right-click the table, select Copy, and then right-click again and select Paste. Name the new table **PortfolioHist**, and then, under Paste Options, choose Structure. Add a "HistDate" Date/Time column to the PortfolioHist table and include it in the Primary Key (i.e., make the Primary Key for the PortfolioHist table a combination key of PortfolioID and HistDate). Repeat this step for the other tables.

Next, create a new C# console application in Visual Studio. In the *Program.cs* file, include the following using directives:

```
using System.Data;
using System.Data.OleDb;
```

Then, add the following connection string property (adjust the path to the Access database file):

```
private string ConnStr =
"Provider=Microsoft.ACE.OLEDB.12.0;Data Source=..\\..\\Path 3.accdb";
```

Like previous code in this book, instantiate a `Program` object and call its `Run` method that we will create shortly:

```
static void Main(string[] args)
{
    Program p = new Program();
    p.Run();
}
```

The `Run` method instantiates a `Dictionary` object with the origin data tables and their corresponding history data tables. For each entry in the `Dictionary`, the `Run` method populates the data from the Access database (using the `FillDataSet` method), copies the data into the history data table (using the `CopyData` method), and finally populates the Access database with the new history rows (using the `UpdateDataSet` method):

```
public void Run()
{
    DataSet ds = null;
    Dictionary<string, string> histTables = new Dictionary<string, string>()
    {
        {"Bond","BondHist"},
        {"Loan","LoanHist"},
        {"Company","CompanyHist"},
        {"Portfolio","PortfolioHist"},
        {"Index","IndexHist"}
    };

    int rowsUpdated = 0;
    foreach(string origtable in histTables.Keys)
    {
        ds = FillDataSet(origtable,histTables[origtable]);
        CopyData(ds, origtable, histTables[origtable]);
        rowsUpdated+= UpdateDataSet(ds, histTables[origtable]);
    }
    Console.WriteLine(rowsUpdated + " rows updated");

}
```

The `FillDataSet` method populates the data for the origin table and then retrieves the schema for the history table. Because we are inserting data only into the history table, we require only the schema. The schema is used in the `CopyTable` method to ensure that the history table contains the same columns as the origin table:

```
private DataSet FillDataSet(string table, string histTable)
{
    DataSet ds = new DataSet();
    using (OleDbConnection conn = new OleDbConnection(ConnStr))
    {
        string cmdStr = "SELECT * FROM [" + table+"]";
```

```
        OleDbCommand cmd = new OleDbCommand(cmdStr, conn);
        OleDbDataAdapter da = new OleDbDataAdapter(cmd);
        conn.Open();
        da.Fill(ds, table);

        cmdStr = "SELECT * FROM " + histTable;
        cmd = new OleDbCommand(cmdStr, conn);
        da = new OleDbDataAdapter(cmd);
        da.FillSchema(ds, SchemaType.Source, histTable);

        conn.Close();
    }
    return ds;
}
```

The `CopyData` method iterates through all the rows in the origin table, creates a new corresponding row in the history table, sets the HistDate column to today's date, and copies over all corresponding columns:

```
private void CopyData(DataSet ds, string origtable, string histTable)
{
    foreach(DataRow row in ds.Tables[origtable].Rows)
    {
        DataRow newrow = ds.Tables[histTable].NewRow();
        newrow["HistDate"] = DateTime.Now;
        foreach(DataColumn dc in ds.Tables[origtable].Columns)
        {
            if(row.IsNull(dc) == false &&
                ds.Tables[histTable].Columns.Contains(dc.ColumnName))
            {
                newrow[dc.ColumnName] = row[dc];
            }
        }
        ds.Tables[histTable].Rows.Add(newrow);
    }
}
```

Finally, the `UpdateDataSet` method updates the history table in the Access database and returns the number of added rows:

```
private int UpdateDataSet(DataSet ds, string table)
{
    int rowc = 0;
    using (OleDbConnection conn = new OleDbConnection(ConnStr))
    {
        string cmdStr = "SELECT * FROM " + table;

        OleDbCommand cmd = new OleDbCommand(cmdStr, conn);
        OleDbDataAdapter da = new OleDbDataAdapter();
        da.SelectCommand = cmd;
        OleDbCommandBuilder cb = new OleDbCommandBuilder(da);
        cb.QuotePrefix = "[";
        cb.QuoteSuffix = "]";
```

```
        conn.Open();
        da.UpdateCommand = cb.GetUpdateCommand();
        da.InsertCommand = cb.GetInsertCommand();
        rowc = da.Update(ds, table);

        conn.Close();
    }
    return rowc;
}
```

Summary

This chapter walked you through some of the basic concepts that you'll need for the chapters that follow. In addition, we populated the Portfolio worksheet/table and then demonstrated how to connect the information from one central worksheet/table to the other worksheets and tables that you created in Chapter 3. Finally, we covered techniques for maintaining a history of the data and analysis created in this book. The next three chapters dive into relative value, risk, and market financial data analysis.

CHAPTER 6

Relative-Value Analysis

There are two essential ways to look at the value, or worth, of an investment. The first way is determining the investment's intrinsic value. Basically, intrinsic value is how much you think an investment is worth in isolation; it might be different than its market value. For instance, even though a bond might have a market price of $40, the net present value (NPV) of the expected cashflows, under your base case assumptions, are worth at least $50. Quantifying risks and developing the different assumptions (scenarios) and their probabilities requires a comprehensive understanding of the investment's fundamentals and is at the core of financial analysis. Relative value, on the other hand, compares an investment's risk-adjusted returns against other potential investments to determine if the investment is rich, cheap, or fair. In other words, all things being equal, a risky investment that is expected to return 15 percent is rich to a less risky investment that is also expected to return 15 percent. Similarly, although a bond might seem cheap because it has a market value of $40 and an intrinsic value of $50, there might be cheaper bonds with similar risk that have a market value of $40 and an intrinsic value of $60.

The key to determining relative value is isolating and quantifying the differences between investments. For instance, comparing two almost identical bonds issued by the same company with different coupons and maturity dates comes down to quantifying the value of extra duration. Furthermore, quantifying differences can be very subjective. For example, if two houses in the same neighborhood were very similar but one had a pool, some would view that as positive, whereas others would view it as negative. Unfortunately, there are generally many differences between investments that are difficult to quantify. This book cannot teach you how to do fundamental research or determine an investment's intrinsic value, but it does cover several techniques to determine relative value by isolating and quantify differences between similar investments.

Relative value is used in one of the more common approaches for establishing the market value of a security. In many cases, the only way to value a security is to compare it to a recently priced (or traded) security for which the market has already established a value. The process begins by finding the most recent and relevant open-market transaction and using it as a benchmark for the unpriced security. For instance, if a security was recently issued at a nine percent yield, and a similar security was coming to market, the security coming to market should price wide of a nine percent yield if there are factors that make it more risky or tighter than nine percent if the security is deemed to have less risk.

This chapter covers methods for comparing bonds, loans, and equities to their peers and the broader market using either Microsoft Excel, Access, or C#. Like previous sections, this chapter is broken down into three paths. However, it's recommended that you read the explanations in Path 1 (Excel) to better understand the implementations of Access and C#.

Path 1: Excel

The following walks you through the relative value techniques in Excel.

Correlation and Regression in Excel

When comparing a security to an index or another security, it's helpful to understand their correlation. Correlation informs us about the relationship between two investments (positive, negative, or none) and the strength of their relationship. A positive correlation means that the value of both securities will move in the same direction. For instance, a company that produces cars and a company that produces raw materials used in car production are likely to be positively correlated. A negative correlation means that the value of both securities move in opposite directions. For example, as the price of oil changes, the value of oil producers is likely to be negatively correlated to companies that are oil consumers such as airlines and trucking companies. The strength of their relationship, measured by the correlation coefficient, informs us as to how closely the two investments move in the same (positive correlation) or opposite (negative correlation) direction.

Determining correlation between investments is important for a few reasons. First, while your portfolio might contain several different investments, *if they are all highly correlated, you lose all the benefits of diversification*. Second, measuring the correlation between investments is used to determining appropriate hedges by finding investments that are negatively correlated. Third—and the focus of this chapter—it will help find suitable benchmark securities. For instance, it would not make sense to measure the performance of Microsoft stock against the Russell 3000 Restaurant Index.

Regression is like correlation except that regression gives you an equation that can be used to make predictions on the value of one investment given the value of another. For instance, the regression equation can predict the change in Microsoft stock if the Russell 3000 Technology index fell by 10 percent. Obviously, the correlation isn't perfect, so the prediction will not be, either. Nevertheless, there are methods to measure how well the regression equation fits historical data.

This section walks you through the process of determining the correlation and regression equation in Excel between two investments. In addition, it demonstrates how to build a correlation matrix like the output of the Bloomberg Peer Correlation screen shown in Figure 3-9.

1. Add a new a new Excel worksheet called "Regression."

   (You'll see this table later in Figure 6-2.)

   In this worksheet, columns A through C are going to contain the daily prices and price changes for Microsoft (MSFT) equity and columns E through G are going to contain the daily prices and price changes for the Russell 3000 Technology Index (RGUST). Column J will contain the labels for our output (Start Date, Correlation, etc.), and column K will contain the values that correspond to those labels.

2. In cell A1, enter the name of an index or equity ticker.

   For this example, use "MSFT Equity" for Microsoft Corporation.

3. In the first row in column E (cell E1), enter the name of the index or equity ticker of the other investment.

   For this example, use "RGUST Index" for the Russell 3000 Technology Index.

4. A few columns over, in cell J1, use the following formula to label the output table (which will read "Regression of MSFT Equity to RGUST Index"):

   ```
   ="Regression of " &A1&" to " &E1
   ```

5. In cell J2, enter the label "Start Date" and in the cell next to it (K2), enter the following formula to get a date 12-months prior to today:

   ```
   =EDATE(TODAY(),-12)
   ```

6. Enter the following formula in cell A2:

   ```
   =BDH(A1,"PX_LAST",$K$2,"","sort=D")
   ```

   This formula pulls in historical prices, sorted from latest to earliest, from the Start Date to today for MSFT Equity.

7. Similarly, in cell E2, pull the historical prices for RGUST Index by entering this formula:

   ```
   =BDH(E1,"PX_LAST",$K$2,"","sort=D")
   ```

8. Enter the following formula in cell C2:

```
=(B2-B3)/B3
```

This formula is used to calculate the percentage daily change in MSFT Equity price.

9. Copy the formula from step 8 down (excluding the final row because the formula requires a cell with a value beneath the current cell).

10. Similarly, for RGUST Index, use the following formula in cell G2 to calculate its percentage daily change and copy it down:

```
=(F2-F3)/F3
```

The next set of formulas are used to fill out the output table in columns J and K. The label for each of these formulas should be put in the J column and the formula itself should be put in the K column.

11. Label cell J3 "Correlation."

12. Enter the following formula in cell K3 (adjusting for rows that contain values):

```
=CORREL(C2:C253,G2:G253)
```

This formula is used to calculate the correlation coefficient between the daily price changes of MSFT Equity and RGUST Index, using the CORREL function.

The CORREL function returns the *correlation coefficient*, which is a number between −1 and 1 that indicates the strength of the linear relationship between MSFT Equity and RGUST Index. A value of 1 indicates that both securities are perfectly positively correlated, and a value of −1 indicates that both securities are perfectly negatively correlated. Although there isn't a hard line that separates weak, moderate, or strong correlation coefficient values, generally you want values between 0.7 and 1 or between −0.7 and −1 for a strong correlation. In this case, the resulting correlation is 0.83 (it might vary depending on the dates used).

Knowing the correlation between two securities is valuable, but linear regression models the relationship between two securities, and we can use it to predict the change in one security given the change in another. To help visualize this relationship, insert a scatter chart into the worksheet using the values in the G column for series X, and the values in the C column for series Y. Next, right-click the series data on the chart and then, on the shortcut menu that opens, select Add Trendline. In the Format Trendline dialog box that displays, select Linear and check the "Display Equation on chart" and "Display R-Squared value on chart" boxes. The result should look like Figure 6-1.

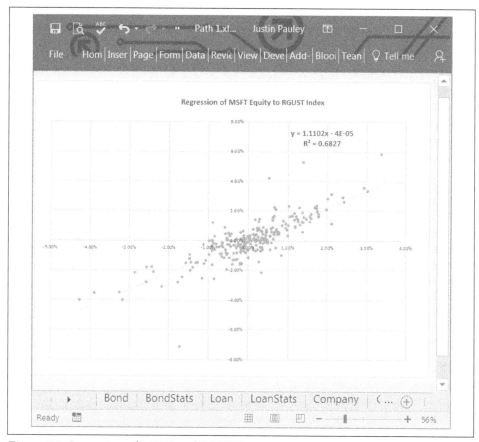

Figure 6-1. Regression of MSFT and RGUST

The regression formula, displayed as "*y*=1.1102x—4E-05" and shown as a line through the data, means that for every 1 percent movement of *x* (Russell 3000 Technology Index), *y* (Microsoft Equity) will move approximately 1.11 percent (the 4E-05 is scientific notation for 4×10^{-5}, essentially zero). The 1.11x is the slope of the regression line and it is also the *Beta* of the security relative to the index. Beta can also be calculated via the SLOPE function in Excel by passing the daily changes for the security and index as arguments.

The next output (label in cell J4, formula in cell K4) is *R Square*, a number between zero and one that indicates how well the regression equation fits the historical data. An R Square of one indicates that the regression equation perfectly fits the data. Calculate the R Square in cell K4 using the following formula (adjust for cells with values):

```
=RSQ(C2:C253,G2:G253)
```

The result of the RSQ formula should match the number on the chart, in my example 0.6827. Ideally, the R Square number would be closer to one, but, as you can see in Figure 6-1, the regression line does not fit the data perfectly.

The next formula in our output (cells J5 and K5) is *Significance F*, which gives you the probability that the regression equation fits the data by chance. For instance, a Significance F value of 15% means that there is a 15 percent chance that the regression equation fit purely by chance. A Significance F of more than 10 percent means you probably shouldn't use the regression equation. In this case, the Significance F is 3.36×10^{-64}, essentially zero. Here is the formula to calculate Significance F:

```
=FDIST(INDEX(LINEST(C2:C253,G2:G253,1,1),4,1),1,
INDEX(LINEST(C2:C253,G2:G253,1,1),4,2))
```

Similarly, we need to calculate the *P-value*, which tells us if the value of Russell 3000 Technology Index meaningfully influences Microsoft equity. Like Significance F, a lower P-value is better and should be less than 5 percent. In this case, the P-value is 3.4×10^{-64}, essentially zero. Unfortunately, there isn't an easy way to calculate this in Excel. Instead, we break it up into three calculations. The first calculation, placed in cells J6 and K6, is simply the number of observations used in the correlation and regression analysis:

```
=COUNT(C2:C253)
```

The second calculation, *t Stat*, is placed in cells J7 and K7:

```
=(K3*SQRT(K6-2))/(SQRT(1-K3^2))
```

Finally, the third calculation, placed in cells J8 and K8, gives you the P-value:

```
=TDIST(K7,K6-2,2)
```

You can use the resulting worksheet (see Figure 6-2) to show the correlation and regression between any two investments. For instance, changing RGUST Index to S5INFT Index (the S&P 500 Information Technology Sector Index GICS Level 1), shows a higher correlation (0.84), a higher R Square (0.71), and a Significance F and P-value around zero.

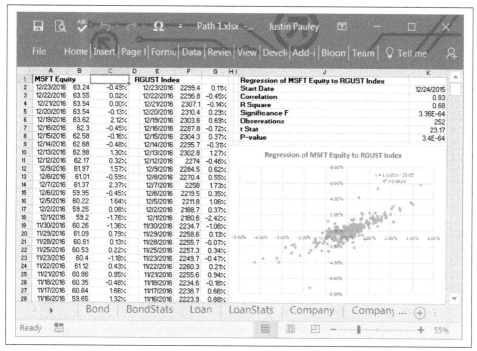

Figure 6-2. A regression worksheet

Instead of repeatedly changing the securities to compare correlation values, we can create a matrix that can compare multiple securities simultaneously. Starting in cell M3, list several securities in sequential rows. Then, similarly, in cell N2, list several securities or indices across sequential columns. The same security can exist in both the row group and the column group. In cell M2, enter the start date for the historical data, or use the formula from earlier to pull one year prior to today:

```
=EDATE(TODAY(),-12)
```

Finally, use the following array formula in cell N3 to calculate the correlation between the securities that intersect at that cell (N2 and M3); because this is an array formula, you must press Ctrl-Shift-Enter in the formula bar after you enter it:

```
=CORREL(
BDH($M3,"chg_pct_1d",$M$2,"","dates=hide","array=true","PER=CD","FILL=PNA",
"CDR=US"),
BDH(N$2,"chg_pct_1d",$M$2,"","dates=hide","array=true","PER=CD","FILL=PNA",
"CDR=US"))
```

The prior array formula uses the Bloomberg BDH function to pull the historical one-day price changes from both securities as an array and passes them to the CORREL function as parameters. The PER, FILL, and CDR arguments (detailed in Chapter 3) ensure that the dates line up. Copy this formula into all the cells in the matrix. Finally, select the cells with the CORREL formula, and then, on the Home tab on the ribbon, click Conditional Formatting, and choose the first option under Color Scales to give the matrix a heat map effect, highlighting strong correlations in darker shades of green and low correlations in darker shades of red. As expected, Figure 6-3 shows a correlation of one where the intersecting names are the same (MSFT Equity and MSFT Equity in cell N3).

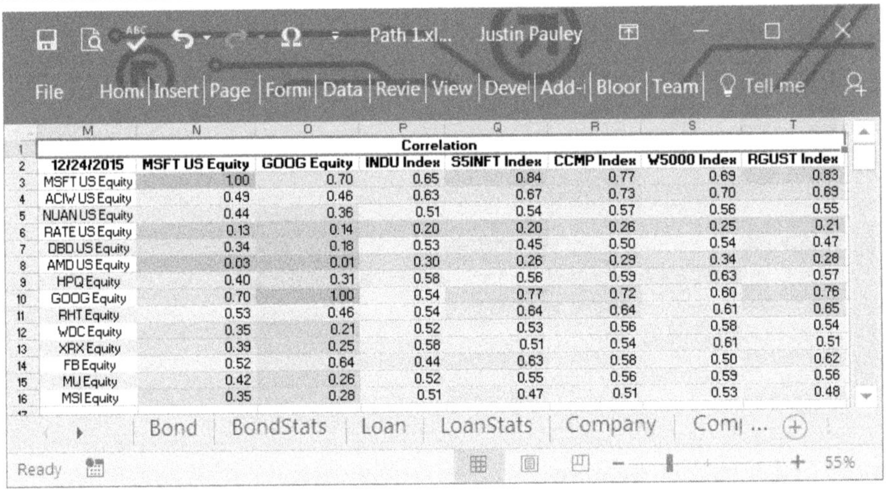

Correlation							
12/24/2015	MSFT US Equity	GOOG Equity	INDU Index	S5INFT Index	CCMP Index	W5000 Index	RGUST Index
MSFT US Equity	1.00	0.70	0.65	0.84	0.77	0.69	0.83
ACIW US Equity	0.49	0.46	0.63	0.67	0.73	0.70	0.69
NUAN US Equity	0.44	0.36	0.51	0.54	0.57	0.56	0.55
RATE US Equity	0.13	0.14	0.20	0.20	0.26	0.25	0.21
DBD US Equity	0.34	0.18	0.53	0.45	0.50	0.54	0.47
AMD US Equity	0.03	0.01	0.30	0.26	0.29	0.34	0.28
HPQ Equity	0.40	0.31	0.58	0.56	0.59	0.63	0.57
GOOG Equity	0.70	1.00	0.54	0.77	0.72	0.60	0.76
RHT Equity	0.53	0.46	0.54	0.64	0.64	0.61	0.65
WDC Equity	0.35	0.21	0.52	0.53	0.56	0.58	0.54
XRX Equity	0.39	0.25	0.58	0.51	0.54	0.61	0.51
FB Equity	0.52	0.64	0.44	0.63	0.58	0.50	0.62
MU Equity	0.42	0.26	0.52	0.55	0.56	0.59	0.56
MSI Equity	0.35	0.28	0.51	0.47	0.51	0.53	0.48

Figure 6-3. Correlation matrix

You can create a matrix for R Square in the same way, except you use the RSQ formula instead of the CORREL formula.

Peer Groups

Our next step in comparing investments is separating the securities in the Loan, Bond, and Company worksheets into peer groups based on their similarities. Determining the appropriate group for a security is subjective and not always easy. For example, you could group the bonds by their sector, rating, months until maturity, or some combination of attributes. The objective is to come up with a cohort that should have similar risk and return characteristics that intuitively makes sense to use as a comparison among members. It is up to you if you want to be specific, such as, "financial software development companies," or "high-yield technology bonds with five years or more until maturity," or broader, such as, "short investment-grade corporate bonds." These groups can always be refined later.

Begin by reviewing the Category column in the Company worksheet that was discussed earlier in this book. This column should contain the categorization that makes most sense to you. Spending time reading each company's description and understanding at least a little about why it exists is a very important step that will help you come up with a category that makes more sense than the sector columns returned by Bloomberg. Make sure that you add a reference to the Category column from the Company worksheet to the Bond and Loan worksheets using the technique from "References and Overrides" on page 47 in Chapter 3.

Next, in the Bond worksheet, add a column called "Months Until Maturity," which we will use to help classify investments as long or short. Populate the column using the following formula, which returns the number of months until maturity:

```
=DATEDIF(TODAY(),[@Maturity],"m")
```

Next, still in the Bond worksheet, add a column called "Peer Groups," which will contain a group for each bond. As I mentioned, determining the appropriate peer group is subjective, but I suggest first sorting by the new Months Until Maturity column and drawing a line in the sand to identify "short" bonds. Because shorter-performing bonds tend to have similar performance characteristics, I have grouped all bonds maturing within four years (48 months) as either "Short HY" if they are not rated "CCC+" or lower or "Short CCC" if they are. Additionally, I grouped all other "CCC+" or lower-rated bonds as "CCC Corp" and, for the remainder, I used an abbreviation of the company's category, such as "FinTech" for financial technology companies. I recommend coming up with your own classifications and use the company's category and the bond's yield as a guide to grouping similar bonds. Repeat this step for the Loan worksheet.

Ratings

Numerical columns such as Spread, Yield, Coupon, and so on are easy to aggregate and compare, but you cannot take an average of a rating. Additionally, ratings cannot simply be converted into linear numbers (AAA = 1, AA+ = 2, etc.), because they represent probabilities of default which are nonlinear. Fortunately, Moody's provides a solution called "Rating Factor" (RF). Moody's RF is an approximate numerical representation of Moody's corporate idealized 10-year cumulative probability of default rate. Dividing the Rating Factors, shown in Table 6-1, by 10,000 gives you the idealized 10-year cumulative probability of default rate. For instance, a bond rated Baa1 (RF of 260) has a 10-year probability of default rate of 2.6 percent (260 divided by 10,000).

Table 6-1. Moody's Rating Factor (source: Moody's Investors Service, Inc.)

Rating	Rating factor
Aaa	1
Aa1	10
Aa2	20
Aa3	40

Rating	Rating factor
A1	70
A2	120
A3	180
Baa1	260
Baa2	360
Baa3	610
Ba1	940
Ba2	1,350
Ba3	1,766
B1	2,220
B2	2,720
B3	3,490
Caa1	4,770
Caa2	6,500
Caa3	8,070
Ca	10,000
C	10,000

To incorporate this into our workbook, create a new worksheet called "RF" and add the contents of Table 6-1 into columns A and B. Next, in the Company, Loan, and Bond worksheets, add a column called "RF" and populate it with the following formula:

```
=IFERROR(VLOOKUP(IF(ISERR(FIND(" ",[@[Moody''s Rating]])),[@[Moody''s Rating]],
LEFT([@[Moody''s Rating]],FIND(" ",[@[Moody''s Rating]])-1)),RF!A:B,2,FALSE),"")
```

This formula checks to see whether the rating column has a space in it (Bloomberg might have returned rating watch information along with the rating, and we want to exclude that). If it has a space, grab the content before the space; otherwise grab the entire cell and use it to VLOOKUP the Rating Factor from the RF worksheet. If the RF does not exist on the RF worksheet (because the rating has been withdrawn [WR] or is not populated), the formula will return an empty string.

Stats Worksheets

In this section, we are going to create new worksheets that will contain the median and standard deviation values for several attributes broken down by Peer Group. This worksheet will help put data into context, and identify trends and potential issues. Begin by creating a new worksheet called "BondStats." On the BondStats worksheet, starting in cell A1, create an Excel table called "MedianBondStats," with the following column headers:

- Peer Group
- Count
- YTD Px Chg
- 3M Px Chg
- YAS Spread
- YAS Yield
- Fixed Coupon
- Months Until Maturity
- RF

In the Peer Group column, list all the distinct groups listed in the Peer Group column in the Bond worksheet. (Hint, you can paste the entire row of Peer Groups and use the Remove Duplicates button on the Data tab.) In the Count column, use the following formula to count the number of bonds in each group:

```
=COUNTIF(Bond[Peer Group],[@[Peer Group]])
```

In the YTD Px Chg column, use the following array formula to calculate the median year-to-date price change for each group. Because it is an array formula, you must press Ctrl-Shift-Enter after typing the formula.

```
=MEDIAN(IF(Bond[Peer Group]=[@[Peer Group]],Bond[YTD Px Chg]))
```

Repeat this process with the other columns. For instance, the 3M Px Chg column should have the following array formula:

```
=MEDIAN(IF(Bond[Peer Group]=[@[Peer Group]],Bond[3M Px Chg]))
```

When this is complete, your BondStats worksheet should resemble Figure 6-4.

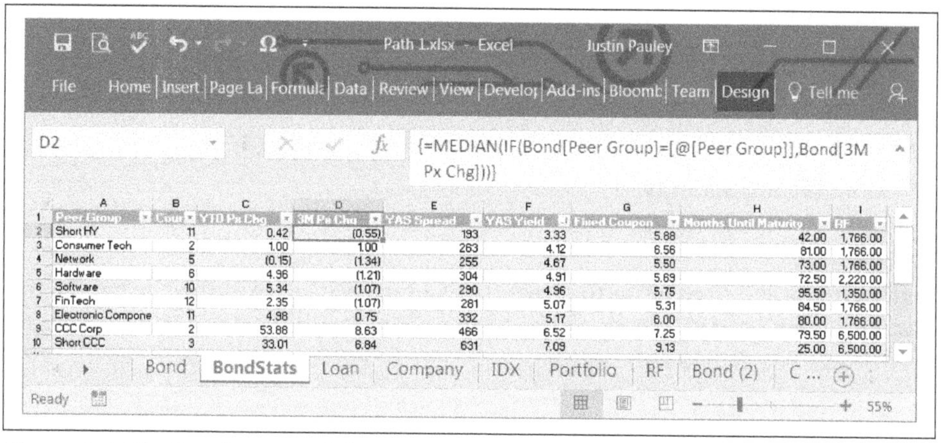

Figure 6-4. The BondStats worksheet

Before moving forward, take the time to think about what this data shows and make sure it makes sense. For instance, as expected, the Short HY group has the lowest yield because, all things being equal, shorter bonds are less risk and should yield less. Likewise, the CCC groups should have the highest risk and they have the highest yields (and highest rating factors). The year-to-date price change of 53 percent for the CCC Corp group looks suspiciously high, but a quick check of the two bonds in the group show that, indeed, both have almost doubled since the beginning of the year. The more bonds that you include in the data, the more meaningful this worksheet will become.

Next, to the right of the MedianBondStats Excel table, create another table called "StdDevBondStats," which will inform you to the amount of dispersion in the data. This table should be identical to the MedianBondStats table, except instead of the MEDIAN function, you use the STDEV array function:

```
=STDEV(IF(Bond[Peer Group]=[@[Peer Group]],Bond[YAS Spread]))
```

Next, to the right of the StdDevBondStats Excel table, create another identical table called "AvgBondStats," which will calculate averages instead of medians or standard deviations. This table should be identical to the other two except it uses AVERAGE array function instead of MEDIAN or STDEV:

```
=AVERAGE(IF(Bond[Peer Group]=[@[Peer Group]],Bond[YAS Spread]))
```

Next, repeat the steps to create the LoanStats worksheet, but use the following column headers:

- Peer Group
- Count
- YTD Px Chg
- 3M Px Chg
- DM
- Yield
- Margin
- Months Until Maturity
- RF

Finally, repeat the steps again to create the "CompanyStats" worksheet using the following column headers. Notice on the CompanyStats worksheet that instead of using Peer Group, you should use Category.

- Category
- Count

- Market Cap
- Total Debt
- Total Debt/EBITDA
- Net Debt/EBITDA
- FCF/Total Debt
- 52 Week High Chg
- 52 Week Low Chg
- YTD Px Chg
- 3M Px Chg
- 12M Total Return

It is important to take a step back from creating these worksheets to understand what the data is telling you. Try sorting by each column and see if anything stands out. Are there any groups that are outperforming/underperforming? Does the difference between year-to-date statistics and last-three-months statistics show any trends? These median statistics are the first of many useful methods for slicing and dicing the data we collect.

Side by Side

In this next step, we bring the median stats that we calculated in the BondStats, Loan-Stats, and CompanyStats worksheets back into our Bond, Loan, and Company worksheets. This allows us to compare individual securities with the medians for their cohort side by side. We use the MEDIAN function instead of AVERAGE to avoid issues with large outliers.

Begin by inserting a column in the Bond table to the right of the RF column: right-click the column to the right of the RF column, and then, on the Insert tab, select "Table Column to the Left." Label this column "Median RF" and populate it with the following formula:

```
=INDEX(MedianBondStats[RF],MATCH([@[Peer Group]],MedianBondStats[Peer Group],0))
```

This formula is like the one used to pull columns from the Company worksheet, except in this case, it pulls the RF column from the MedianBondStats table where the current row's Peer Group cell matches the Peer Group in the MedianBondStats table. It is recommended that you highlight this column to distinguish it as a column containing median information for the Peer Group, not data about the current bond. The result should look like Figure 6-5.

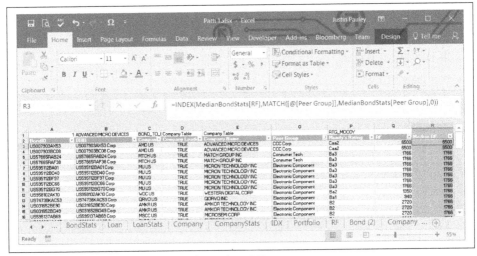

Figure 6-5. The Bond worksheet with Median RF

Repeat that step to add the other columns from MedianBondStats table into the Bond table. For instance, here's the formula for adding Median Fixed Coupon column:

```
=INDEX(MedianBondStats[Fixed Coupon],MATCH([@[Peer Group]],
MedianBondStats[Peer Group],0))
```

After you add each of the columns from MedianBondStats, take a moment to review the Bond table. As you scroll, sort, or filter the data, you can use the median data to put each security into context. For instance, you might have noticed before that one bond had an above average YTD price change, but now you might recognize that it is in-line with its peers. Alternatively, if it is outperforming its peers, you can quantify the amount.

Repeat this process to add columns from MedianLoanStats to the Loan table by using formulas such as this one:

```
=INDEX(MedianLoanStats[Margin],MATCH([@[Peer Group]],
MedianLoanStats[Peer Group],0))
```

Then, repeat the process to add columns from MedianCompanyStats to the Company table with formulas using Category instead of Peer Group:

```
=INDEX(MedianCompanyStats[12M Total Return],MATCH([@Category],
MedianCompanyStats[Category],0))
```

After you complete this process, review each of the tables by sorting by Peer Group (or Category in the Company table) and comparing each security to its cohort. Putting each of these performance metrics into context is an important part of determining relative value. You might notice, for instance, a security that has strong fundamentals and improving technicals but is trading at a lower price because it is rated

CCC by one agency. Or, perhaps, one security has lagged the rally that other securities in its cohort have experienced. You can make numerous valuable observations when carrying out this type of comparison. As the underlying data changes or Peer Groups are changed, the median stats will update automatically.

Indices

In addition to comparing securities to their peer group, it's valuable to compare them to indices to measure performance against a more established benchmark. Each security can be measured against one index or multiple indices, depending on your analysis. In this section, we demonstrate how to compare equities in the Company worksheet to an index. You can duplicate this technique to compare a security to multiple indices, or expand it to the Loan and Bond worksheets.

First, add a column to the Company worksheet labeled "IndexID." In this column, place the IndexID from the IDX worksheet of the index that you want to use as comparison for each equity. Next, add three additional columns: "Index YTD Px Change," "Index 3M Px Change," and "Index 12M Total Return." Next, in the Index YTD Px Change column, use the INDEX function to pull the YTD Px Change column from the IDX worksheet for the given IndexID:

```
=INDEX(IDX[YTD Px Change],MATCH([@IndexID],IDX[IndexID],0))
```

Repeat this step to pull in the 3M Px Change and 12M Total Return columns from the IDX worksheet into the Company worksheet. Optionally, you can add a column, "Index Correlation," that returns the correlation between the company and the Index using data from the last calendar year with the following array formula (requires Ctrl-Shift-Enter):

```
=CORREL(BDH([@BBID],"chg_pct_1d","-1CY","","dates=hide","array=true"),
BDH(INDEX(IDX[BBID],MATCH([@IndexID],IDX[IndexID],0)),
"chg_pct_1d","-1CY","","dates=hide","array=true"))
```

After the index information is in the Company worksheet, you can organize the Index columns next to the company columns and compare performance side by side.

Weighted Z-Score

With so many different metrics and countless differences between investments, it is difficult to sort securities from "best" to "worst." For instance, one bond might have a higher coupon, but a worse rating. Moreover, some of these values are in percentages, whereas others, like rating factor, are entirely different units. One technique to simplify these different metrics into one "score" is by using a *z-score* (also known as a standard score). Z-scores measure the number of standard deviations between a data point and the mean (average). In other words, to normalize these different metrics, z-scores measure how much better or worse a metric is from the average. Z-score is calculated by dividing the difference between the value and the average by the standard deviation, as follows:

- Z = (Value—Average of all values) / Standard Deviation of all values

For example, if a bond had a coupon of 8%, the average coupon of all bonds was 5.63%, and the standard deviation of coupons for all bonds was 1.13%, the bond's coupon has a z-score of 2.09—z = (8%-5.63%)/1.13%. This z-score means that the coupon is two standard deviations above the mean. Z-scores can also be negative; a z-score of –1 means that the value is one standard deviation below the mean.

Although determining the number of standard deviations one value is from the mean is useful, the z-score can help synthesize the value of multiple attributes into a single score by taking a weighted average of the z-scores, where the weights are assigned based on how important one metric is relative to the others. For instance, if we calculated the z-score for a bond's coupon, rating, and number of months until maturity, we could take a weighted average of those z-scores and assign a higher weight to the coupon z-score to favor bonds with higher coupons.

Unfortunately, adding z-scores to the Bond, Loan, and Company worksheets takes several steps:

1. In the BondStats worksheet, to the right of the AvgBondStats table, add four new column headers labeled Field, Mean, StdDev, and Weight.

2. Under the Field column header, list all the fields to compare, such as YTD Px Chg, 3M Px Chg, YAS Spread, YAS Yield, Fixed Coupon, Months Until Maturity, and RF.

3. Under the Mean column header, calculate the average of each of these columns in the Bond table using the AVERAGE function. For instance, next to "YTD Px Chg" use the following formula:

   ```
   =AVERAGE(Bond[YTD Px Chg])
   ```

4. Likewise, in the StdDev column, calculate the standard deviation for each column using the STDEV function. For instance, next to YAS Yield in the StdDev column use the following formula:

   ```
   =STDEV(Bond[YAS Yield])
   ```

5. Under the Weight column, enter a percentage weight such that the sum of all the weights adds up to 100 percent.

   You can change these weights later, and it might be easier to begin with equal weights for each field.

   The resulting table should resemble Figure 6-6.

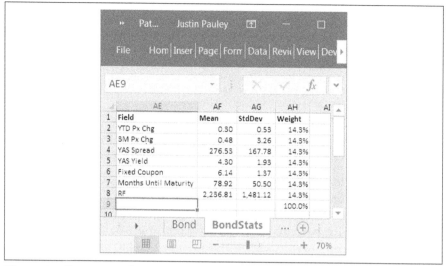

Figure 6-6. Z-score weight table

6. Using the Name box in the upper-left corner, define a name for each cell in the Mean, StdDev, and Weight columns.

   Each defined name should begin with "Bond," followed by the field name, and conclude with the column header. For instance, name the cell containing the mean of YTDPxChg column "BondYTDPxChgMean," and name the cell containing the weight for the Fixed Coupon column "BondFixedCouponWeight."

   Even though it is a bit annoying to name each cell in the table, it will make it a lot easier to construct the complicated z-score calculation in the Bond worksheet.

7. After each cell in the new table is named, add a new column in the Bond worksheet labeled "z-score."

8. In this column, add all the z-scores multiplied by their weights for columns where higher values are better, and subtract the z-scores multiplied by their weights for columns where lower values are better.

   For example, the formula should begin with the calculation for YTD Px Change's z-score, multiplied by its assigned weight:

   ```
   =(([@[YTD Px Chg]]-BondYTDPxChgMean)/BondYTDPxChgStdev*BondYTDPxChgWeight)
   ```

9. Add the next field, 3M Px Chg, to the formula so that it becomes:

   ```
   =(([@[YTD Px Chg]]-BondYTDPxChgMean)/BondYTDPxChgStdev*BondYTDPxChgWeight)+
   (([@[3M Px Chg]]-Bond3MPxChgMean)/Bond3MPxChgStdev*Bond3MPxChgWeight)
   ```

After adding the rest of the columns, the final formula should look like this:

```
=((([@[YTD Px Chg]]-BondYTDPxChgMean)/BondYTDPxChgStdev*BondYTDPxChgWeight)
+((([@[3M Px Chg]]-Bond3MPxChgMean)/Bond3MPxChgStdev*Bond3MPxChgWeight)
+((([@[YAS Spread]]-BondYASSpreadMean)/BondYASSpreadStdev*BondYASSpreadWeight)
+((([@[YAS Yield]]-BondYASYieldMean)/BondYASYieldStdev*BondYASYieldWeight)
+((([@[Fixed Coupon]]-BondFixedCouponMean)/
BondFixedCouponStdev*BondFixedCouponWeight)
-((([@[Months Until Maturity]]-BondMonthsUntilMatMean)/
BondMonthsUntilMatStdev*BondMonthsUntilMatWeight)
-((([@RF]-BondRFMean)/BondRFStdev*BondRFWeight)
```

Notice that the weighted z-scores for Months Until Maturity and RF are subtracted instead of added because these values are better if they are lower.

Now you can sort the z-score column from highest to lowest value ("best" to "worst"). Take the time to adjust the weights and notice the impact on the z-score column. For instance, if all of the weights were changed to zero, except Months Until Maturity, which was set to 100 percent, the highest z-score would be the shortest bond. Try adjusting all the scores to zero, setting Fixed Coupon and RF each to 50 percent, and sorting the z-score column again. The top of the list should have high coupons, but ones with lower ratings should be pushed lower on the list. You can repeat the z-score analysis for the Loan and Company worksheets.

Like any of the different analyses in this book, investment decisions should not be made based on the z-score alone. It is a tool for highlighting investment ideas and providing context to a wealth of data.

Path 2: Access

Because the tables in the Access database are linked to the Excel workbook, follow the steps in the previous section (Path 1) to update both the Excel workbook and Access database tables. The calculations for correlation, regression, and median performed in Excel are not necessary to duplicate in Access, but it is helpful to understand how to do so. This section covers the Microsoft Access implementation of techniques covered in Excel (Path 1).

Just as the prior section added columns to multiple worksheets (Bond, Loan, Company), the linked Access tables will also contain these new columns. As a result, the queries used to maintain a history (BondHistQuery, CompanyHistQuery, etc.) will fail unless the corresponding history tables (BondHist, CompanyHist, etc.) are also modified to match the same columns (schema).

Correlation and Regression in Access

For the purposes of this section, we are going to create a simplified table called "Comp" that will contain historical daily price changes for two securities. Follow the schema in Table 6-2 to create the Comp table (by selecting "Table" under the "Create" menu in Microsoft Access). This table will only be used as an example for this section, it will not be referenced later.

Table 6-2. Comp table schema

Field name	Data type
HistDate	Date/Time (set as Primary Key)
X	Number (set Field Size to Double)
Y	Number (set Field Size to Double)

Open the newly created Comp table and populate it with values. Populate X and Y columns with daily price change values (percentage) of different securities; alternatively copy and paste the values (using Paste Append in Access) of columns A (HistDate column), G (X column), and C (Y column) from the Regression worksheet to match the Excel results.

To calculate the *correlation* between the X and Y columns, use the following query:

```
SELECT (Avg(X * Y) - Avg(X) * Avg(Y)) / (StDevP(X) * StDevP(Y)) AS Correlation
FROM Comp;
```

To calculate the regression equation, start by calculating the *regression coefficient* by using the following query:

```
select (Avg(X * Y) - Avg(X) * Avg(Y)) / VarP(X) AS RegressCoeff from Comp;
```

Then, calculate the *intercept* using the following:

```
select Avg(Y) - ((Avg(X * Y) - Avg(X) * Avg(Y)) / VarP(X))
* Avg(X) AS Intercept from Comp;
```

Use the two results to create the regression equation: Y = RegressCoeff * X + Intercept. Using the data from the Regression worksheet as an example, to predict the value of Microsoft stock, given the value of the Russell 3000 Technology Index, multiply the value of Russell 3000 Technology Index by the regression coefficient and add the intercept.

To determine how well the regression equation fits the historical data, calculate R Square using the following query:

```
select (Avg(X * Y) - Avg(X) * Avg(Y)) ^ 2 / (VarP(X) * VarP(Y)) as RSquare
from Comp;
```

Median in Access

Unfortunately, because median is not a standard aggregate function included in Access, it requires some Visual Basic for Applications (VBA) code to calculate. Fortunately, Microsoft does provide the necessary code (*https://msdn.microsoft.com/en-us/library/dd789431(v=office.12).aspx*).

To begin, in Access, on the Create tab, click Module. Then, in the code window, insert the following code function from Microsoft, and then close the Visual Basic window:

```
Public Function DMedian( _
  ByVal strField As String, ByVal strDomain As String, _
  Optional ByVal strCriteria As String) As Variant

    ' Purpose:
    '     To calculate the median value
    '     for a field in a table or query.
    ' In:
    '     strField: the field.
    '     strDomain: the table or query.
    '     strCriteria: an optional WHERE clause to
    '                  apply to the table or query.
    ' Out:
    '     Return value: the median, if successful;
    '                   Otherwise, an Error value.

    Dim db As DAO.Database
    Dim rstDomain As DAO.Recordset
    Dim strSQL As String
    Dim varMedian As Variant
    Dim intFieldType As Integer
    Dim intRecords As Integer

    Const errAppTypeError = 3169

    On Error GoTo HandleErr

    Set db = CurrentDb()

    ' Initialize return value.
    varMedian = Null

    ' Build SQL string for recordset.
    strSQL = "SELECT " & strField & " FROM " & strDomain

    ' Only use a WHERE clause if one is passed in.
    If Len(strCriteria) > 0 Then
        strSQL = strSQL & " WHERE " & strCriteria
    End If

    strSQL = strSQL & " ORDER BY " & strField
```

```
        Set rstDomain = db.OpenRecordset(strSQL, dbOpenSnapshot)

        ' Check the data type of the median field.
        intFieldType = rstDomain.Fields(strField).Type
        Select Case intFieldType
        Case dbByte, dbInteger, dbLong, _
          dbCurrency, dbSingle, dbDouble, dbDate
            ' Numeric field.
          If Not rstDomain.EOF Then
              rstDomain.MoveLast
              intRecords = rstDomain.RecordCount
              ' Start from the first record.
              rstDomain.MoveFirst

              If (intRecords Mod 2) = 0 Then
                  ' Even number of records.
                  ' No middle record, so move to the
                  ' record right before the middle.
                  rstDomain.Move ((intRecords \ 2) - 1)
                  varMedian = rstDomain.Fields(strField)
                  ' Now move to the next record, the
                  ' one right after the middle.
                  rstDomain.MoveNext
                  ' And average the two values.
                  varMedian = _
                    (varMedian + rstDomain.Fields(strField)) / 2
                  ' Make sure you return a date, even when
                  ' averaging two dates.
                  If intFieldType = dbDate And Not IsNull(varMedian) Then
                      varMedian = CDate(varMedian)
                  End If
              Else
                  ' Odd number or records.
                  ' Move to the middle record and return its value.
                  rstDomain.Move ((intRecords \ 2))
                  varMedian = rstDomain.Fields(strField)
              End If
          Else
              ' No records; return Null.
              varMedian = Null
          End If
        Case Else
            ' Non-numeric field; so raise an app error.
            Err.Raise errAppTypeError
        End Select

        DMedian = varMedian

ExitHere:
    On Error Resume Next
    rstDomain.Close
    Set rstDomain = Nothing
```

```
    Exit Function

HandleErr:
    ' Return an error value.
    DMedian = CVErr(Err.Number)
    Resume ExitHere
End Function
```

The DMedian function takes three arguments: the name of the column, the name of the table, and, optionally, where clause criteria. Note that each parameter is "quoted" and column names should be within brackets ([and]). For instance, to calculate the median RF value in the Bond table where the YAS Spread was wider than 250 bps, use the following query:

```
select dMedian("rf","Bond","[YAS Spread] > 250")
```

Path 3: C#

This section covers the C# implementation of the techniques covered in Excel (Path 1). If you haven't done so already, I recommend that you read the Excel section for a more in-depth explanation of these calculations and their purpose.

Correlation and Regression

This section creates an application that pulls historical daily price changes from Bloomberg for two securities and calculates their correlation, regression equation, and R Square. This code requires the use of a popular mathematical library, MathNet. Start a new console application and add a reference to MathNet by right-clicking References in the new project and selecting Manage NuGet Packages. Search for Math-Net.Numerics and then click Install. In addition, add a reference to the Bloomberg libraries used in Chapter 3.

In *Program.cs*, begin by adding the following using directives:

```
using Element = Bloomberglp.Blpapi.Element;
using Message = Bloomberglp.Blpapi.Message;
using Name = Bloomberglp.Blpapi.Name;
using Request = Bloomberglp.Blpapi.Request;
using Service = Bloomberglp.Blpapi.Service;
using Session = Bloomberglp.Blpapi.Session;
using DataType = Bloomberglp.Blpapi.Schema.Datatype;
using SessionOptions = Bloomberglp.Blpapi.SessionOptions;
using InvalidRequestException =
        Bloomberglp.Blpapi.InvalidRequestException;
using Datetime = Bloomberglp.Blpapi.Datetime;
using System.Collections;
using MathNet.Numerics.Statistics;
using MathNet.Numerics;
```

Next, in the `Program` class, add the typical Bloomberg statements used in previous examples:

```
private static readonly Name SECURITY_DATA = new Name("securityData");
private static readonly Name SECURITY = new Name("security");
private static readonly Name FIELD_DATA = new Name("fieldData");
private static readonly Name RESPONSE_ERROR = new Name("responseError");
private static readonly Name SECURITY_ERROR = new Name("securityError");
private static readonly Name FIELD_EXCEPTIONS = new Name("fieldExceptions");
private static readonly Name FIELD_ID = new Name("fieldId");
private static readonly Name ERROR_INFO = new Name("errorInfo");
private static readonly Name CATEGORY = new Name("category");
private static readonly Name MESSAGE = new Name("message");
private static readonly Name DATE = new Name("date");
```

Add the body of the `Main` function that instantiates the `Program` class and calls a `Run` method.

```
static void Main(string[] args)
{
    Program p = new Program();
    p.Run();
}
```

The `Run` method retrieves historical data points from Bloomberg and then uses Math-Net to calculate the correlation, intercept, slope, and R Square. The `Run` method gets the historical Bloomberg data from the `GetHistory` method (defined later) that will return a `Dictionary` containing date–value pairs for the specific security, field, and starting date. The end date will always be today. After the data points are returned from `GetHistory`, MathNet's library is used to calculate the necessary statistics:

```
public void Run()
{

    //Declare the securities to compare X,Y
    string secY = "/ticker/MSFT US Equity";
    string secX = "/ticker/S5INFT Index";
    //Declare the field to use to compare
    string field = "chg_pct_1d"; // One day price change

    //Declare the starting date, end date is today.
    DateTime startDate = new DateTime(2015, 12, 24);

    //Retrieve the historical points from Bloomberg
    Dictionary<DateTime, double> resultY = GetHistory(secY, field, startDate);
    Dictionary<DateTime, double> resultX = GetHistory(secX, field, startDate);

    //Use MathNet to calculate the correlation
    double correlation = Correlation.Pearson(resultY.Values, resultX.Values);

    //Use MathNet to calculate the intercept and slope
    Tuple<double, double> p = Fit.Line(resultX.Values.ToArray(),
```

```
    resultY.Values.ToArray());
    double intercept = p.Item1;
    double slope = p.Item2;

    //Use MathNet to calculate the R Square
    double rsqr =
    GoodnessOfFit.RSquared(resultX.Values.Select(x => intercept + slope * x),
    resultY.Values);

    Console.WriteLine("Correlation is " + correlation.ToString());
    Console.WriteLine("Regression equation is y="
    + slope.ToString() + "x+" + intercept.ToString());
    Console.WriteLine("R Square is " + rsqr.ToString());
    Console.ReadLine();

}
```

The GetHistory method looks like the previous Bloomberg examples, except that it passes a Dictionary object to ProcessHistoryResponse to store the results of the request:

```
private Dictionary<DateTime, double> GetHistory
    (string security, string field, DateTime startDate)
{

    Dictionary<DateTime, double> date2value = new Dictionary<DateTime, double>();
    SessionOptions sessionOptions = new SessionOptions();
    Session session = new Session();
    bool sessionStarted = session.Start();
    if (!sessionStarted)
    {
        System.Console.Error.WriteLine("Failed to start session.");
        return null;
    }
    if (!session.OpenService("//blp/refdata"))
    {
        System.Console.Error.WriteLine("Failed to open //blp/refdata");
        return null;
    }

    Service refDataService = session.GetService("//blp/refdata");
    Request request = refDataService.CreateRequest("HistoricalDataRequest");

    Element securities = request.GetElement("securities");
    securities.AppendValue(security);
    Element fields = request.GetElement("fields");
    fields.AppendValue(field);

    request.Set("startDate", startDate.ToString("yyyyMMdd"));

    try
    {
```

```
        session.SendRequest(request, null);
    }
    catch (InvalidRequestException e)
    {
        System.Console.WriteLine(e.ToString());
    }

    bool done = false;
    while (!done)
    {
        Event eventObj = session.NextEvent();
        if (eventObj.Type == Event.EventType.PARTIAL_RESPONSE)
        {
            ProcessHistoryResponse(eventObj, date2value);
        }
        else if (eventObj.Type == Event.EventType.RESPONSE)
        {
            ProcessHistoryResponse(eventObj, date2value);
            done = true;
        }
        else
        {
            foreach (Message msg in eventObj)
            {
                System.Console.WriteLine(msg.AsElement);
                if (eventObj.Type == Event.EventType.SESSION_STATUS)
                {
                    if (msg.MessageType.Equals("SessionTerminated"))
                    {
                        done = true;
                    }
                }
            }
        }
    }
    session.Stop();
    return date2value;
}
```

Similarly, the `ProcessHistoryResponse` method is like the one used in Chapter 3, except that it populates the `Dictionary` object parameter with the dates and values from the Bloomberg request:

```
private void ProcessHistoryResponse(Event eventObj, Dictionary<DateTime, double>
date2value)
{
    foreach (Message msg in eventObj)
    {
        if (msg.HasElement(RESPONSE_ERROR))
        {
            Element error = msg.GetElement(RESPONSE_ERROR);
            Console.WriteLine("Request failed: "
```

```
            + error.GetElementAsString(CATEGORY) +
            " (" + error.GetElementAsString(MESSAGE) + ")");
            continue;
    }


    Element securityData = msg.GetElement(SECURITY_DATA);
    string security = securityData.GetElement(SECURITY).GetValueAsString();
    Console.WriteLine(security);

    Element fieldData = securityData.GetElement(FIELD_DATA);

    for (int i = 0; i < fieldData.NumValues; i++)
    {
        Element element = fieldData.GetValueAsElement(i);
        DateTime date = element.GetElementAsDatetime(DATE).ToSystemDateTime();
        double? value = null;
        for (int f = 0; f < element.NumElements; f++)
        {
            Element field = element.GetElement(f);
            if (!field.Name.Equals(DATE))
            {
                if (field.Datatype == DataType.FLOAT32)
                    value = Convert.ToDouble(field.GetValueAsFloat32());
                else if (field.Datatype == DataType.FLOAT64)
                    value = field.GetValueAsFloat64();
            }
        }
        if (value != null)
            date2value.Add(date, value.Value);
    }


    }
}
```

Peer Groups

As we did in Path 1, this section walks you through how to add a "Peer Groups" column to the Bond and Loan tables, create and populate new tables to hold summary statistics about the Bond, Loan, and Company tables, and query the summary statistics side by side with their respective securities.

The first step is to add a "PeerGroup" column to both the Bond and Loan tables in Access with the type "Short Text." Then, as described in Path 1, populate the new PeerGroup columns with the appropriate peer group for each security.

Ratings

Next, we need to incorporate Moody's RF as discussed earlier in this chapter. Begin by creating a new table called "RF" using the schema described in Table 6-3. After you've created that, populate the RF table with the contents of Table 6-1.

Table 6-3. RF table schema

Field name	Data type
Rating (Primary Key)	Short Text
Factor	Number

You can join the RF table to your Bond or Loan table by using a query like the following:

```
Select SecurityDes,MoodyRating,Factor
from Bond b
left outer join RF on RF.Rating=
iif(instr(b.MoodyRating," ")>0,left(b.MoodyRating,instr(b.MoodyRating," ")-1),
b.MoodyRating)
```

This query selects the description, Moody's rating, and the Moody's rating factor for each bond in the Bond table. The `iif` function is used in the join argument to remove any rating watch information from the MoodyRating column.

Stats Tables

This section covers creating and populating tables with aggregate statistics about each peer group. First, we need to create tables to store the different aggregate statistics such as median, mean, and standard deviation. Begin by creating a new table called "MedianBondStats" using the schema in Table 6-4. You can add more columns to this table that you want to aggregate, but they should have exactly the same name and case as those in the Bond table.

Table 6-4. MedianBondStats table schema

Field name	Data type
PeerGroup (Primary Key)	Short Text
Count	Number
PxChgYTD	Number (Field Size Double)
PxChg3M	Number (Field Size Double)
YASSpread	Number (Field Size Double)
YASYield	Number (Field Size Double)
FixedCpn	Number (Field Size Double)
MonthsUntilMaturity	Number (Field Size Double)
RF	Number

Next, copy and paste this table twice, creating identical tables called "MeanBondStats" and "StdevBondStats."

Repeat these steps to create MedianLoanStats, MeanLoanStats, and StdevLoanStats tables using the schema from Table 6-5.

Table 6-5. MedianLoanStats table schema

Field name	Data type
PeerGroup (Primary Key)	Short Text
Count	Number
PxChgYTD	Number (Field Size Double)
PxChg3M	Number (Field Size Double)
DM	Number (Field Size Double)
Yield	Number (Field Size Double)
Margin	Number (Field Size Double)
MonthsUntilMaturity	Number (Field Size Double)
RF	Number

Repeat these steps once more to create MedianCompanyStats, MeanCompanyStats, and StdevCompanyStats using the schema from Table 6-6.

Table 6-6. MedianCompanyStats table schema

Field name	Data type
Category (Primary Key)	Short Text
Count	Number
MarketCap	Number (Field Size Double)
TotalDebt	Number (Field Size Double)
TotalDebtToEBITDA	Number (Field Size Double)
NetDebtToEBITDA	Number (Field Size Double)
FCFToTotalDebt	Number (Field Size Double)
YrHi	Number (Field Size Double)
YrLow	Number (Field Size Double)
PxChgYTD	Number (Field Size Double)
PxChg3M	Number (Field Size Double)
TotalReturn12M	Number (Field Size Double)

Next, create a new C# console application that will populate these tables. The code that follows loops through the Bond, Loan, and Company tables categorizing the data into lists by Peer Group (or Category for Company table) and column name. Then, it aggregates the lists by median, average (mean), and standard deviation. Finally, it inserts or updates the median, mean, and standard deviation tables with the aggregated statistics.

Like earlier code sets that connect to our Access database, start the program by declaring a connection string, and calling the `Program` class's `Run` method in the `Main` function:

```
private string ConnStr =
"Provider=Microsoft.ACE.OLEDB.12.0;Data Source=..\\..\\Path 3.accdb";
static void Main(string[] args)
{
    Program p = new Program();
    p.Run();
}
```

Next, define the `Run` method and call a `ProcessTable` method, passing as arguments the name of the table and the column by which to group. The `ProcessTable` method returns the number of rows updated in the median, average, and standard deviation tables.

```
public void Run()
{
    int rowc = 0;
    rowc += ProcessTable("Bond", "PeerGroup");
    rowc += ProcessTable("Loan", "PeerGroup");
    rowc += ProcessTable("Company", "Category");

    Console.WriteLine(rowc + " rows updated");
}
```

The `ProcessTable` method takes all of the data from a table (table parameter), groups the data together by the PeerGroup column (or Category column for the Company table), calculates the median, mean, and standard deviation of the values, and stores those statistics in the MedianStats, MeanStats, and StdevStats tables (such as Median-BondStats).

The `ProcessTable` method starts by defining the name of the aggregate tables and populates them from the database by calling `FillDataSet`. The `FillDataSet` method, defined later, populates the `DataSet` object with the contents of each of the tables passed as arguments. In addition, it excludes rows that are missing a Peer Group or Category and adds the RF and MonthsUntilMaturity columns when appropriate using SQL.

Next, the `ProcessTable` method passes the dataset, names of the tables, and column to group by to the `CategorizeData` method (defined later), that will return a multidimensional array, breaking the table's data down by Peer Group (or Category for the Company table) and column name.

The variable `peergroup2column2values` has a complicated type declaration, so let's break it down. This object contains a list of Peer Groups, and for each Peer Group, it contains a list of column names, and for each combination of Peer Group and column name, the object contains a list of values in the database. In other words, it allows you to reference all of the YASSpread double values for the Peer Group "Short CCC" by iterating through peergroup2column2values["Short CCC"]["YAS Spread"].

Next, the ProcessTable method iterates through the list of Peer Groups, referencing the existing rows in the median, mean, and standard deviation tables for that Peer Group, and, if the row doesn't exist, it creates it.

Then, the method iterates through the list of columns associated with the Peer Group, and calculates the median, standard deviation, mean, and count for the values in our Dictionary object. Finally, the method sets the corresponding values in the appropriate rows and updates the dataset using the UpdateDataSet method (defined later).

Let's see how this looks in code:

```
public int ProcessTable(string table, string groupBy)
{
    string mediantable = "Median" + table + "Stats";
    string meantable = "Mean" + table + "Stats";
    string stdevtable = "Stdev" + table + "Stats";

    //Get data for table, median, mean, and stddev tables
    // from the Access database
    DataSet ds = FillDataSet(table, mediantable, meantable, stdevtable);

    // This Data structure will hold a Dictionary
    // of Peer Groups -> Column -> Values
    // For instance, to get all of the Price values for the Tech peer group
    // you would iterate through the
    // Double List peergroup2column2values["Tech"]["Price"]
    Dictionary<string, Dictionary<string, List<double>>> peergroup2column2values =
    CategorizeData(ds, table, mediantable, groupBy);

    foreach (string peergroup in peergroup2column2values.Keys)
    {
        DataRow medianRow = null;
        DataRow meanRow = null;
        DataRow stdDevRow = null;

        //Find the rows for this Peer Group in the median, mean, and stdDev tables
        medianRow =
        ds.Tables[mediantable].AsEnumerable().
        SingleOrDefault(x => x.Field<string>(groupBy) == peergroup);
        meanRow =
        ds.Tables[meantable].AsEnumerable().
        SingleOrDefault(x => x.Field<string>(groupBy) == peergroup);
        stdDevRow =
        ds.Tables[stdevtable].AsEnumerable().
        SingleOrDefault(x => x.Field<string>(groupBy) == peergroup);

        //If they couldn't be found, add them.
```

```csharp
        if (medianRow == null)
        {
            medianRow = ds.Tables[mediantable].NewRow();
            medianRow[groupBy] = peergroup;
            ds.Tables[mediantable].Rows.Add(medianRow);
        }

        if (meanRow == null)
        {
            meanRow = ds.Tables[meantable].NewRow();
            meanRow[groupBy] = peergroup;
            ds.Tables[meantable].Rows.Add(meanRow);
        }

        if (stdDevRow == null)
        {
            stdDevRow = ds.Tables[stdevtable].NewRow();
            stdDevRow[groupBy] = peergroup;
            ds.Tables[stdevtable].Rows.Add(stdDevRow);
        }

        foreach (string column in peergroup2column2values[peergroup].Keys)
        {
            // For each column in each peer group, calculate the
            // median, stddev, mean, and count.
            double median = GetMedian(peergroup2column2values[peergroup][column]);
            double stddev =
            GetStandardDev(peergroup2column2values[peergroup][column]);
            double mean = peergroup2column2values[peergroup][column].Average();
            int count = peergroup2column2values[peergroup][column].Count;

            // put the statistics in their correct tables
            meanRow[column] = mean;
            medianRow[column] = median;
            if (Double.IsNaN(stddev))
                stdDevRow[column] = DBNull.Value;
            else
                stdDevRow[column] = stddev;

            meanRow["Count"] = count;
            medianRow["Count"] = count;
            stdDevRow["Count"] = count;
        }
    }

    int rowc = UpdateDataSet(ds, mediantable, meantable, stdevtable);
    return rowc;

}
```

The `CategorizeData` method groups a table's data by its Peer Group and column name and returns the data to the `ProcessTable` method. It includes only columns that also exist in the corresponding MedianStats table.

The `CategorizeData` method also adds a "Total" PeerGroup to the `Dictonary` object that will aggregate all the values for each Peer Group. This makes it possible for you to view the median, average, and standard deviation of all the values across all Peer Groups:

```
private Dictionary<string, Dictionary<string,
List<double>>> CategorizeData(
DataSet ds, string table, string mediantable, string groupBy)
{
    //Create an instance of the data structure
    Dictionary<string, Dictionary<string, List<double>>> peergroup2column2values
    = new Dictionary<string, Dictionary<string, List<double>>>();
    // Add a Total peer group
    peergroup2column2values.Add("Total", new Dictionary<string, List<double>>());

    foreach (DataRow row in ds.Tables[table].Rows)
    {
        //Get the PeerGroup value from each row
        // (or category for Company table)
        string peergroup = (string)row[groupBy];
        foreach (DataColumn dc in ds.Tables[table].Columns)
        {
            // Loop through each column
            // If the column also exists in the MedianTable
            // add it to the peergroup2column2values dictionary
            string columnName = dc.ColumnName;
            if (
                ds.Tables[mediantable].Columns.Contains(columnName)
                && row.IsNull(dc) == false
                && columnName != groupBy
                )
            {
                if (peergroup2column2values.ContainsKey(peergroup) == false)
                    peergroup2column2values.Add(peergroup,
                    new Dictionary<string, List<double>>());

                if (peergroup2column2values[peergroup].
                ContainsKey(columnName) == false)
                    peergroup2column2values[peergroup].
                    Add(columnName, new List<double>());

                if (peergroup2column2values["Total"].
                ContainsKey(columnName) == false)
                    peergroup2column2values["Total"].
                    Add(columnName, new List<double>());

                peergroup2column2values[peergroup][columnName].
```

```
            Add(Convert.ToDouble(row[dc]));
            peergroup2column2values["Total"][columnName].
            Add(Convert.ToDouble(row[dc]));

        }
      }
    }
    return peergroup2column2values;
  }
```

The next method is `FillDataSet`, which populates the `DataSet` object with the contents from the Access Database. Which query you use depends on the table being populated. The Loan and Bond table query are the same; select every column from the Bond or Loan table, including the Moody's rating factor from the RF table, and include the number of months until Maturity column using the `DATEDIFF` function. The query for the Company table is similar except there is no maturity. The other tables (the median, mean, and standard deviation tables) simply select each column:

```
private DataSet FillDataSet(params string[] tables)
{
    DataSet ds = new DataSet();
    using (OleDbConnection conn = new OleDbConnection(ConnStr))
    {
        conn.Open();
        foreach (string table in tables)
        {
            string cmdStr = null;

            switch (table.ToUpper())
            {
                case "LOAN":
                case "BOND":
                    cmdStr= "Select b.*,Factor as RF,
                    DATEDIFF(\"m\",now(),b.Maturity) as MonthsUntilMaturity";
                    cmdStr += " from " + table+ " b";
                    cmdStr += " left outer join RF on RF.Rating =
                    iif(instr(b.MoodyRating, \" \") > 0,
                    left(b.MoodyRating,
                    instr(b.MoodyRating, \" \") - 1), b.MoodyRating)";
                    cmdStr += " where b.PeerGroup is not null";
                    break;
                case "COMPANY":
                    cmdStr = "Select b.*,Factor as RF";
                    cmdStr += " from " + table + " b";
                    cmdStr += " left outer join RF on RF.Rating =
                    iif(instr(b.MoodyRating, \" \") > 0,
                    left(b.MoodyRating,
                    instr(b.MoodyRating, \" \") - 1), b.MoodyRating)";
                    cmdStr += " where b.Category is not null";
                    break;
                default:
```

```
                    cmdStr = "SELECT * FROM [" + table + "]";
                    break;
            }

            OleDbCommand cmd = new OleDbCommand(cmdStr, conn);
            OleDbDataAdapter da = new OleDbDataAdapter(cmd);
            da.Fill(ds, table);
        }
        conn.Close();
    }
    return ds;
}
```

The final three methods are the same as previous code examples:

```
private int UpdateDataSet(DataSet ds,params string[] tables)
{
    int rowc = 0;
    using (OleDbConnection conn = new OleDbConnection(ConnStr))
    {
        conn.Open();
        foreach (string table in tables)
        {
            string cmdStr = "SELECT * FROM " + table;

            OleDbCommand cmd = new OleDbCommand(cmdStr, conn);
            OleDbDataAdapter da = new OleDbDataAdapter();
            da.SelectCommand = cmd;
            OleDbCommandBuilder cb = new OleDbCommandBuilder(da);
            cb.QuotePrefix = "[";
            cb.QuoteSuffix = "]";
            da.UpdateCommand = cb.GetUpdateCommand();
            da.InsertCommand = cb.GetInsertCommand();
            da.DeleteCommand = cb.GetDeleteCommand();
            rowc += da.Update(ds, table);
        }
        conn.Close();
    }
    return rowc;
}

public static double GetMedian(List<double> list)
{
    double median = 0;
    if (list.Count != 0)
    {
        // create new instance of list
        // so source list isnt modified
        // List should be ordered.
        List<double> sortedList = list.OrderBy(x => x).ToList();
        int size = sortedList.Count;
        int mid = size / 2;
        if (size % 2 != 0)
```

```
                median = sortedList[mid];
            else
                median = (sortedList[mid] + sortedList[mid - 1]) / 2;
        }
        return median;
    }
    public static double GetStandardDev(List<double> list)
    {
        double stdev = 0;
        if (list.Count != 0)
        {
            double average = list.Average();
            stdev =
            Math.Sqrt((list.Sum(x => Math.Pow(x - average, 2))) / (list.Count() - 1));
        }
        return stdev;
    }
}
```

Figure 6-7 shows the resulting MedianBondStats table. As expected, the CCC groups have a median RF of 6,500, a higher spread, yield, and the YTD price change shows that these CCCs outperformed during 2016.

Figure 6-7. MedianBondStats table

Side by Side

Now that we have the aggregate statistics in our database, we can line them up against individual securities to compare each security to its peers. The following query joins the Bond table to the MedianBondStats table, alternating columns between the Bond table and the MedianBondStats table. It's ordered by PeerGroup to make it easier to see the different securities within the same group:

```
SELECT Bond.BondID, Bond.SecurityDes, Bond.PeerGroup, Bond.PxChgYTD,
MedianBondStats.PxChgYTD, Bond.PxChg3M,
MedianBondStats.PxChg3M, MedianBondStats.YASSpread, Bond.YASYield,
MedianBondStats.YASYield
FROM Bond INNER JOIN MedianBondStats
ON Bond.PeerGroup = MedianBondStats.PeerGroup
ORDER BY Bond.PeerGroup;
```

Similarly, add a column to the Company table called "IndexID" and populate it with
the IndexID from the Index table that corresponds to a relevant index for that company. The following query returns each company and alternates between that company's performance metric and its corresponding index's performance metric:

```
SELECT Company.CompanyName, Index.IndexName, Company.Price, Index.Price,
Company.YrHi, Index.YrHi, Company.YrLow, Index.YrLow, Company.PxChgYTD,
Index.PxChgYTD, Company.PxChg3M, Index.PxChg3M, Company.TotalReturn12M,
Index.TotalReturn12M
FROM Company INNER JOIN [Index] ON Company.IndexID = Index.IndexID;
```

Weighted Z-Score

To add a weighted z-score to your analysis, begin by creating a table to store the different weightings. For example, Table 6-7 contains the schema for BondZWeights that
will contain the z-score weightings for the Bond table. This table contains only one
row and does not require a Primary Key.

Table 6-7. BondZWeights schema

Field name	Data type
PxChgYTD	Number (Field Size Double)
PxChg3M	Number (Field Size Double)
YASSpread	Number (Field Size Double)
YASYield	Number (Field Size Double)
FixedCpn	Number (Field Size Double)
MonthsUntilMaturity	Number (Field Size Double)
RF	Number (Field Size Double)

Populate this table with percentage weights that add up to 100 percent. The higher the
value, the bigger the impact that field will have on the z-score. After the weights are in
the database, you have all the necessary numbers to calculate the z-score in a query:

```
SELECT
b.BBID,
b.SecurityDes,
b.PxChgYTD,
b.PxChg3M,
b.YASSpread,
b.YASYield,
b.FixedCpn,
```

```
(select Factor from RF where RF.Rating=
iif(instr(b.MoodyRating, " ") > 0,
left(b.MoodyRating, instr(b.MoodyRating, " ") - 1),
b.MoodyRating))  as RatingFactor,
DATEDIFF("m",now(),b.Maturity) as MonthsTilMaturity,

((b.PxChgYTD-mean.PxChgYTD)/sd.PxChgYTD*z.PxChgYTD)
+((b.PxChg3M-mean.PxChg3M)/sd.PxChg3M*z.PxChg3M)
+((b.YASSpread-mean.YASSpread)/sd.YASSpread*z.YASSpread)
+((b.YASYield-mean.YASYield)/sd.YASYield*z.YASYield)
+((b.FixedCpn-mean.FixedCpn)/sd.FixedCpn*z.FixedCpn)
-(((select Factor from RF where RF.Rating=
iif(instr(b.MoodyRating, " ") > 0,
left(b.MoodyRating, instr(b.MoodyRating, " ") - 1),
b.MoodyRating))-mean.RF)/sd.RF*z.RF)
-((DATEDIFF("m",now(),b.Maturity)-mean.MonthsUntilMaturity)/
sd.MonthsUntilMaturity*z.MonthsUntilMaturity) AS WeightedZScore

FROM Bond AS b, MeanBondStats AS mean, StdevBondStats AS sd, BondZWeights AS z
WHERE mean.PeerGroup='Total' and sd.PeerGroup='Total';
```

This query returns each bond, along with the metrics included in the z-score, and a calculation of the z-score using the "Total" PeerGroup from the MeanBondStats and StdevBondStats weighted by the weights in the BondZWeights table.

Summary

This chapter presented the tools and techniques to take financial data about a security and compare it to its peers and the broader market to determine its relative value. Using your insight to assign appropriate Peer Groups and z-score weights will take your analysis from a simple data dump to a valuable tool for finding new investments and evaluating existing ones. Additionally, being mindful of the correlation between securities is helpful for portfolio construction and hedging. Chapter 7 examines risk analysis and covers comparing securities within a portfolio instead of to other potential investments.

Portfolio Risk Analysis

Everyone has a plan 'til they get punched in the mouth.
—Mike Tyson

This chapter covers three different techniques for measuring the risk and return of a portfolio of investments. First, we examine measuring risk by calculating the variance and standard deviation of a portfolio. Though this calculation might be complicated and requires matrix multiplication of correlation coefficients, it is a useful way to measure risk and the benefits of diversification. Moreover, you can use the portfolio standard deviation combined with expected return to calculate the portfolio's *Sharpe Ratio*. The Sharpe Ratio is a traditional method for measuring the risk-adjusted return of a portfolio.

The second, and easier, technique to measure risk is breaking down the individual positions into different "buckets." This technique can be useful in highlighting unseen concentrations and trends. For instance, by grouping positions into buckets by maturity, you can quickly determine the percentage of the portfolio that has near-term maturities. Some characteristics, such as ratings, might not be the focus of your investment decisions but can affect liquidity and price volatility.

The final technique is to establish thresholds for different metrics that can be easily monitored for breaches. For instance, this approach demonstrates how to highlight positions for which the price has moved significantly or is currently at the end of the 52-week range. It can also highlight positions for which a loan's call protection is ending or a bond's maturity is near and its market price is indicating a potential default.

As with the discussion of Relative Value in Chapter 6, the explanation of these techniques and their purpose will be detailed in the Microsoft Excel section (Path 1), whereas the Microsoft Access and C# sections (Paths 2 and 3) will contain only details on implementation. I recommend that you read the first section on Excel.

Path 1: Excel

This section covers the Excel implementation, If you're following Path 2, all the techniques should be implemented in Excel, as shown in this section, and will be accessible in Access through the linked tables.

Variance, Volatility, and Standard Deviation

Before diving into the complicated calculations, it is important to understand a few terms. In the financial world, both *variance* and *standard deviation* are measurements of *volatility* and risk. Standard deviation and variance are related terms; in fact, standard deviation is simply the square root of variance. A portfolio's variance is a function of the individual position's size relative to the portfolio size (or "weight"), the standard deviation (volatility) of the position's historical returns, and the correlation (or covariance) between each position in the portfolio. Incorporating the correlation among positions is important because it measures the benefits of diversification. Without getting into too much math, we are going to measure the risk of our portfolio by calculating the standard deviation.

When most people talk about the standard deviation of a portfolio, they are generally referring to the standard deviation of historical returns. Calculating the standard deviation of historical portfolio returns measures the volatility of those historical returns. The focus of this chapter is understanding current risk of a portfolio as it is today by calculating its current standard deviation. Complicating things a bit more, the calculation for the current standard deviation uses the historical standard deviation for each underlying position.

Unfortunately, calculating standard deviation of a portfolio is not simple and requires several steps. The first set of steps creates a table that summarizes the data returned from Bloomberg:

1. Create a new worksheet titled **PortfolioStats**.

   This worksheet will use the Bloomberg BDH function to pull down the historical monthly prices for each position, calculate annualized returns and standard deviations, and produce a summary table including the expected return, standard deviation, and Sharpe Ratio for the portfolio.

2. On the PortfolioStats worksheet, enter **Start Date** and **End Date** into cells A1 and A2. In cells B1 and B2, enter the starting and ending dates for the price history. For example, set B1 to **1/31/1990**, and B2 to **1/16/2017**.

3. Across row 6, starting in cell A6 and ending in cell H6, enter the labels **Posi tionID**, **BBID**, **Historical Return**, **StdDev**, **Weight**, **WtdStd**, **Forecasted Return**, and **Return**.

4. Starting in cell A7, under the PositionID heading that was created in the previous step, enter numbers, starting at **1** and ending with the highest PositionID from the Positions worksheet, down sequential rows. For instance, cell A7 should contain **1**, cell A8 should contain **2**, and so on.

5. In cell B7 (under the BBID column header), enter the following formula and copy it down to the last row used in step 4:

```
=IFERROR(INDEX(Portfolio[BBID],MATCH(A7,Portfolio[PositionID],0)),"")
```

This formula pulls the Bloomberg ID (BBID) from the Portfolio worksheet where the PositionID (in column A) matches the PositionID from the Position Excel table.

Figure 7-5 shows the final version, which might help make sense of the formulas shown in steps 1 through 5. The next steps pull the necessary information from Bloomberg used to populate the summary table created in the previous three steps.

6. In cell J2, enter the following formula:

```
=VLOOKUP(ROUNDDOWN(COLUMN()/6,0),$A:$B,2,FALSE)
```

This formula uses the column number to pull the BBID from column B. For instance, because column J is the 10th column, and 10 divided by 6, rounded down, equals 1, it will pull the first position. Likewise, the next position history will be in column P, which is the 16th column, which will result in the second position (16 divided by 6, rounded down, equals 2).

7. Place the following formula in cell J3:

```
=BDH(J2,"px_last",$B$1,$B$2,"PER=CM")
```

This formula will populate columns J and K with monthly historical prices for BBID retrieved in step 6 using the start and end date from step 2.

8. In cell L4, enter the following formula and copy it down to L500:

```
=IF(K4>0,(K4-K3)/K3,"")
```

This formula simply calculates the monthly change in price. If historical price isn't in column K, it will display an empty cell. It is still important that this is copied down 500 rows or more (if you used an earlier start date), even if the history for this security doesn't go back that far because this formula will be copied and used on other securities that might have a longer history.

9. In sequential rows, starting in cell M4 and ending in cell M10, enter the following labels: **Starting Price**, **Ending Price**, **Day Count**, **Return**, **Annualized Return**, **Standard Deviation**, and **Annualized Standard Deviation**.

10. In cell N4, enter the following formula:

    `=VLOOKUP(MIN(J:J),J:K,2,FALSE)`

    This formula returns the starting price by using the minimum date in a VLOOKUP. Column J contains the historical dates.

11. In cell N5, enter the following formula:

    `=VLOOKUP(MAX(J:J),J:K,2,FALSE)`

    Similarly, this returns the ending price by using the maximum date in a VLOOKUP.

12. In cell N6, enter the following formula:

    `=MAX(J:J)-MIN(J:J)`

    This formula calculates the number of days between the starting date and ending date (which might differ from the start date and end date entered in step 2 because not every security goes back to 1990 or the start date you used).

13. In cell N7, enter the following formula:

    `=(N5-N4)/N4`

    This formula calculates the return between the starting price and ending price.

14. In cell N8, enter the following formula:

    `=(1+N7)^(365/N6)-1`

    This is the formula to annualize a return number.

15. In cell N9, enter the following formula:

    `=STDEV(L:L)`

    This formula returns the standard deviation of the monthly price changes.

16. In cell N10, enter the following formula:

    `=N9*SQRT(12)`

    This annualizes the standard deviation from step 15.

17. Copy columns J through N and paste it into cell P1. Repeat this step, copying all five columns, and pasting them to the right after skipping a column. The five columns (J through N) should be pasted into column P, V, AB, AH, and so on until each position is displayed.

    Because the formula in cell J2 uses the column number to return the corresponding BBID, you can copy and paste the five columns and they should automatically display the next corresponding BBID.

After you complete steps 6 through 17, your worksheet should look like that shown in Figure 7-1.

J	K	L	M	N	O	P	Q	R
1								
2 FDC US Equity					DBD US Equity			
3 10/30/2015	15.84					1/31/1990	8.52	
4 11/30/2015	16.80	6.06%	Starting Price	15.84		2/28/1990	8.79	3.19% Starting
5 12/31/2015	16.02	-4.64%	Ending Price	15.62		3/30/1990	9.01	2.53% Ending
6 1/29/2016	13.37	-16.54%	Day Count	546.00		4/30/1990	8.02	-10.96% Day Ci
7 2/29/2016	12.50	-6.51%	Return	-1.39%		5/31/1990	8.67	8.00% Return
8 3/31/2016	12.94	3.52%	Annualized Return	-0.93%		6/29/1990	8.72	0.57% Annua
9 4/29/2016	11.39	-11.98%	Standard Deviation	8.60%		7/31/1990	8.99	3.12% Stand.
10 5/31/2016	12.53	10.01%	Annualized Standard Deviat	29.79%		8/31/1990	7.14	-20.60% Annua
11 6/30/2016	11.07	-11.65%				9/28/1990	7.16	0.35%
12 7/29/2016	12.40	12.01%				10/31/1990	6.12	-14.48%
13 8/31/2016	13.92	12.26%				11/30/1990	6.96	13.71%
14 9/30/2016	13.16	-5.46%				12/31/1990	6.91	-0.71%
15 10/31/2016	13.99	6.31%				1/31/1991	7.56	9.29%
16 11/30/2016	14.57	4.15%				2/28/1991	7.56	0.00%
17 12/30/2016	14.19	-2.61%				3/28/1991	7.60	0.65%
18 1/31/2017	15.34	8.10%				4/30/1991	7.80	2.60%
19 2/28/2017	16.10	4.95%				5/31/1991	8.32	6.65%
20 3/31/2017	15.50	-3.73%				6/28/1991	7.90	-5.05%

Portfolio Correlation | PortfolioScenarios | **PortfolioStats** | Ret ...

Ready   55%

Figure 7-1. PortfolioStats worksheet

Now that the historical data from Bloomberg is retrieved and each position's annualized return and standard deviation are calculated, follow the next steps to put them into the summary table.

18. In cell C7, enter the following formula and copy it down to the last row used in column A:

    `=IF(B7="","",OFFSET($N$8,0,(A7-1)*6))`

    Like the formula in J2, this formula uses the Position ID to determine the location of the Annualized Return number for each position. The OFFSET function is defined in more detail in step 28.

19. In cell D7, enter the following formula and copy it down to the last row used in column A:

    `=IF(B7="","",OFFSET($N$10,0,(A7-1)*6))`

    Similarly, this formula is used to retrieve the Annualized Standard Deviation of each position using its Position ID to reference the appropriate column. For example, when Position ID in column A is two (in cell A8), (A8-1)*6 will equal six and the OFFSET function will look at the column N plus six columns to the right, which is the location of the second position's calculation results.

20. In cell E7, enter the following formula and copy it down to the last row used in column A:

```
=IFERROR(INDEX(Portfolio[% Of Portfolio],
MATCH(A7,Portfolio[PositionID],0)),"")
```

Like the formula used to retrieve the BBID, this formula returns the Weight (or percentage of total market value) this position represents of the entire portfolio from the Excel Position table.

21. In cell F7, enter the following formula and copy it down to the last row used in column A:

    ```
    =IF(E7<>"",E7*D7,"")
    ```

    This simply weights the standard deviation by the market value of the position.

    Now that we have a table (starting in cell C6) containing the standard deviations of historical returns for each position in the portfolio, we need to calculate the correlation between each position. It is a lot cleaner if we create the correlation matrix in another worksheet.

22. Create a worksheet called **Portfolio Correlation**.

23. In column A, starting in row 3 (cell A3), enter numbers, starting at 1 and ending with the highest PositionID from the Positions worksheet, down sequential rows. For instance, cell A4 should contain the number 2, and cell A5 should contain the number 3, and so on.

24. Like step 23, enter PositionID numbers across columns starting by putting the number 1 in cell C1 and the number 2 in cell D1, and so on.

25. In cell B3, enter the following formula and copy it down to the last row with a PositionID:

    ```
    =IFERROR(VLOOKUP(A3,PortfolioStats!A:B,2,FALSE),"")
    ```

    This formula will pull the BBID from the PortfolioStats worksheet for the PositionID in column A.

26. In cell C2, enter the following formula and copy it across columns to the last column with a PositionID:

    ```
    =IFERROR(VLOOKUP(C1,PortfolioStats!$A:$B,2,FALSE),"")
    ```

    Like step 25, this formula pulls the BBID from PortfolioStats worksheet for the PositionID in row 1. The result of steps 25 and 26 should be a matrix of positions in the portfolio with the Bloomberg IDs (BBIDs) across the top and the left side.

27. In cell B2, enter a date that will be used as the starting date for calculating the correlation between the positions that intersect at each cell in the matrix.

    Each cell in the matrix will contain the correlation between the two securities (BBIDs) that intersect at that cell. For instance, cell D4 will contain the correlation between the security listed in cell D2 and the security listed in B4. The correlation calculation, in step 28, will use the historical return data from the

PortfolioStats worksheet for both securities. Therefore, it is important that the date placed in cell B2 exists in the historical returns for every security in the portfolio.

28. In cell C3, enter the following formula and copy it across columns and down rows such that it is in every cell that has a corresponding BBID in row 2 and column B:

```
=IF(AND($B3<>"",C$2<>""),
CORREL(OFFSET(PortfolioStats!$A:$A,
MATCH($B$2,OFFSET(PortfolioStats!$A:$A,0,(6*C$1)+3),0)-1,(6*C$1)+5,10,1),
OFFSET(PortfolioStats!$A:$A,MATCH($B$2,
OFFSET(PortfolioStats!$A:$A,0,(6*$A3)+3),0)-1,(6*$A3)+5,10,1)),"")
```

This is a complicated formula, so let's break it down.

1. If BBIDs don't exist in row header and column header, display a blank cell.

2. CORREL is the correlation function. It takes two arrays of historical price changes. The function uses the OFFSET and MATCH functions to find the correct array for the PositionIDs found in the column and row headers.

3. The first argument to the CORREL function is:

```
OFFSET(PortfolioStats!$A:$A,
MATCH($B$2,OFFSET(PortfolioStats!$A:$A,0,(6*C$1)+3),0)-1,(6*C$1)+5,10,1)
```

4. The OFFSET function takes three parameters: the first is a starting point (in this case the entire first column of the PortfolioStats worksheet); the second argument is the number of rows to move down; and the last is the number of columns to move over. The last argument is calculated using the same technique from PortfolioStats to determine a value at a fixed location based on the PositionID.

5. To figure out the number of rows to move down (the second argument to the OFFSET function), we use the MATCH function:

```
MATCH($B$2,OFFSET(PortfolioStats!$A:$A,0,(6*C$1)+3),0)
```

6. The MATCH function is used to tell the outer OFFSET function the number of rows to move down to find the starting correlation date (entered in cell B2, step 27). The MATCH function takes three parameters: the date to look up (cell B2), the array to look through, and a type (which is zero).

7. To figure out the array to look through for the date, the formula uses another OFFSET function that returns the date column for the given PositionID.

8. The second function to the CORREL function is the same as the first, except the inner functions reference the PositionID for the given row instead of the given column.

The resulting matrix containing the correlation between each security should look like Figure 7-2 (here, we added conditional formatting).

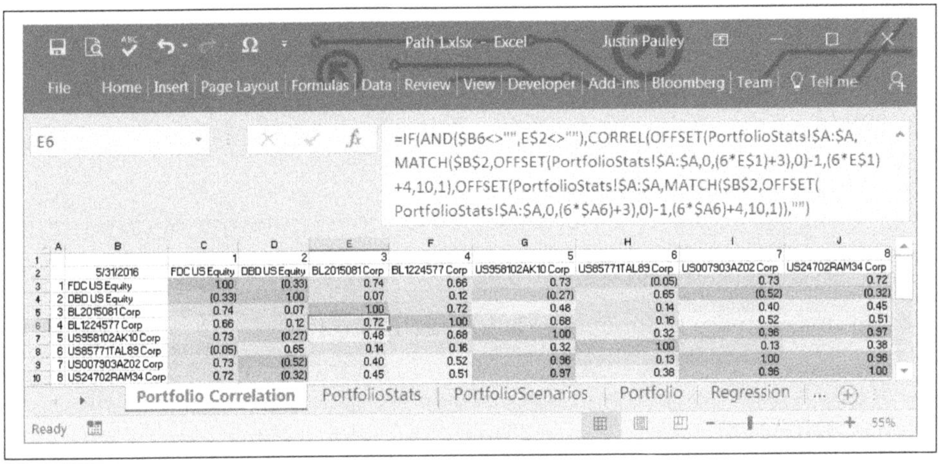

Figure 7-2. Portfolio correlation matrix

With the portfolio correlation matrix complete, the next step is to calculate the portfolio's standard deviation. Remember that the portfolio's standard deviation is the square root of its variance, which is a function of each position's weight, standard deviation of historical returns, and correlation to every other position. The actual formula for variance is shown in Figure 7-3. Without getting too deep in the math, we are going to use MMULT function to do the matrix multiplication between the WtdStd column on the table in PortfolioStats worksheet with the correlation matrix on the Portfolio Correlation worksheet.

$$
Variance = \begin{bmatrix} w_1\sigma_1 & \cdots & w_n\sigma_n \end{bmatrix} \times \begin{bmatrix} 1 & \rho_{12} & \cdots & \rho_{1n} \\ \rho_{21} & 1 & \cdots & \rho_{2n} \\ \vdots & \vdots & \ddots & \vdots \\ \rho_{n1} & \cdots & \cdots & 1 \end{bmatrix} \times \begin{bmatrix} w_1\sigma_1 \\ \vdots \\ w_n\sigma_n \end{bmatrix}
$$

$$w_n\sigma_n = position\ weight\ x\ position\ standard\ deviation$$
$$\rho_{12} = correlation\ between\ position\ one\ and\ two$$

Figure 7-3. Formula for variance

29. On the PortfolioStats worksheet, in cell D1, add the label **StdDev**.

30. In cell E1, enter the following formula:

```
=SQRT(MMULT(MMULT(TRANSPOSE(F7:F14),'Portfolio Correlation'!C3:J10),
PortfolioStats!F7:F14))
```

This formula uses matrix multiplication to calculate variance by multiplying the weighted standard deviations in the WtdStd column (transposed) by the correlation matrix and then multiplying by the weighted standard deviations again (not transposed). The formula takes the square root of the resulting variance to return the standard deviation.

The resulting standard deviation can be used to determine how much adding or removing a position increases or decreases the risk of your portfolio (higher standard deviation means higher risk) as well as to compare the risk of the portfolio over time or against other portfolios.

Sharpe Ratio with Historical or Forecasted Returns

The *Sharpe Ratio*, developed by Nobel laureate William F. Sharpe, measures the risk-adjusted return of a portfolio. Essentially, the Sharpe Ratio informs as to whether the returns from a portfolio are coming from additional risk or better investments. A higher Sharpe Ratio means the portfolio is earning a higher return with less risk. Although the standard deviation calculation (from previous section) is useful in understanding the volatility and risk of a portfolio, you can use the Sharpe Ratio to measure the volatility relative to the potential return. The formula (shown in Figure 7-4) is simply dividing the difference between the average portfolio return and the risk-free rate by the standard deviation of the portfolio; however, there are a few nuances worth discussing.

$$Sharpe\ Ratio = \frac{\bar{R}_p - R_f}{\sigma_p}$$

$$\bar{R}_p = Portfolio\ Return$$
$$R_f = Risk\ Free\ Rate$$
$$\sigma_p = Portfolio\ Standard\ Deviation$$

Figure 7-4. The formula to calculate the Sharpe Ratio

Like the note on standard deviation, the more common and simplified use of the Sharpe Ratio is calculated using historical portfolio returns (and the standard deviation of those returns) instead of expected portfolio returns and current standard deviation. Because the focus is on the current risk-adjusted return, we need to use the return and standard deviation of the current portfolio. Fortunately, we have already calculated the standard deviation in the previous section of this chapter. The risk-free rate is typically the yield on US treasury securities that should match the duration of the portfolio (equity portfolios should consider the longest treasury security). In practice, many participants use shorter rates such as three-month London Interbank Offered Rate (LIBOR).

Unfortunately, determining future returns is more difficult than using historical portfolio returns. There are few sensible approaches for coming up with the portfolio return to use in the Sharpe Ratio formula. First, especially for equities, the historical annualized returns (which were calculated in the last section, in column C of PortfolioStats worksheet) might be the only proxy for future returns (although, most certainly not a guarantee). Second, for fixed income, it might make sense to use one of the many yield calculations, such as yield-to-maturity or yield-to-worst. Finally, and most optimal, develop different scenarios and assign probabilities to calculate a probability weighted return.

The next steps are to create a worksheet to calculate probability weighted returns and the Sharpe Ratio using either historical or probability weighted returns.

31. Create a new worksheet called **PortfolioScenarios**.

32. Label cell A1 **PositionID** and list the PositionIDs sequentially down the rows in column A (cell A2 should contain 1, cell A3 should contain 2, and so on).

33. Convert the Excel range into an Excel table and name it **PortfolioScenario**.

34. Label cell B1 **Description** and place the following formula in cell B2 and copy it down to the final PositionID in column A:

    ```
    =IFERROR(INDEX(Portfolio[Description],MATCH(A2,Portfolio[PositionID],0)),"")
    ```

    This formula pulls the Description column from the Portfolio worksheet by matching the PositionID from column A to the PositionID column in the Portfolio table.

35. Label cell C1 **SecurityID** and then, in cell C2, place the following formula and copy it down to the final PositionID in column A:

    ```
    =IFERROR(INDEX(Portfolio[SecurityID],MATCH(A2,Portfolio[PositionID],0)),"")
    ```

    This formula pulls the SecurityID from the Portfolio worksheet.

36. Label cell D1 **Type** and populate the column with the following formula:

    ```
    =IFERROR(INDEX(Portfolio[Type],MATCH(A2,Portfolio[PositionID],0)),"")
    ```

37. Label cell E1 **Coupon/Margin** and populate the column with the following formula:

    ```
    =IF([@Type]="Loan",INDEX(Loan[Margin],MATCH([@SecurityID],
    Loan[LoanID],0)),IF([@Type]="Bond",INDEX(Bond[Fixed Coupon],
    MATCH([@SecurityID],Bond[BondID],0)),""))
    ```

This formula pulls the Margin column from the Loan worksheet if the security is a loan, or, if the security is a bond, it will pull the Coupon column. If the security is neither a loan nor a bond, it will return an empty cell.

38. Label cell F1 **Yield** and populate the column with the following formula:

```
=IF([@Type]="Loan",INDEX(Loan[Yield],MATCH([@SecurityID],
Loan[LoanID],0)),IF([@Type]="Bond",INDEX(Bond[YAS Yield],
MATCH([@SecurityID],Bond[BondID],0)),""))
```

Like the Coupon/Margin column, this formula will pull the Yield column for bonds or loans.

39. Label cell G1 **12M Equity Total Return** and populate the column with the following formula:

```
=IF([@Type]="Equity",INDEX(Company[12M Total Return],
MATCH([@SecurityID],Company[CompanyID],0)),"")
```

This formula pulls the 12M Total Return column for equities.

40. Label cells H1, I1, and J1: **Best Return**, **Average Return**, and **Worst Return**, respectively.

41. Using the values from columns E through G as a guide, populate columns H, I, and J manually with your best educated guess for the best, average, and worst case returns for each position.

For instance, in a best-case scenario an equity position might return 30 percent whereas a loan trading at par without call protection may have very little upside.

42. Label cells K, L, and M as **Best Probability**, **Average Probability**, and **Worst Probability**, respectively.

43. Populate columns K, L, and M manually with your best educated guess for the probabilities for best-, average-, and worst-case outcomes. The sum of columns K, L, and M should equal 100 percent.

44. Label cell N1 **Forecasted Return** and populate the column with the following formula:

```
=[@[Best Return]]*[@[Best Probability]]+
[@[Average Return]]*[@[Average Probability]]+
[@[Worst Return]]*[@[Worst Probability]]
```

This formula returns a probability weighted return based on the potential outcomes and probabilities provided in columns H through M.

The resulting PortfolioScenarios worksheet containing the forecasted return should look like Figure 7-5.

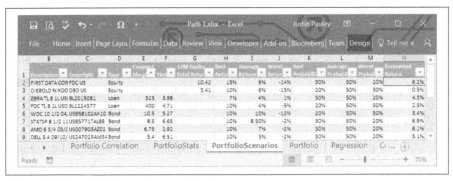

Figure 7-5. PortfolioScenarios worksheet

Now that we've calculated our forecasted returns, we can incorporate them back into the PortfolioStats worksheet and calculate the Sharpe Ratio.

45. On the PortfolioStats worksheet, in cell A3, enter the label **Risk Free Rate** and place the following formula in cell B3:

    ```
    =BDP("CT10 Govt","ASK_YIELD")/100
    ```

This formula retrieves the current yield on the current 10-year US Treasury note. You can replace this formula with any value you want to use as the risk-free rate for your portfolio. It should have similar duration to your positions.

46. Label cell A4 **Use Forecasted** and in cell B4 enter **TRUE**.

This cell will be used to toggle between using historical or forecasted returns in the Sharpe Ratio.

47. On the PortfolioStats worksheet, in cell G7, under the header Forecasted Return place the following formula and copy it down:

    ```
    =IFERROR(INDEX(PortfolioScenario[Forecasted Return],
    MATCH(A7,PortfolioScenario[PositionID],0)),"")
    ```

This formula uses the PositionID to retrieve the Forecasted Return from the PortfolioScenarios worksheet.

48. Under the Return header, in cell H7, enter the following formula and copy it down:

    ```
    =IF($B$4=TRUE,G7,C7)
    ```

This column will contain either the values from the Historical Return column or the Forecasted Return column depending on the value in cell B4.

49. Label cell D2 **Return** and enter the following formula in cell E2:

    `=SUMPRODUCT(H7:H45,E7:E45)` (if you have more than 45 rows, adjust the formula).

This formula returns the weighted average return of the portfolio using either historical or forecasted returns based on the value in cell B4.

50. Label cell D3 **Sharpe Ratio** and enter the following formula in cell E3 to calculate the Sharpe Ratio:

    ```
    =(E2-B3)/E1
    ```

As a rule of thumb, a Sharpe Ratio of one is good, two is very good, and three is excellent. However, Sharpe Ratios make more sense in relative terms, when either comparing different portfolios, or making changes to positions in a single portfolio. As such, it can be a powerful tool for testing hypothetical trades. The Sharpe Ratio should not be the only technique used to determine if one investment is better than another; it is merely a data point in an overall investment analysis. Furthermore, the Sharpe Ratio works best with normally distributed returns and is also influenced by the various inputs into its calculation including the period used for the underlying position returns. Figure 7-6 shows the resulting table on the PortfolioStats worksheet.

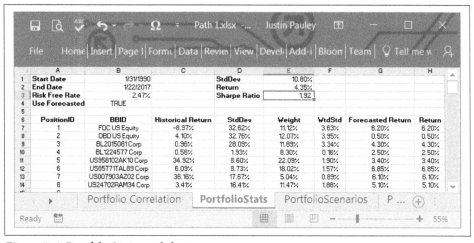

Figure 7-6. PortfolioStats worksheet

Portfolio Breakdown

This section covers techniques to breakdown the positions within a portfolio into multiple categories or "buckets." Deconstructing the portfolio can highlight risks that would be otherwise difficult to see by looking at each position individually. For instance, without aggregating the portfolio, you might not notice an overweight sector, the percent of the portfolio that loses its call protection in the next six months, the amount of CCC rated positions, and so on. This section also discusses categorizing financial data into ranges, such as price, market capitalization, and by months until maturity. Although this section provides many examples, an important part of financial analysis is developing your own view on how financial information, specifically risk metrics, are viewed.

The following steps enhance the Portfolio worksheet by pulling additional details from the relevant Bond, Loan, and Company worksheets. It is then a lot easier to summarize data from one table rather than pulling from multiple worksheets. Take note of the established pattern of pulling all security-level information into each of the Bond, Loan, and Company worksheets, performing all calculations on those respective worksheets, and then pulling the resulting columns into the Portfolio worksheet. The next part of the pattern will be summarizing the data from the Portfolio worksheet.

The first set of columns apply more to fixed income (bond and loan) securities; equity columns will come in the next group of steps.

1. Add a column to the Portfolio table on the Portfolio worksheet called "Months Until Maturity" and populate the column with the following formula:

    ```
    =IF([@Type]="Loan",INDEX(Loan[Months Until Maturity],
    MATCH([@SecurityID],Loan[LoanID],0)),
    IF([@Type]="Bond",INDEX(Bond[Months Until Maturity],
    MATCH([@SecurityID],Bond[BondID],0)),""))
    ```

    This formula pulls the data from the Months Until Maturity column from the Loan or Bond worksheets, depending on the Type column in the Portfolio worksheet. Equity securities do not have maturity dates and will display a blank cell.

2. Add another column called **Coupon Type**, and then enter the following formula:

    ```
    =IF([@Type]="Loan",INDEX(Loan[Coupon Type],
    MATCH([@SecurityID],Loan[LoanID],0)),IF([@Type]="Bond",
    INDEX(Bond[Coupon Type],MATCH([@SecurityID],Bond[BondID],0)),""))
    ```

    This formula pulls the Coupon Type (fixed or floating) from the Bond and Loan tables. Equity securities do not have coupons and will display a blank cell.

3. Add another column called **Coupon/Margin**, and then enter the following formula:

    ```
    =IF([@Type]="Loan",INDEX(Loan[Margin],MATCH([@SecurityID],
    Loan[LoanID],0)),IF([@Type]="Bond",INDEX(Bond[Fixed Coupon],
    MATCH([@SecurityID],Bond[BondID],0)),""))
    ```

    This formula pulls either the Margin column from the Loan worksheet or the Coupon from the Bond worksheet.

4. Add another column called **Yield**, and then enter the following formula:

    ```
    =IF([@Type]="Loan",INDEX(Loan[Yield],MATCH([@SecurityID],Loan[LoanID],0)),
    IF([@Type]="Bond",INDEX(Bond[YAS Yield],MATCH([@SecurityID],
    Bond[BondID],0)),""))
    ```

This formula pulls the Yield column on loans, YAS Yield for bonds, and empty cell for equities.

5. Add another column called **Callable Ever**, and then enter the following formula:

```
=IF([@Type]="Loan",INDEX(Loan[Callable?],MATCH([@SecurityID],
Loan[LoanID],0)),
IF([@Type]="Bond",INDEX(Bond[Callable?],MATCH([@SecurityID],
Bond[BondID],0)),""))
```

This formula returns the "Y" or "N" from the "Callable?" columns on the Bond and Loan tables that indicates if the security can ever be optionally prepaid before the maturity date.

6. Add another column called **Callable Now**, and then enter the following formula:

```
=IF([@Type]="Loan",IFERROR(INDEX(Loan[Next Call Date],MATCH([@SecurityID],
Loan[LoanID],0))<= TODAY(),FALSE),IF([@Type]="Bond",
IFERROR(INDEX(Bond[Next Call Date],MATCH([@SecurityID],
Bond[BondID],0))<= TODAY(),FALSE),""))
```

This formula adds a bit of complexity by checking the value of the "Next Call Date" from the Bond and Loan worksheets to see if it is less than or equal to today's date (returned from the Excel TODAY() function). The result of this formula is TRUE if the security can currently be optionally redeemed.

7. Add another column called **Callable Next 6 Months**, and then enter the following formula:

```
=IF([@Type]="Loan",IFERROR(EDATE(INDEX(Loan[Next Call Date],
MATCH([@SecurityID],Loan[LoanID],0)),-6)<= TODAY(),FALSE),
IF([@Type]="Bond",IFERROR(EDATE(INDEX(Bond[Next Call Date],
MATCH([@SecurityID],Bond[BondID],0)),-6)<= TODAY(),FALSE),""))
```

Like step 6, this formula subtracts six months from the Next Call Date using the Excel EDATE function and compares the resulting date to today's date. The result is TRUE if the security is callable within six months from today's date.

8. Add a column called **Facility Rating**, and then enter the following formula:

```
=IF([@Type]="Loan",INDEX(Loan[Moody''s Rating],MATCH([@SecurityID],
Loan[LoanID],0)),IF([@Type]="Bond",INDEX(Bond[Moody''s Rating],
MATCH([@SecurityID],Bond[BondID],0)),""))
```

This formula pulls in the Moody's rating from the Bond or Loan worksheet. Although companies have corporate family ratings, this rating is specific to the loan facility or bond. Because loans generally have priority over other debt in a bankruptcy, they can have higher ratings than the company.

9. Add a column called **Facility RF**, and then enter the following formula:

```
=IF([@Type]="Loan",INDEX(Loan[RF],MATCH([@SecurityID],Loan[LoanID],0)),
IF([@Type]="Bond",INDEX(Bond[RF],MATCH([@SecurityID],
Bond[BondID],0)),""))
```

This formula returns the Moody's rating factor for the Moody's rating that will be useful in categorizing the ratings of portfolio. Moody's rating factor is described in Chapter 6.

The next set of columns pull data from the Company worksheet; for bonds and loans, these columns reference the issuer of the securities. For instance, Company Rating returns AMD's corporate rating, which might be different from the rating on AMD's bonds or loans.

10. Add a column called **CompanyID**, and then enter the following formula:

    ```
    =IF([@Type]="Loan",
    INDEX(Loan[CompanyID],MATCH([@SecurityID],Loan[LoanID],0)),
    IF([@Type]="Bond",INDEX(Bond[CompanyID],MATCH([@SecurityID],
    Bond[BondID],0)),[@SecurityID]))
    ```

    For bonds and loans, this formula returns the CompanyID column from the Bond and Loan worksheets. Equities display the SecurityID column, which is equivalent to their CompanyID. The following steps pull fields from the Company worksheet using this field to identify the correct company.

11. Add a column called **Category**, and then enter the following formula:

    ```
    =INDEX(Company[Category],MATCH([@CompanyID],Company[CompanyID],0))
    ```

    This formula pulls the Category column from the Company worksheet based on the CompanyID (from step 10).

12. Add a column called **Company Rating**, and then enter the following formula:

    ```
    =INDEX(Company[Moody''s Rating],MATCH([@CompanyID],Company[CompanyID],0))
    ```

    This formula returns the Company's Moody's rating (the corporate family rating).

13. Add a column called **Company RF**, and then enter the following formula:

    ```
    =INDEX(Company[RF],MATCH([@CompanyID],Company[CompanyID],0))
    ```

    This formula returns the Moody's rating factor for the corporate family rating (from step 12).

14. Add a column called **Company Market Cap**, and then enter the following formula:

    ```
    =INDEX(Company[Market Cap],MATCH([@CompanyID],Company[CompanyID],0))
    ```

    This formula returns the Market Cap value for each company.

15. Add a column called **Total Debt/EBITDA**, and then enter the following formula:

    ```
    =INDEX(Company[Total Debt/EBITDA],MATCH([@CompanyID],Company[CompanyID],0))
    ```

    This formula returns the Total Debt/EBITDA for each company.

Now that the Portfolio worksheet has a lot more detail, we can break down the data to highlight potential risks. The next set of steps creates a separate worksheet called PortfolioBreakdown, which will contain several Excel tables that will slice and dice the information from the Portfolio table. In each case, the market value (MV) of the positions is used to measure the real risk of the position. These tables are on another worksheet to avoid having to move them around when the Portfolio table grows in either rows or columns.

16. Create a new worksheet called **PortfolioBreakdown**.

17. Starting in cell A1, create an Excel table with the following column headers (cells A1, B1, and C1): **Type, MV, % of Portfolio**, and the following row headers (cells A2, A3, and A4): **Bond, Loan**, and **Equity**.

    This table groups positions by their type, sums their respective market values, and expresses their exposure as a percentage of the overall portfolio. Make sure that you have converted this range into an Excel table using the Table option on the Insert tab on the Excel ribbon, or selecting the range and pressing Ctrl-T.

18. In the MV column, enter the following formula:

    ```
    =SUMIF(Portfolio[Type],[@Type],Portfolio[MarketValue])
    ```

    This formula sums the market value column from the Portfolio worksheet where the types (in cells A2, A3, and A4 of the PortfolioBreakdown worksheet) match the types in the Portfolio worksheet.

19. On the Design tab, click Table Style Options, and then select Total Row to add a total row to the Excel table. On the total row, in the MV column, click to open the drop-down menu, and then select Sum to display the sum of the MV column.

    This step adds a total row to the MV column, and the resulting number should match the total market value of all positions in the Portfolio worksheet. It is important that these numbers tie to ensure you are accurately including all positions.

20. In the "% of Portfolio" column, divide each row's MV cell by the total number in the total row (from step 19, cell B5 in Figure 7-7).

    This step shows you the percentage each type of security makes up of the total portfolio. The percentages in the "% of Portfolio" should total 100 percent.

    The previous four steps (steps 17 through 20) are important steps that are going to be repeated several times in this section. Your Excel table should look like Figure 7-7. For brevity, some of the future steps are going to combine these prior four steps into a single step of "create an Excel table with the following column and row headers."

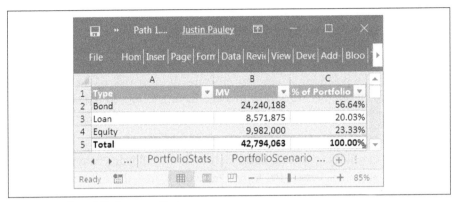

Figure 7-7. Portfolio by security type

The next steps break down the bond and loan portion of the portfolio by coupon type (fixed or floating) instead of security type. In addition, it will include a column that displays the weighted average coupon or margin of the securities.

21. Add an Excel table (with total row) to PortfolioBreakdown with the following column headers (across columns): **Coupon Type**, **Market Value**, **% of Fixed Income**, and **Weighted Avg Cpn/Margin**, and the row headers (down rows): **Fixed**, and **Floating**.

22. In the Market Value column, enter the following formula:

```
=SUMPRODUCT(N(Portfolio[Type]<>"Equity"),
N(Portfolio[Coupon Type]=[@[Coupon Type]]),Portfolio[MarketValue])
```

This formula totals the Market Value of nonequity positions by their coupon type.

The total of the Market Value column (in the total row) should match the sum of Bond and Loan market values from the Excel table created in the prior steps.

23. The "% of Fixed Income" column should divide the Market Value column for Fixed and Float by the total in the total row.

Because the only positions included in this table are fixed income (bonds and loans), the percentages do not reflect the entire portfolio.

24. The Weighted Avg Cpn/Margin column should contain the following formula:

```
=SUMPRODUCT(N(Portfolio[Type]<>"Equity"),
N(Portfolio[Coupon Type]=[@[Coupon Type]]),Portfolio[Coupon/Margin],
Portfolio[MarketValue])/[@[Market Value]]
```

This formula weights the market value of each position by its Coupon/Margin from the Portfolio worksheet broken down by Coupon Type. It does not make sense to total this column in the total row.

The next steps summarize the call protection of the fixed income positions. In addition, we calculate the average price for each category. Generally, securities that are callable can be redeemed at par (price of 100) by the issuer and, therefore, premium securities that trade above par are at risk of being called.

The formulas in the Market Value column are not all going to be the same to avoid double counting securities. Step 26 shows the different formulas to be placed at the intersection of Market Value and the different call protection categories.

25. Add an Excel table with the column headers: Call Protection, Market Value, % of Fixed Income, and Average Price, and the following row headers: Callable Now, Callable in 6MO, Callable Later, Not Callable.

26. In the Market Value column (which should sum to the total amount of fixed income positions), use the following formulas for the different call protection categories:

- Callable Now should sum the market value where Callable Ever and Now are true:

    ```
    =SUMPRODUCT(N(Portfolio[Type]<>"Equity"),
    N(Portfolio[Callable Ever]="Y"),N(Portfolio[Callable Now]=TRUE),
    Portfolio[MarketValue])
    ```

- Because we don't want to double count currently callable securities, Callable in 6MO should include only securities that are not callable now but are callable in six months:

    ```
    =SUMPRODUCT(N(Portfolio[Type]<>"Equity"),
    N(Portfolio[Callable Ever]="Y"),N(Portfolio[Callable Now]=FALSE),
    N(Portfolio[Callable Next 6 Months]=TRUE),Portfolio[MarketValue])
    ```

- Callable Later are securities that are callable but aren't callable now or in six months:

    ```
    =SUMPRODUCT(N(Portfolio[Type]<>"Equity"),
    N(Portfolio[Callable Ever]="Y"),N(Portfolio[Callable Now]=FALSE),
    N(Portfolio[Callable Next 6 Months]=FALSE),Portfolio[MarketValue])
    ```

- Not Callable are securities where Callable Ever is false:

    ```
    =SUMPRODUCT(N(Portfolio[Type]<>"Equity"),
    N(Portfolio[Callable Ever]="N"),Portfolio[MarketValue])
    ```

27. The "% of Fixed Income" column should simply divide each cell in the Market Value column by the total Market Value in the total row.

28. The Average Price column is going to mimic the SUMPRODUCT formula used in the Market Value column, except include the Price column and divide by the Market Value column to produce the weighted average price. For instance, for Callable in 6MO, use this:

```
=SUMPRODUCT(N(Portfolio[Type]<>"Equity"),N(Portfolio[Callable Ever]="Y"),
N(Portfolio[Callable Now]=FALSE),
N(Portfolio[Callable Next 6 Months]=TRUE),Portfolio[MarketValue],
Portfolio[Price])/[@[Market Value]]
```

The next Excel table separates the portfolio by Category and security type demonstrating how to break down the portfolio by multiple fields.

29. Add an Excel table with the column headers: **Category**, **Bond**, **Loan**, **Equity**, **Total**, and **% of Portfolio**. The row headers should include the distinct list of values in the Category column of the Portfolio worksheet.

30. In the Bond column, enter the following formula:

```
=SUMPRODUCT(N(Portfolio[Type]="Bond"),N(Portfolio[Category]=[@Category]),
Portfolio[MarketValue])
```

This formula sums the market value exposure for Bond positions that match the intersecting category.

31. In the Loan column, enter the following formula:

```
=SUMPRODUCT(N(Portfolio[Type]="Loan"),N(Portfolio[Category]=[@Category]),
Portfolio[MarketValue])
```

This is the same as step 30 but totals the exposure for Loans.

32. In the Equity column, enter the following formula:

```
=SUMPRODUCT(N(Portfolio[Type]="Equity"),
N(Portfolio[Category]=[@Category]),Portfolio[MarketValue])
```

33. In the Total column, add the Bond, Loan, and Equity columns.

The sum of this column should be equivalent to the total market value of the portfolio.

34. In the "% of Portfolio" column, divide the value in the Total column by the sum of the Total column (in the total row).

The resulting three Excel tables should look like Figure 7-8. Note that the first two tables deal only with the fixed income (bond and loan) portion of the portfolio, whereas the last table breaks down the entire portfolio. Therefore, the total balance in the first two should match as well as match the summation of cells B25 and C25.

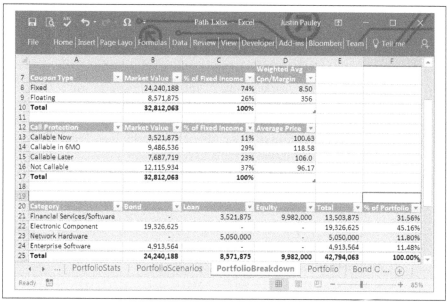

Figure 7-8. Additional PortfolioBreakdown tables

The next three Excel tables break down the portfolio by Moody's rating. In the following examples, the rating factor is used to bucket several ratings together into more significant categories (AAA-A, CCC and Lower, etc.). I should also note that, although we are referencing Moody's ratings, we are using the rating categories more commonly associated with other rating agencies (S&P, Fitch, etc.) because it is more commonly used. The steps to create the first table, which breaks down the facility rating of fixed income positions, will be repeated to break down the equity corporate family issuer ratings and the corporate family ratings of all positions.

35. Add an Excel table with the column headers: **Fixed Income Facility**, **Max RF**, **Bonds**, **Loans**, **Total**, and **% of Fixed Income**, and row headers: **AAA-A**, **BBB**, **B**, **CCC and Lower**, and **Not Rated**.

36. Populate the Max RF column with the following rating factors in sequential rows: **180**, **610**, **1766**, **3490**, **10000**. The Not Rated row should be empty.

The easiest way to view a portfolio broken down by ratings is by significant categories, and the easiest way to break individual ratings into those categories is by using their rating factors. The Max RF column contains the maximum rating factor in the group. For instance, Table 6-1 shows that the maximum rating factor for AAA-A is 180, and from 180 to 610 is all the BBB ratings (Baa1 to Baa3). But for the second row, replace I1 with I2, I1 with I3 in the third row, and so on.

37. In the Bonds column, enter the following formula:

```
=SUMPRODUCT(N(Portfolio[Type]="Bond"),
N(Portfolio[Facility RF]<=[@[Max RF]]),
N(Portfolio[Facility RF]>I1),Portfolio[MarketValue])
```

This formula sums the market value of the Bond positions where the position's rating factor is between the current Max RF and the Max RF of the row above the current one. For instance, the BBB row sum the market value for Bonds with rating factors that are less than or equal to 610 but greater than 180. Please note that you must change the I1 in the formula to the location of the column header Max RF, as you drag the formula down it will reference the Max RF of the row above it. For the first row (AAA-A), the formula references the header row which is fine because there nothing higher than AAA rating.

38. Repeat step 37 to populate the Loans column, except use "Loan" instead of "Bond", such as:

```
=SUMPRODUCT(N(Portfolio[Type]="Loan"),
N(Portfolio[Facility RF]<=[@[Max RF]]),
N(Portfolio[Facility RF]>I1),Portfolio[MarketValue])
```

Like the Bond column, this sums the market value of Loan positions across the rating stack.

39. In the Total column, add the market value of the Bonds and Loans column:

```
=[@Loans]+[@Bonds]
```

This total should match the sum of market value for Loans and Bonds.

40. In the "% of Fixed Income" column, divide each Total column entry by the total of the Total column (in the total row). These should add up to 100%.

The next steps create a table that summarizes the corporate family ratings for the equity positions.

41. Like the previous table, create an Excel table with the following column headers: **Equity Corp Rating**, **Max RF**, **Market Value**, and **% of Equity**, with row headers: **AAA-A**, **BBB**, **B**, **CCC and Lower**, and **Not Rated**.

42. Populate the Max RF column with the following rating factors in sequential rows: **180**, **610**, **1766**, **3490**, **10000**. The Not Rated row should be empty.

43. The Market Value column should contain the following formula:

```
=SUMPRODUCT(N(Portfolio[Type]="Equity"),
N(Portfolio[Company RF]<=[@[Max RF]]),
N(Portfolio[Company RF]>I10),Portfolio[MarketValue])
```

This is the same formula as the previous Excel table, except that it filters on Equity positions and references the Company RF instead of the Facility RF.

44. The "% of Equity" column should divide the Market Value column by the total of the Market Value column (in the total row). This should add up to 100 percent.

    The final ratings based table breaks down the corporate family ratings of all positions. Even though a bond or a loan can have a different facility rating than its issuer, the issuer's rating (corporate family rating) is still important in determining the risk, and potentially liquidity, of the security.

45. Like the previous table, create an Excel table with the following column headers: **Portfolio Corp Ratio**, **Max RF**, **Market Value**, and **% of Portfolio**, and with row headers: **AAA-A**, **BBB**, **B**, **CCC and Lower**, and **Not Rated**.

46. Populate the Max RF column with the following rating factors in sequential rows: **180, 610, 1766, 3490, 10000**. The Not Rated row should be empty.

47. Like step 43, populate the Market Value column with the following:

    ```
    =SUMPRODUCT(N(Portfolio[Company RF]<=[@[Max RF]]),
     N(Portfolio[Company RF]>I19),Portfolio[MarketValue])
    ```

48. Repeat step 44 to populate the "% of Portfolio"

    The resulting rating breakdown tables should look like Figure 7-9.

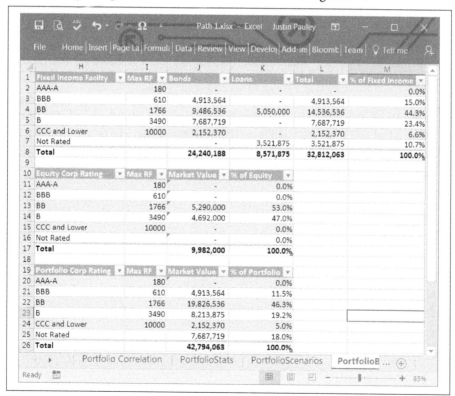

Figure 7-9. Ratings breakdown tables

In the final set of examples, we break down the portfolio by bands of price, months until maturity, total debt, and so on. Because the steps are very similar for each table, only one full example is provided, but you can easily repeat it for any metric with ranges.

The following steps group the portfolio market value for equity positions by price.

49. Create an Excel table with the following column headers: **Equity Price**, **End Price**, **Market Value**, and **% of Equity**, and the following row headers: **0**, **15**, **25**, **40**.

50. In the End Price column, enter the following prices sequentially: **15, 25, 40, 150**

    The price bands in the Equity Price and End Price columns should read 0-15, 15-25, 25-40, 40-150. The final price used (in this example, 150) should be high enough to include the maximum price of any equity position.

51. In the Market Value column, enter the following formula:

    ```
    =SUMPRODUCT(N(Portfolio[Type]="Equity"),
    N(Portfolio[Price]<=[@[End Price]]),
    N(Portfolio[Price]>[@[Equity Price]]),Portfolio[MarketValue])
    ```

    This formula sums the market value of equity positions for which the price is less than or equal to the End Price but greater than the Equity Price.

52. In the "% of Equity" field, divide the Market Value column by the total of the Market Value column. It should total 100 percent.

    You can use these last four steps to summarize any metric by different ranges. Simply by repeating the last four steps using the Months Until Maturity field instead of the Price field will highlight positions that are nearing their maturity and exposure to long-dated securities. Figure 7-10 demonstrates various examples of range-based Excel tables.

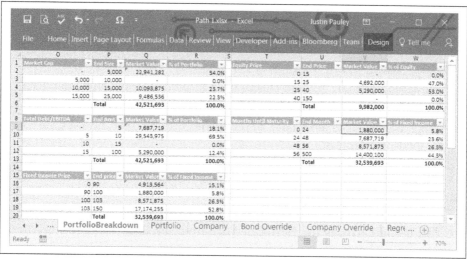

Figure 7-10. Range-based tables

Warning Signs

The third and last technique discussed in this chapter is establishing warning signs in your portfolio to highlight specific trends or changes that might require attention. For instance, you might want to be notified if a position's price drops more than five percent in three months, a rating is CCC, a security trading below par is maturing soon, and so on. This section establishes these warnings by adding warning columns to the portfolio worksheet that are conditionally highlighted. This section contains only a few examples, but there are endless warning columns that you can establish depending on your needs.

The first warning column is going to highlight positions that have a maturity in the next 24 months, and the price of the security is trading less than par. Discounted fixed income securities should accrete to par as they approach maturity; as such, those trading at a discount close to maturity should be reviewed. If you find this formula too sensitive, you can adjust it to a lower price threshold.

1. Add a column to the Portfolio table called **Maturity Warning**.

2. Populate the column with the following formula:

   ```
   =AND([@[Months Until Maturity]]<=24,[@Price]<100)
   ```

   This formula checks the Months Until Maturity column for fixed income positions that are maturing in 24 months or less and for which the price is less than par. It will return TRUE for those discounted positions with short-term maturities.

3. Select the column, and then, on the ribbon, click the Home tab. In the Styles group, click the Conditional Formatting button, point to Highlight Cell Rules, and then choose Equals To. In the text box on the left, type **TRUE**, and then choose a color highlight option, such as "Light Red Fill with Dark Red Text."

The second warning column checks fixed income securities that are callable in the next six months that are trading at a premium to their call price.

4. Add a column called **Next Call Price** to the Portfolio table and populate it with the following formula:

```
=IF([@[Callable Ever]]="Y",IF([@Type]="Loan",INDEX(Loan[Next Call Price],
MATCH([@SecurityID],Loan[LoanID],0)),IF([@Type]="Bond",
INDEX(Bond[Next Call Price],MATCH([@SecurityID],
Bond[BondID],0)),"")),"")
```

This formula returns the Next Call Price from the Loan or Bond worksheets; otherwise, it leaves an empty cell.

5. Add a column called **Call Warning** and populate it with the following formula:

```
=AND([@[Callable Next 6 Months]]=TRUE,[@Price]>[@[Next Call Price]])
```

This formula returns TRUE if the security is callable in the next six months and the price is trading higher than the Next Call Price.

6. Apply the conditional formatting in the same fashion as step 3.

The third warning column simply highlights positions for which the Moody's facility or corporate family rating is CCC or lower.

7. Add a column called **CCC Warning** with the following formula:

```
=OR(LEFT([@[Facility Rating]],1)="C",LEFT([@[Company Rating]],1)="C")
```

This formula checks the first letter of the Facility Rating and Company Rating and returns TRUE if either one of them begins with the letter "C." Apply the appropriate conditional formatting.

The final warning column highlights positions for which the price dropped five percent or more in the last three months.

8. Add a column called **3M Px Change** and populate the column with the following formula:

```
=IF([@Type]="Equity",INDEX(Company[3M Px Change],
MATCH([@SecurityID],Company[CompanyID],0)),IF([@Type]="Loan",
INDEX(Loan[3M Px Chg],MATCH([@SecurityID],Loan[LoanID],0)),
IF([@Type]="Bond",INDEX(Bond[3M Px Chg],MATCH([@SecurityID],
Bond[BondID],0)))))
```

This formula pulls the 3M Px Change column from the appropriate Bond, Loan, or Company worksheet.

9. Add a column called **Price Warning** and populate the column with the following formula:

```
=[@[3M Px Change]]<-5
```

This formula returns TRUE if the 3M Px Change is a drop greater than five percent (i.e., a change less than –5). As a reminder, Bloomberg returns percentages as whole numbers for this field. Apply appropriate conditional formatting.

Alternatively, you can base the Price Warning on the three-month price change relative to either its benchmark (for equities) or the median three-month price change for the security's peer-group described in Chapter 6. This will be helpful if the entire market has sold off five percent and you want to highlight only idiosyncratic issues. To accomplish this, add the company's benchmark's three-month price difference using the following:

```
=IF([Type]="Equity",INDEX(Company[Index 3M Px Change],
MATCH([SecurityID],Company[CompanyID],0)),"")
```

Then, add the median three-month price change for the security's peer group using:

```
=IF([@Type]="Equity",INDEX(Company[Median 3M Px Chg],
MATCH([@SecurityID],Company[CompanyID],0)),IF([@Type]="Loan",
INDEX(Loan[Median 3M Px Chg],MATCH([@SecurityID],Loan[LoanID],0)),
IF([@Type]="Bond",INDEX(Bond[Median 3M Px Chg],
MATCH([@SecurityID],Bond[BondID],0)))))
```

Finally, you can adjust the Price Warning column as you see fit. For instance, you could have it set to TRUE only when the difference between the security's three-month price change and the median peer group three-month price change is below negative five percent.

The resulting table should look like Figure 7-11 (the numbers are adjusted for demonstration purposes).

Figure 7-11. Portfolio warning columns

Path 2: Access

This section expands upon the lessons covered in the Excel section (Path 1). Specifically, this section demonstrates how to use queries to view the portfolio breakdown tables as well as check for positions with warning signs.

Portfolio Breakdown

Microsoft Access makes it a lot easier to analyze and group data; complicated Excel formulas are replaced with simple queries. For instance, in Access you can re-create the multistep process with complicated formulas used to display the breakdown of portfolio positions by asset class by using the following query:

```
SELECT
Type,
Format(Sum(MarketValue),"#,##0") AS MV,
FormatPercent(sum([% Of Portfolio]),2) as PctofPortfolio
FROM Portfolio
WHERE Type Is Not Null
GROUP BY Type;
```

This query groups rows in the Portfolio table by the Type column and sums the MarketValue and "% of Portfolio" columns. We use the `Format` and `FormatPercent` functions to properly format the results shown in Figure 7-12.

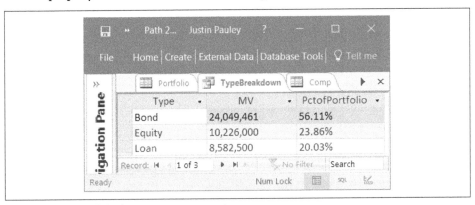

Figure 7-12. Portfolio by security type in Access

Similarly, you can use the following query to break down the fixed income securities by coupon type:

```
SELECT
[Coupon Type],
Format(sum(MarketValue),"#,##0") as MV,
FormatPercent(Sum(MarketValue)/(select sum(marketvalue) from Portfolio
where type ='Bond' or type='loan'),0) as PctOfFI,
format(Sum(MarketValue * [Coupon/Margin])/Sum(MarketValue),
```

```
iif([Coupon Type]="Floating", "#,##0", "0.00")) as WtdAvg
from Portfolio
where (type='bond' or type='loan') and [Coupon Type] is not null
Group by [Coupon Type]
```

In this query, the sum of the MarketValue column is divided by a subquery that returns the total market value of all fixed income assets to display the percentage of fixed income assets. Additionally, this query calculates the weighted average Coupon/Margin by dividing the product of MarketValue and Coupon/Margin columns by the sum of MarketValue. We use the IIF function to display floating margins without any trailing decimal places because it is already in basis points.

The query to re-create the Excel table displaying the breakdown by call protection is a bit more complicated. Because each row in the resulting table has a slightly different calculation, we use a UNION to combine several slightly different queries:

```
SELECT
'Callable Now' as CallProtection,
Format(sum(MarketValue),"#,##0") as MV,
FormatPercent(Sum(MarketValue)/(select sum(marketvalue) from Portfolio
where type ='Bond' or type='loan'),0) as PctOfFI,
format(Sum(MarketValue * [Price])/Sum(MarketValue),"0.00") as WtdAvgPx
from Portfolio
where Type <> 'Equity'
and [callable ever]='Y' and [callable now]=True

UNION

SELECT
'Callable In 6MO' as CallProtection,
Format(sum(MarketValue),"#,##0") as MV,
FormatPercent(Sum(MarketValue)/(select sum(marketvalue) from Portfolio
where type ='Bond' or type='loan'),0) as PctOfFI,
format(Sum(MarketValue * [Price])/Sum(MarketValue),"0.00") as WtdAvgPx
from Portfolio
where Type <> 'Equity'
and [callable ever]='Y' and [callable now]=False and [callable next 6 months]=true

UNION

SELECT
'Callable Later' as CallProtection,
Format(sum(MarketValue),"#,##0") as MV,
FormatPercent(Sum(MarketValue)/(select sum(marketvalue) from Portfolio
where type ='Bond' or type='loan'),0) as PctOfFI,
format(Sum(MarketValue * [Price])/Sum(MarketValue),"0.00") as WtdAvgPx
from Portfolio
where Type <> 'Equity'
and [callable ever]='Y' and [callable now]=False
and [callable next 6 months]=false
```

```
UNION

SELECT
'Not Callable' as CallProtection,
Format(sum(MarketValue),"#,##0") as MV,
FormatPercent(Sum(MarketValue)/(select sum(marketvalue) from Portfolio
where type ='Bond' or type='loan'),0) as PctOfFI,
format(Sum(MarketValue * [Price])/Sum(MarketValue),"0.00") as WtdAvgPx
from Portfolio
where Type <> 'Equity'
and [callable ever]='N'
```

This query implements the identical logic from the Excel workbook and uses the same aggregate functions discussed earlier to display the percentage of fixed income assets and weighted average price.

Even though the previous query used UNIONs to separate logic in each row of the table, you can use the IIF function to separate logic used in each column of a table. The following query, which breaks down the portfolio by Category and asset class, uses the IIF function to filter the positions that are included in each column:

```
SELECT
Category,
Format(sum(iif(Type='Bond',MarketValue,0)),"#,##0") as Bond,
Format(sum(iif(Type='Loan',MarketValue,0)),"#,##0") as Loan,
Format(sum(iif(Type='Equity',MarketValue,0)),"#,##0") as Equity,
Format(sum(MarketValue),"#,##0") as Total,
FormatPercent(sum([% Of Portfolio]),2) as PctofPortfolio
from Portfolio
where Category is not null
Group by Category
```

The next query, which breaks down the portfolio by Facility Rating using rating factors, combines the prior two techniques by using UNIONs to connect different queries filtering by rating factors and IIF functions to filter columns by security type:

```
SELECT
'AAA-A' as Rating,
1 as Ord,
Format(sum(iif(Type='Bond',MarketValue,0)),"#,##0") as Bond,
Format(sum(iif(Type='Loan',MarketValue,0)),"#,##0") as Loan,
Format(sum(MarketValue),"#,##0") as Total,
FormatPercent(Sum(MarketValue)/(select sum(marketvalue) from Portfolio
where type ='Bond' or type='loan'),0) as PctOfFI
from Portfolio
where [Facility RF] <= 180
and Type <> 'Equity'

UNION

SELECT
'BBB' as Rating,
```

```
2 as Ord,
Format(sum(iif(Type='Bond',MarketValue,0)),"#,##0") as Bond,
Format(sum(iif(Type='Loan',MarketValue,0)),"#,##0") as Loan,
Format(sum(MarketValue),"#,##0") as Total,
FormatPercent(Sum(MarketValue)/(select sum(marketvalue) from Portfolio
where type ='Bond' or type='loan'),0) as PctOfFI
from Portfolio
where [Facility RF] >180 and [Facility RF] <= 610
and Type <> 'Equity'

UNION

SELECT
'BB' as Rating,
3 as Ord,
Format(sum(iif(Type='Bond',MarketValue,0)),"#,##0") as Bond,
Format(sum(iif(Type='Loan',MarketValue,0)),"#,##0") as Loan,
Format(sum(MarketValue),"#,##0") as Total,
FormatPercent(Sum(MarketValue)/(select sum(marketvalue) from Portfolio
where type ='Bond' or type='loan'),0) as PctOfFI
from Portfolio
where [Facility RF] >610 and [Facility RF] <= 1766
and Type <> 'Equity'

UNION

SELECT
'B' as Rating,
4 as Ord,
Format(sum(iif(Type='Bond',MarketValue,0)),"#,##0") as Bond,
Format(sum(iif(Type='Loan',MarketValue,0)),"#,##0") as Loan,
Format(sum(MarketValue),"#,##0") as Total,
FormatPercent(Sum(MarketValue)/(select sum(marketvalue) from Portfolio
where type ='Bond' or type='loan'),0) as PctOfFI
from Portfolio
where [Facility RF] >1766 and [Facility RF] <= 3490
and Type <> 'Equity'

UNION

SELECT
'CCC and Lower' as Rating,
5 as Ord,
Format(sum(iif(Type='Bond',MarketValue,0)),"#,##0") as Bond,
Format(sum(iif(Type='Loan',MarketValue,0)),"#,##0") as Loan,
Format(sum(MarketValue),"#,##0") as Total,
FormatPercent(Sum(MarketValue)/(select sum(marketvalue) from Portfolio
where type ='Bond' or type='loan'),0) as PctOfFI
from Portfolio
where [Facility RF] >3490 and [Facility RF] <= 10000
and Type <> 'Equity'
```

```
UNION
SELECT
'Not Rated' as Rating,
6 as Ord,
Format(sum(iif(Type='Bond',MarketValue,0)),"#,##0") as Bond,
Format(sum(iif(Type='Loan',MarketValue,0)),"#,##0") as Loan,
Format(sum(MarketValue),"#,##0") as Total,
FormatPercent(Sum(MarketValue)/(select sum(marketvalue) from Portfolio
where type ='Bond' or type='loan'),0) as PctOfFI
from Portfolio
where [Facility RF] is null
and Type <> 'Equity'
order by Ord
```

This query incorporates an order column called Ord to control the order in which the rows are displayed. As Figure 7-13 shows, the resulting table can be sorted by the Ord column to display the rating categories in the correct order.

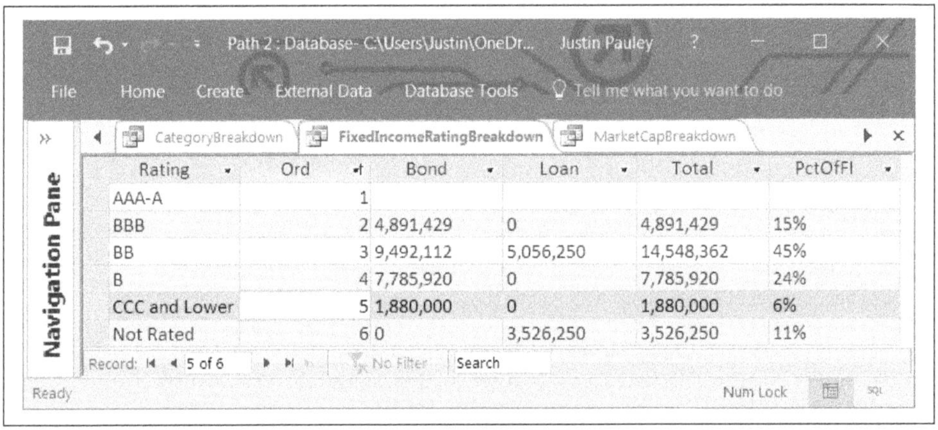

Figure 7-13. Ratings breakdown sorted by Ord

The final query in this section uses UNIONs to break down the portfolio into Market Cap ranges. You can use this technique to break down the portfolio by other columns. It also uses an Ord column to control the order in which the rows are displayed:

```
SELECT
'0 - 5,000' as MarketCap,
1 as Ord,
Format(Sum(MarketValue),"#,##0") AS MV,
FormatPercent(sum([% Of Portfolio]),2) as PctofPortfolio
from Portfolio
where [Company Market Cap] between 0 and 5000
UNION
SELECT
'5,000-10,000' as MarketCap,
2 as Ord,
```

```
Format(Sum(MarketValue),"#,##0") AS MV,
FormatPercent(sum([% Of Portfolio]),2) as PctofPortfolio
from Portfolio
where [Company Market Cap] between 5000 and 10000
UNION
SELECT
'10,000-15,000' as MarketCap,
3 as Ord,
Format(Sum(MarketValue),"#,##0") AS MV,
FormatPercent(sum([% Of Portfolio]),2) as PctofPortfolio
from Portfolio
where [Company Market Cap] between 10000and 15000
UNION
SELECT
'15,000-25,000' as MarketCap,
4 as Ord,
Format(Sum(MarketValue),"#,##0") AS MV,
FormatPercent(sum([% Of Portfolio]),2) as PctofPortfolio
from Portfolio
where [Company Market Cap] between 15000 and 25000
order by ord
```

Warning Signs

This section covers how to turn a simple query into a basic report that highlights rows with the warnings established in the Excel Portfolio worksheet. The following query displays the warning columns, followed by the rest of the column in Excel Portfolio linked table for which any of the warning columns are true:

```
SELECT
[Maturity Warning],
[Call Warning],
[CCC Warning],
[Price Warning],
*
from Portfolio
where [Maturity Warning]=true
or [Call Warning]=true
or [CCC Warning]=true
or [Price Warning]=true
```

After executing this query, on the ribbon, on the Create tab, click Report to create a report using the results of the query. Next, in Design view, to add conditional formatting to the report, select the Warning columns. Then, on the Format tab, click the Control Formatting button, and then select Conditional Formatting. Add a rule that changes the format when the cell value is equal to "Yes." The resulting report should look like Figure 7-14.

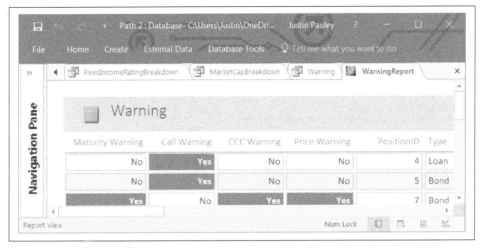

Figure 7-14. Warning Report

Depending on your preference, you can also establish different macros to print or send this report by email using the Macros option on the Create tab.

Path 3: C#

This section covers the C# implementation of the techniques covered in the prior Excel (Path 1) section. This section is also a good example of converting a very complicated task in Excel into a straightforward application.

Sharpe Ratio with Historical or Forecasted Returns

This section walks you through the creation of a C# console application that calculates the weighted average annualized portfolio return using either historical or forecasted returns, the portfolio's standard deviation, and the portfolio's Sharpe Ratio. The steps are straightforward:

1. Query the database for position information.
2. Use Bloomberg to calculate each position's historical return and standard deviation.
3. Construct a correlation matrix to calculate the portfolio standard deviation.
4. Calculate the Sharpe Ratio.

Before beginning the C# code, use the schema listed in Table 7-1 to create a database table named "PortfolioScenarios" that contains scenarios like the PortfolioScenarios worksheet in the Excel implementation (see Figure 7-5). Populate the table for each position.

Table 7-1. PortfolioScenarios schema

Field name	Data type
PositionID (Primary Key)	Number
BestReturn	Number (double)
AverageReturn	Number (double)
WorstReturn	Number (double)
BestProbability	Number (double)
AverageProbability	Number (double)
WorstProbability	Number (double)

Create a new C# console application and, as with previous examples, add the appropriate references to the Bloomberg API as well as MathNet. Add a DataSet Item called ADS to the project. And add two TableAdapters to the ADS DataSet connected to your Access database.

The first TableAdapter is called `Portfolio`, with the following query:

```
SELECT
p.PositionID, p.Type, p.SecurityID, p.[Size], a.BBID,a.Price
FROM Portfolio p
inner join
(
    select BondID as SecurityID,Price,BBID from Bond
    UNION
    select LoanID as SecurityID,Price,BBID from Loan
    UNION
    select CompanyID as SecurityID,Price,BBID from Company
) a on a.SecurityID=p.SecurityID
```

The second TableAdapter is called `PortfolioScenarios`, with the following query:

```
SELECT PositionID, BestReturn, AverageReturn, WorstReturn, BestProbability,
AverageProbability, WorstProbability,
BestReturn * BestProbability +
AverageReturn * AverageProbability +
WorstReturn * WorstProbability AS ForecastedReturn
FROM      PortfolioScenarios
```

Add the following using directives to *Program.cs*:

```
using Event = Bloomberglp.Blpapi.Event;
using Element = Bloomberglp.Blpapi.Element;
using Message = Bloomberglp.Blpapi.Message;
using Name = Bloomberglp.Blpapi.Name;
using Request = Bloomberglp.Blpapi.Request;
using Service = Bloomberglp.Blpapi.Service;
using Session = Bloomberglp.Blpapi.Session;
using DataType = Bloomberglp.Blpapi.Schema.Datatype;
using SessionOptions = Bloomberglp.Blpapi.SessionOptions;
using InvalidRequestException =
```

```
            Bloomberglp.Blpapi.InvalidRequestException;
    using System.Data;


    using MathNet.Numerics.LinearAlgebra;
    using MathNet.Numerics.Statistics;
```

Declare the following variables in the `Program` class:

```
    private ADS DS = new ADS();
    private static readonly Name SECURITY_DATA = new Name("securityData");
    private static readonly Name SECURITY = new Name("security");
    private static readonly Name FIELD_DATA = new Name("fieldData");
    private static readonly Name RESPONSE_ERROR = new Name("responseError");
    private static readonly Name SECURITY_ERROR = new Name("securityError");
    private static readonly Name FIELD_EXCEPTIONS = new Name("fieldExceptions");
    private static readonly Name FIELD_ID = new Name("fieldId");
    private static readonly Name ERROR_INFO = new Name("errorInfo");
    private static readonly Name CATEGORY = new Name("category");
    private static readonly Name MESSAGE = new Name("message");
    private static readonly Name DATE = new Name("date");

    //Date range for historical price changes
    private DateTime StartDate = new DateTime(1990, 1, 31);
    private DateTime EndDate = DateTime.Now;

    //Start Date for correlation matrix
    private DateTime CorrelationDate = new DateTime(2016, 6, 30);

    //UseForecasted=true -> use PortfolioScenarios Table
    //UseForecasted=false -> use historical annualzied returns
    private bool UseForecasted = true;
```

Declare a class called `PositionStat` that will store the calculation results from the Bloomberg data as well as the historical price changes used for the correlation.

```
    private class PositionStat
    {
        public int PositionID = 0;
        public double StartingPrice = 0;
        public double EndingPrice = 0;
        public double DayCount = 0;
        public double HistoricalReturn = 0;
        public double AnnualizedReturn = 0;
        public double StdDev = 0;
        public double AnnualizedStdDev = 0;
        public double MarketValue = 0;
        public double Weight = 0;
        public double ForecastedReturn = 0;
        public double Return = 0;
        public Dictionary<DateTime, double> Hist = new Dictionary<DateTime, double>();
    }
```

Declare a `List` collection to contain a list of `PositionStat`:

```
List<PositionStat> Stats = new List<PositionStat>();
```

Instantiate an instance of `Program` in the `Main` method and call the `Go` method that controls the basic flow of the program:

```
static void Main(string[] args)
{
    new Program().Go();
}
private void Go()
{
    // Populate DS with data from Access Database
    FillDataSet();
    //Populate Stats collection using data from Bloomberg
    PopulatePositionStats();
    //Use Stats collection to calculate portfolio Standard Deviation
    double StdDev = CalcStdDev();
    // Calculate weighted average return of portfolio
    double Return = Stats.Sum(x => x.Weight * x.Return);
    //Fetch the 10-year US treasury yield for risk free rate
    Dictionary<DateTime, double> riskfree =
    GetHistory("CT10 Govt", "ASK_YIELD", DateTime.Now.AddDays(-1),false);
    //Calculate Sharpe Ratio
    double Sharpe = (Return - riskfree.ElementAt(0).Value/100) / StdDev;
    //Output
    Console.WriteLine("Std Dev: "+StdDev.ToString("p2"));
    Console.WriteLine("Return: " + Return.ToString("p2"));
    Console.WriteLine("Sharpe Ratio: " + Sharpe.ToString("p2"));
}
```

The `FillDataSet` method populates the `DS` variable with data from the Access database:

```
private void FillDataSet()
{

    using (ADSTableAdapters.PortfolioScenariosTableAdapter ta =
    new ADSTableAdapters.PortfolioScenariosTableAdapter())
    {
        ta.Fill(DS.PortfolioScenarios);
        ta.Connection.Close();
    }
    using (ADSTableAdapters.PortfolioTableAdapter ta =
    new ADSTableAdapters.PortfolioTableAdapter())
    {
        ta.Fill(DS.Portfolio);
        ta.Connection.Close();
    }
}
```

The `PopulatePositionStats` function iterates through each position in the `DS` dataset that was populated from `FillDataSet`, requests historical prices from Bloomberg, and populates the `Stats` collection with calculated data:

```
private void PopulatePositionStats()
{
    //Iterate through the positions
    foreach (ADS.PortfolioRow position in DS.Portfolio.OrderBy(x => x.PositionID))
    {
        // Populates prices variable with historical dates
        // and prices from Bloomberg
        // GetHistory(Bloomberg ID, Bloomberg Field, Historical Start Date,
        // Fetch Monthly Data?)
        Dictionary<DateTime, double> prices =
        GetHistory(position.BBID, "PX_LAST", StartDate, true);

        // If less than two historical dates are returned
        // there is not much that can be done.
        // Error handling should be added in the event there
        // are less than 2 positions
        if (prices.Count > 2)
        {
            PositionStat stat = new PositionStat();
            stat.PositionID = position.PositionID;

            // price on the earliest date returned
            stat.StartingPrice = prices.OrderBy(x => x.Key).First().Value;

            //price on the latest date returned
            stat.EndingPrice = prices.OrderByDescending(x => x.Key).First().Value;
            // number of days returned
            stat.DayCount =
            (prices.OrderByDescending(x => x.Key).First().Key -
            prices.OrderBy(x => x.Key).First().Key).TotalDays - 1;
            stat.HistoricalReturn =
            (stat.EndingPrice - stat.StartingPrice) / stat.StartingPrice;
            //annualize historical returns
            stat.AnnualizedReturn = Math.Pow(1 + stat.HistoricalReturn, 365 /
            stat.DayCount) - 1;

            // Loop through returned prices
            // populate Hist property with
            // monthly price change
            for (int i = 1; i < prices.Count; i++)
            {
                DateTime currDate = prices.OrderBy(x => x.Key).ElementAt(i).Key;
                DateTime prevDate =
                prices.OrderBy(x => x.Key).ElementAt(i - 1).Key;
                double currPx = prices[currDate];
                double prevPx = prices[prevDate];
                double chgPx = (currPx - prevPx) / prevPx;
                stat.Hist.Add(currDate, chgPx);
```

```
        }

        //Calculate standard deviation of monthly price changes
        stat.StdDev = Statistics.StandardDeviation(stat.Hist.Values);
        //annualize standard deviation
        stat.AnnualizedStdDev = stat.StdDev * Math.Sqrt(12);

        //Calculate Market Value of the position
        double price = 0;
        if (position.Type.ToUpper() == "EQUITY")
            price = position.Price;
        else
            price = position.Price / 100;
        stat.MarketValue = price * (double)position.Size;

        // find the position in the PortfolioScenarios table
        // Populate the ForecastedReturn property of stat with
        // data from the Access database
        ADS.PortfolioScenariosRow scenario =
        DS.PortfolioScenarios.FindByPositionID(stat.PositionID);
        stat.ForecastedReturn = scenario.ForecastedReturn;

        //set stat.Return depending on if we are
        // looking at forecasted returns
        // or annualized historical returns
        if (UseForecasted)
            stat.Return = stat.ForecastedReturn;
        else
            stat.Return = stat.AnnualizedReturn;

        Stats.Add(stat);

    }
}
// Once market value is calculated for each position
// loop through and set the Weight property to
// the market value percentage of the portfolio
double totalMV = Stats.Sum(x => x.MarketValue);
foreach (PositionStat stat in Stats)
    stat.Weight = stat.MarketValue / totalMV;
}
```

The GetHistory and ProcessHistoryResponse methods are the same code as the program featured in the correlation section of this book, except that GetHistory accepts a Boolean argument to request monthly prices instead of daily:

```
private Dictionary<DateTime, double> GetHistory (
string security, string field, DateTime startDate, bool monthly)
{

    Dictionary<DateTime, double> date2value = new Dictionary<DateTime, double>();
    SessionOptions sessionOptions = new SessionOptions();
```

```
Session session = new Session();
bool sessionStarted = session.Start();
if (!sessionStarted)
{
    System.Console.Error.WriteLine("Failed to start session.");
    return null;
}
if (!session.OpenService("//blp/refdata"))
{
    System.Console.Error.WriteLine("Failed to open //blp/refdata");
    return null;
}

Service refDataService = session.GetService("//blp/refdata");
Request request = refDataService.CreateRequest("HistoricalDataRequest");

Element securities = request.GetElement("securities");
securities.AppendValue(security);
Element fields = request.GetElement("fields");
fields.AppendValue(field);

request.Set("startDate", startDate.ToString("yyyyMMdd"));

//if Monthly argument is set
//to true, set periodicity to Calendar Month
if (monthly)
{
    request.Set("periodicitySelection", "MONTHLY");
    request.Set("periodicityAdjustment", "CALENDAR");
}

try
{
    session.SendRequest(request, null);
}
catch (InvalidRequestException e)
{
    System.Console.WriteLine(e.ToString());
}

bool done = false;
while (!done)
{
    Event eventObj = session.NextEvent();
    if (eventObj.Type == Event.EventType.PARTIAL_RESPONSE)
    {
        ProcessHistoryResponse(eventObj, date2value);
    }
    else if (eventObj.Type == Event.EventType.RESPONSE)
    {
        ProcessHistoryResponse(eventObj, date2value);
        done = true;
```

```
        }
        else
        {
            foreach (Message msg in eventObj)
            {
                System.Console.WriteLine(msg.AsElement);
                if (eventObj.Type == Event.EventType.SESSION_STATUS)
                {
                    if (msg.MessageType.Equals("SessionTerminated"))
                    {
                        done = true;
                    }
                }
            }
        }
    }
    session.Stop();
    return date2value;

}

private void ProcessHistoryResponse(Event eventObj,
Dictionary<DateTime, double> date2value)
{
    foreach (Message msg in eventObj)
    {
        if (msg.HasElement(RESPONSE_ERROR))
        {
            Element error = msg.GetElement(RESPONSE_ERROR);
            Console.WriteLine("Request failed: " + error.GetElementAsString(CATEGORY) +
            " (" + error.GetElementAsString(MESSAGE) + ")");
            continue;
        }


        Element securityData = msg.GetElement(SECURITY_DATA);
        string security = securityData.GetElement(SECURITY).GetValueAsString();
        Console.WriteLine(security);

        Element fieldData = securityData.GetElement(FIELD_DATA);

        for (int i = 0; i < fieldData.NumValues; i++)
        {
            Element element = fieldData.GetValueAsElement(i);
            DateTime date = element.GetElementAsDatetime(DATE).ToSystemDateTime();
            double? value = null;
            for (int f = 0; f < element.NumElements; f++)
            {
                Element field = element.GetElement(f);
                if (!field.Name.Equals(DATE))
                {
                    if (field.Datatype == DataType.FLOAT32)
```

```
                value = Convert.ToDouble(field.GetValueAsFloat32());
            else if (field.Datatype == DataType.FLOAT64)
                value = field.GetValueAsFloat64();
        }
    }
    if (value != null)
        date2value.Add(date, value.Value);
}


    }
}
```

The `CalcStdDev` method populates a matrix with the correlations between every posi-tion combination. Then, it multiplies the correlation matrix by the vector of weighted standard deviations of each position:

```
private double CalcStdDev()
{
    int count = Stats.Count;
    //Matrix to store the correlation between each position
    Matrix<double> corrMatrix = Matrix<double>.Build.Dense(count, count);

    //Vector to store the weighted standard deviation of each position
    // where the weight is the percentage the position makes up
    // of the portfolio and the standard deviation
    // is the annualized standard deviation of historical returns.
    Vector<double> weightVector = Vector<double>.Build.Dense(count);

    for (int i = 0; i < count; i++)
    {
        weightVector[i] = Stats[i].Weight * Stats[i].AnnualizedStdDev;
        for (int j = 0; j < count; j++)
        {
            corrMatrix[i, j] = GetCorrelation(Stats[i], Stats[j]);
        }
    }

    //Matrix multiplication
    Vector<double> variance =
    weightVector * corrMatrix * weightVector.ToColumnMatrix();

    return Math.Sqrt(variance[0]);
}
```

The `GetCorrelation` method calculates the correlation between two positions using historical monthly price changes starting from the `CorrelationDate` declared at the start of the application:

```
private double GetCorrelation(PositionStat stat1, PositionStat stat2)
{
    double corr = 0;
```

```
//Get the list of monthly price changes from the first position
// where the date of the price change is greater than or equal to
// the CorrelationDate variable set at the
//start of the program
List<double> set1 = (from stat in stat1.Hist
                        where stat.Key >= CorrelationDate
                        select stat.Value).ToList();
//Like set1, this gets the monthly price changes
// for the second position
List<double> set2 = (from stat in stat2.Hist
                        where stat.Key >= CorrelationDate
                        select stat.Value).ToList();

//MathNet to calculate correlation
corr = Correlation.Pearson(set1, set2);
return corr;
}
```

Portfolio Breakdown and Warning Signs

For the most part, the queries covered in the Access section of this chapter (Path 2) can be easily modified to work with the table structure used by the C# applications. I recommend that you save the Portfolio query in Chapter 5 that calculates each position's market value as "PortfolioQuery" and use that in queries that require market value. For instance, the following query uses a saved Portfolio query to group positions by Type:

```
SELECT
Type,
Format(Sum(MarketValue),"#,##0") AS MV,
FormatPercent(sum(PctofPortfolio),2) as PortfolioPct
FROM PortfolioQuery
WHERE Type Is Not Null
GROUP BY Type;
```

Summary

Chapter 6 focused on relative value of individual securities, whereas this chapter demonstrated different ways to measure risk and return of a portfolio. You should use the techniques in both chapters together to enhance investment decisions. For instance, a security could look attractive from a relative-value perspective, but it might cause your portfolio to have too much concentration in a sector. The scope continues to broaden in Chapter 8, which covers the entire loan market.

CHAPTER 8

Market Analysis

This chapter discusses the importance of incorporating broader market trends into your analysis. For instance, one reason the stock of a retail company looks attractive relative to a technology company's stock is that the general market sentiment has put pressure on the broader retail sector. Although we can easily measure the market sentiment in equity markets, it is more difficult to track in less transparent markets such as high-yield bonds and corporate loans. This chapter demonstrates how to use the data collected from Markit to identify broader trends in the corporate loan market. You can alter the methods used in this chapter to analyze other markets with similar sets of data.

This chapter breaks down the Markit loan data into three sections and demonstrates different types of analysis in each section.

The first section uses the facility update information to identify trends in new issue loans over time. We can use this information to determine the count and volume of loans that have come to market monthly and their average coupon, size, and term (years until maturity). Additionally, this information informs as to sectors that are pricing wide or tight to the general market, implying their risk.

The second section uses recommended update information to identify trends in loan refinancings. Aggregated loan refinancing data shows important information such as the average number of years in maturity extensions as well as the average change in coupon. This information, which we can break down by sector, highlights general trends in the market.

The final section uses the loan market information for a variety of purposes. By using historical prices, we can discern price movement trends by sector, identify outperforming or underperforming loans, and highlight loans that fit a pattern (such as "now trading above $90 but once traded below $70").

Unfortunately, Microsoft Excel has limitations when it comes to analyzing large datasets. For example, the maximum row count is 200,000 with only 125 days of loan price. That notwithstanding, this chapter provides basic examples for each section in Excel and more in-depth analysis in Microsoft Access.

Path 1: Excel

Markit provides a lot of useful loan market data, but, unfortunately, Excel does not handle aggregating large sets of data well. I recommend that you maintain each worksheet diligently and keep only necessary historical data. Furthermore, if the row count is in the thousands, you should not add formulas directly to the Markit data.

New Issue Loan Analysis

Markit's facility update data contains static information about each corporate loan, including its closing date, size, term, and spread. Because most loans are floating-rate instruments, their spread is the margin the loan pays above an index (typically London Interbank Offered Rate [LIBOR]). For example, if a loan's coupon is three-month LIBOR plus 300 bps, its spread is 300 bps. As most new issue loans price around par, their spread is roughly the same as their discount margin (DM) and is also the best indicator of risk. All things being equal, a new loan with a 300 bps spread should be less risky than a loan with a 500 bps spread.

However, as the market's risk appetite changes over time, a loan that priced with a 300 bps spread two months ago, could price with a 500 bps spread today. We can use the observable spreads in the facility update data to track the market sentiment by taking average spread levels over time using the following steps:

1. Create a new worksheet called **New Issue**.

2. Across the columns in row one, add the following labels: **Date**, **Count**, **Total Size**, **Avg Size**, **Term**, **All Spread**, **Healthcare**, **Retail**, and **Oil & Gas**.

3. In column A, under the Date column header, add a monthly date range using the first of each month. For instance, in cell A2, enter the date **2/1/2017**; in cell A3, enter **1/1/2017**; and so on.

4. Convert the Excel range into a table.

5. In the Count column (column B), enter the following formula in each row:

```
=SUMPRODUCT(N(LoanFacilities[Close Date]>=[@Date]),
N(LoanFacilities[Close Date]<=EDATE([@Date],1)-1),
N(LoanFacilities[Currency]="US Dollar"),
N(LoanFacilities[LoanX Facility Category]="Institutional"),
N(LoanFacilities[Status]="Active"),N(LoanFacilities[Initial Spread]>0))
```

This formula assumes you named the Excel table containing the Markit facility data "LoanFacilities." It uses the combination of SUMPRODUCT function and N function to count only rows in the LoanFacilities table that meet defined criteria. The first N function filters out rows for which the Close Date is before the date in column A. The next N function filters out rows for which the Close Date is past the last day of the month (the EDATE function adds one month to the date in column A and then one is subtracted from that date to get to the last date of the month). The next set of filters limit results to Institutional loans (excluding revolvers and pro-rata tranches), USD currency, and Active status, where the spread is populated (excludes some bad rows).

6. In the Total Size column, enter the following formula:

```
=SUMPRODUCT(N(LoanFacilities[Close Date]>=[@Date]),
N(LoanFacilities[Close Date]<=EDATE([@Date],1)-1),
N(LoanFacilities[Currency]="US Dollar"),
N(LoanFacilities[LoanX Facility Category]="Institutional"),
N(LoanFacilities[Status]="Active"),
N(LoanFacilities[Initial Spread]>0),LoanFacilities[Initial Amount])
```

This formula is the same formula as that in step 5, except it added `LoanFacilities[Initial Amount])` as the last parameter which results in the SUMPRODUCT returning the sum of the Initial Amount column for each row that meets the criteria.

7. In the Avg Size column, enter the following formula:

```
=[@[Total Size ($mm)]]/[@Count]
```

This formula simply divides the Total Size column by the Count to calculate the average size of the loans issued during that period.

8. In the Term column, enter the following formula:

```
=SUMPRODUCT(N(LoanFacilities[Close Date]>=[@Date]),
N(LoanFacilities[Close Date]<=EDATE([@Date],1)-1),
N(LoanFacilities[Currency]="US Dollar"),
N(LoanFacilities[LoanX Facility Category]="Institutional"),
N(LoanFacilities[Status]="Active"),
LoanFacilities[Initial Amount],
N(LoanFacilities[Initial Spread]>0),
LoanFacilities[Term])/[@[Total Size]]
```

This is the same formula as that in step 6 except it adds the Term column to the list of arguments of the SUMPRODUCT and divides by the Total Size column which results in a weighted average Term. It is important to weight the different metrics by initial amount (as opposed to taking a simple average) because there are several small loans that could possibly skew the results.

9. In the All Spread column, enter the following formula:

```
=SUMPRODUCT(N(LoanFacilities[Close Date]>=[@Date]),
N(LoanFacilities[Close Date]<=EDATE([@Date],1)-1),
N(LoanFacilities[Currency]="US Dollar"),
N(LoanFacilities[LoanX Facility Category]="Institutional"),
N(LoanFacilities[Status]="Active"),LoanFacilities[Initial Amount],
N(LoanFacilities[Initial Spread]>0),
LoanFacilities[Initial Spread])/[@[Total Size]]
```

Like step 8, this calculates the weighted average Initial Spread.

10. In the Healthcare column, enter the following formula :

```
=SUMPRODUCT(N(LoanFacilities[Close Date]>=[@Date]),
N(LoanFacilities[Close Date]<=EDATE([@Date],1)-1),
N(LoanFacilities[Currency]="US Dollar"),
N(LoanFacilities[LoanX Facility Category]="Institutional"),
N(LoanFacilities[Status]="Active"),LoanFacilities[Initial Amount],
N(LoanFacilities[Initial Spread]>0),LoanFacilities[Initial Spread],
N(LoanFacilities[Industry]="Healthcare"))/
SUMPRODUCT(N(LoanFacilities[Close Date]>=$A2),
N(LoanFacilities[Close Date]<=EDATE([@Date],1)-1),
N(LoanFacilities[Currency]="US Dollar"),
N(LoanFacilities[LoanX Facility Category]="Institutional"),
N(LoanFacilities[Status]="Active"),LoanFacilities[Initial Amount],
N(LoanFacilities[Initial Spread]>0),
N(LoanFacilities[Industry]="Healthcare"))
```

This formula includes the same filters as previous steps but includes a filter for Industry to include only healthcare loans. Additionally, instead of using Total Size as the denominator, we use the total initial amount of all healthcare loans. The total size of all healthcare loans is calculated using the same formulas as the numerator but excluding the Initial Spread number. The result is the weighted average spread of healthcare loans. This formula can result in a divide-by-zero error if no healthcare loans were issued during the period.

11. Use the same formula as the one in step 10 for the Retail and Oil & Gas columns but change the Healthcare filter to **Retailing** and **Oil & Gas**.

This will result in weighted average Retail and Oil & Gas spread columns.

Figure 8-1 presents the resulting table, which highlights that the Healthcare, Retail, and Oil & Gas sectors are generally pricing wide to the overall market. It also shows that the Oil & Gas loans have been generally improving over the past few months.

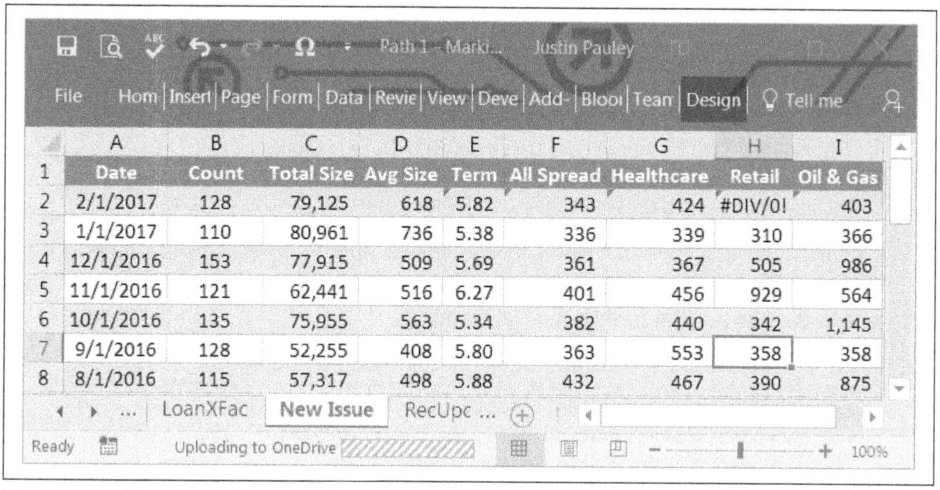

	A	B	C	D	E	F	G	H	I
1	Date	Count	Total Size	Avg Size	Term	All Spread	Healthcare	Retail	Oil & Gas
2	2/1/2017	128	79,125	618	5.82	343	424	#DIV/0!	403
3	1/1/2017	110	80,961	736	5.38	336	339	310	366
4	12/1/2016	153	77,915	509	5.69	361	367	505	986
5	11/1/2016	121	62,441	516	6.27	401	456	929	564
6	10/1/2016	135	75,955	563	5.34	382	440	342	1,145
7	9/1/2016	128	52,255	408	5.80	363	553	358	358
8	8/1/2016	115	57,317	498	5.88	432	467	390	875

Figure 8-1. New issue loan analysis

As I've said several times throughout this book, even though this information can be useful in identifying trends, analysts should always review the underlying loan information to make sure outliers aren't skewing the numbers.

Refinancings

Like a mortgage, companies can refinance their loans (after a non-call period) into new loans at lower spreads and potentially longer maturities. Although a single company refinancing its debt into a lower spread loan is generally a sign of good performance (lenders willing to take less yield to lend to the company), it could also be the company dealing with an upcoming maturity. An upward trend in refinancings will generally correlate with improving market sentiment.

Like its facility update information, Markit's recommended update data can be used as observable pricing points to help identify trends in refinancings. Every time a loan is restructured, refinanced, or paid down Markit assigns a new LoanX ID and notes the change in the recommended update data feed. This feed includes the original and new details for many fields, including spread and maturity. This data can be useful to identify spread compression in each sector as well as the overall market.

The following steps create a new worksheet that aggregates information on refinanced loans:

12. Create a worksheet called **`Refinancings`**.
13. Across the columns in row one, add the following labels: **`Date`**, **`Count`**, **`Size`**, **`Years Extension`**, **`Original Spread`**, **`New Spread`**, **`Spread Change`**, **`Healthcare`**, and **`Retail`**.

14. Like step 3, earlier, under the Date column header (column A), enter monthly dates using the first date of each month.

15. In the Count column, enter the following formula:

```
=SUMPRODUCT(N(LoanUpdates[Inactivation Date]>=[@Date]),
N(LoanUpdates[Inactivation Date] < EDATE([@Date],1)-1),
N(LoanUpdates[InactivationReason]="Refinanced"))
```

This formula assumes that the recommended update Excel table is called Loan-Updates. Like the steps in the last section, this filters out LoanUpdates by rows within the period that have been Refinanced.

16. In the Years Extension column, enter the following formula:

```
=SUMPRODUCT(N(LoanUpdates[Inactivation Date]>=[@Date]),
N(LoanUpdates[Inactivation Date] <= EDATE([@Date],1)-1),
N(LoanUpdates[InactivationReason]="Refinanced"),
N(LoanUpdates[Repl Maturity Date] >= LoanUpdates[Maturity Date]),
LoanUpdates[Initial Amount],
LoanUpdates[Repl Maturity Date]-LoanUpdates[Maturity Date])/
SUMPRODUCT(N(LoanUpdates[Inactivation Date]>=[@Date]),
N(LoanUpdates[Inactivation Date] <= EDATE([@Date],1)-1),
N(LoanUpdates[InactivationReason]="Refinanced"),
N(LoanUpdates[Repl Maturity Date] >= LoanUpdates[Maturity Date]),
LoanUpdates[Initial Amount])/365
```

This formula adds filters to include only rows for which the new maturity date is later than the original maturity date, indicating an extension. It also adds the difference between the new maturity date and the previous maturity date to come up with the weighted average number of days the loans were extended. This number is divided by 365 to display that number in years.

17. In the Original Spread column, enter the following formula:

```
=SUMPRODUCT(N(LoanUpdates[Inactivation Date]>=[@Date]),
N(LoanUpdates[Inactivation Date] <= EDATE([@Date],1)-1),
N(LoanUpdates[InactivationReason]="Refinanced"),
N(LoanUpdates[Repl Initial Spread]>0), N(LoanUpdates[Initial Spread]>0),
LoanUpdates[Initial Amount],LoanUpdates[Initial Spread])/
SUMPRODUCT(N(LoanUpdates[Inactivation Date]>=[@Date]),
N(LoanUpdates[Inactivation Date] <= EDATE([@Date],1)-1),
N(LoanUpdates[InactivationReason]="Refinanced"),
N(LoanUpdates[Repl Initial Spread]>0),
N(LoanUpdates[Initial Spread]>0),LoanUpdates[Initial Amount])
```

This returns the average original spread where both the initial and current spread exist.

18. In the New Spread column, enter the following formula:

```
=SUMPRODUCT(N(LoanUpdates[Inactivation Date]>=[@Date]),
N(LoanUpdates[Inactivation Date] <= EDATE([@Date],1)-1),
```

```
N(LoanUpdates[InactivationReason]="Refinanced"),
N(LoanUpdates[Repl Initial Spread]>0),
N(LoanUpdates[Initial Spread]>0),LoanUpdates[Initial Amount],
LoanUpdates[Repl Initial Spread])/
SUMPRODUCT(N(LoanUpdates[Inactivation Date]>=[@Date]),
N(LoanUpdates[Inactivation Date] <= EDATE([@Date],1)-1),
N(LoanUpdates[InactivationReason]="Refinanced"),
N(LoanUpdates[Repl Initial Spread]>0),
N(LoanUpdates[Initial Spread]>0),LoanUpdates[Initial Amount])
```

Similarly, this returns the weighted average replacement spread.

19. In the Spread Change column, enter the following formula:

```
=SUMPRODUCT(N(LoanUpdates[Inactivation Date]>=[@Date]),
N(LoanUpdates[Inactivation Date] <= EDATE([@Date],1)-1),
N(LoanUpdates[InactivationReason]="Refinanced"),
N(LoanUpdates[Repl Initial Spread]>0),
N(LoanUpdates[Initial Spread]>0),LoanUpdates[Initial Amount],
LoanUpdates[Repl Initial Spread]-LoanUpdates[Initial Spread])/
SUMPRODUCT(N(LoanUpdates[Inactivation Date]>=[@Date]),
N(LoanUpdates[Inactivation Date] <= EDATE([@Date],1)-1),
N(LoanUpdates[InactivationReason]="Refinanced"),
N(LoanUpdates[Repl Initial Spread]>0),
N(LoanUpdates[Initial Spread]>0),LoanUpdates[Initial Amount])
```

This returns the weighted average change in spread.

20. In the Healthcare column, enter the following formula:

```
=SUMPRODUCT(N(LoanUpdates[Inactivation Date]>=[@Date]),
N(LoanUpdates[Inactivation Date] <= EDATE([@Date],1)-1),
N(LoanUpdates[InactivationReason]="Refinanced"),
N(LoanUpdates[Repl Initial Spread]>0),
N(LoanUpdates[Initial Spread]>0),LoanUpdates[Initial Amount],
LoanUpdates[Repl Initial Spread]-LoanUpdates[Initial Spread],
N(LoanUpdates[Industry]="Healthcare"))/
SUMPRODUCT(N(LoanUpdates[Inactivation Date]>=[@Date]),
N(LoanUpdates[Inactivation Date] <= EDATE([@Date],1)-1),
N(LoanUpdates[InactivationReason]="Refinanced"),
N(LoanUpdates[Repl Initial Spread]>0),
N(LoanUpdates[Initial Spread]>0),LoanUpdates[Initial Amount],
N(LoanUpdates[Industry]="Healthcare"))
```

This returns the weighted average change in spread for Healthcare loans. This might return a divide-by-zero error if there were no healthcare refinancings during the period.

21. Place the same formula from step 20 in the Retail column but change Healthcare to **Retailing**.

These steps should result in a table that looks like Figure 8-2. Use the resulting table to identify trends in spread compression across months and sectors.

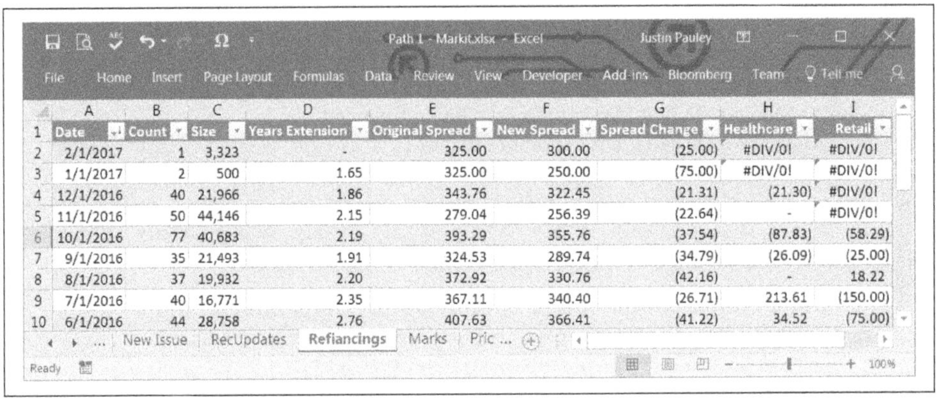

Date	Count	Size	Years Extension	Original Spread	New Spread	Spread Change	Healthcare	Retail
2/1/2017	1	3,323	-	325.00	300.00	(25.00)	#DIV/0!	#DIV/0!
1/1/2017	2	500	1.65	325.00	250.00	(75.00)	#DIV/0!	#DIV/0!
12/1/2016	40	21,966	1.86	343.76	322.45	(21.31)	(21.30)	#DIV/0!
11/1/2016	50	44,146	2.15	279.04	256.39	(22.64)	-	#DIV/0!
10/1/2016	77	40,683	2.19	393.29	355.76	(37.54)	(87.83)	(58.29)
9/1/2016	35	21,493	1.91	324.53	289.74	(34.79)	(26.09)	(25.00)
8/1/2016	37	19,932	2.20	372.92	330.76	(42.16)	-	18.22
7/1/2016	40	16,771	2.35	367.11	340.40	(26.71)	213.61	(150.00)
6/1/2016	44	28,758	2.76	407.63	366.41	(41.22)	34.52	(75.00)

Figure 8-2. Loan refinancing analysis

You can use this data to identify how much interest savings companies are getting (spread tightening/reduction) as well as their ability to extend their loan maturities. Like the loan facility information, analysts should review the underlying recommended updates data for outliers that might skew the results. Note that the spreads are in basis points.

Price History

Markit distributes daily loan prices that it collects from sell-side broker dealers on most of the corporate loan market. In addition to providing bid and offer prices, Markit provides a Depth column that represents the number of price contributors. Depth can be used as a proxy for a loan's liquidity, with a larger depth number signaling greater liquidity. Firms often use this data to mark their positions daily, but the universe of daily loan prices can be used for much more, including the following:

- Overall market metrics, including the change in average daily price change across all loans or by sector and rating
- The average liquidity of a portfolio of loans
- The price range for a loan, indicating its performance in different credit cycles
- Companies that are underperforming or outperforming the market

However, big data presents a big problem. Because Markit delivers the data in "third normal form," the loan pricing data doesn't contain any information about the loan itself other than an identifier (LoanX ID) that can be used to link to the LoanFacilities table. And, as you might find out, linking the information for more than 6,000 loans per day can cause Excel to slow down or crash (mine crashed writing this chapter).

One potential solution to this issue is to use VLOOKUP or INDEX/MATCH functions to add columns from the LoanFacilities table to the LoanPrices table and convert the resulting data from a formula into values (removing the link). However, this solution comes with a few drawbacks:

- Every time you get the daily loan prices from Markit, you must repeat the steps to populate the facility information from the LoanFacilities table.
- By adding data that already exists in another table, thus removing "third normal form," it might introduce data issues. For instance, if the LoanPrices table copied the sector information for a loan from the LoanFacilities table and then the sector information was updated, the information in the LoanPrices table would be incorrect because the data would not be linked.
- There is still no guarantee that simply linking the data using a VLOOKUP will not crash your Excel.

Therefore, I recommend that you use Microsoft Access to perform analysis on large datasets instead of Excel. Nevertheless, for those who want to live dangerously, the following steps demonstrate how to link the industry and size columns from the LoanFacilities table to the LoanPrices table.

22. In the Marks worksheet, add a column to the LoanPrices table called **Industry**, and then enter the following formula:

    ```
    =INDEX(LoanFacilities[Industry],MATCH([@[LoanX ID]],
    LoanFacilities[LoanX ID],0))
    ```

    This formula pulls the Industry information from the LoanFacilities table for the specific LoanX ID.

23. Select every cell under the Industry column header, right-click, and then, on the shortcut menu that opens, select Copy. Then, right-click again and select Paste Values in the same column.

    This overwrites the INDEX formula with the Industry value. Removing the link between the two tables will improve Excel's performance.

24. Add another column to the LoanPrices table called **Initial Amount**, and then enter the following formula:

    ```
    =INDEX(LoanFacilities[Initial Amount],MATCH([@[LoanX ID]],
    LoanFacilities[LoanX ID],0))
    ```

    Like step 22, this formula pulls the Initial Amount column from the LoanFacilities table.

25. Select every cell under the Initial Amount column header, right-click and select Copy, and then right-click again and select Paste Values.

The following steps will demonstrate how to create a running summary of loan price movements for the entire market and by sector.

26. Create a new worksheet called **Price Changes**.

27. In row 1, across columns A through G add the following column headers: **Date**, **Count**, **All**, **% Change**, **Healthcare**, **Retail**, **Oil & Gas**.

28. In cell A2, under the Date column header, add this formula:

    ```
    =MAX(LoanPrices[Mark Date])
    ```

    This returns the latest date in the LoanPrices table.

29. In cell A3, under the cell containing the latest date, place the formula and drag it down for the desired number of days:

    ```
    =MAXIFS(LoanPrices[Mark Date],LoanPrices[Mark Date],"< "&A2)
    ```

    This formula returns the latest pricing date that is less than the row above it. This formula is used to get sequential pricing dates, because the pricing dates might not be consecutive due to weekends and holidays.

30. Convert the Excel range (through column G) into an Excel table

31. In column B, under the Count column header, enter the following formula:

    ```
    =COUNTIF(LoanPrices[Mark Date],[@Date])
    ```

    This function returns the number of loan prices in LoanPrices for each given day.

32. Under the All column header, use the following formula:

    ```
    =SUMPRODUCT(N(LoanPrices[Mark Date]=[@Date]),LoanPrices[Initial Amount],
    LoanPrices[Evaluated Price])/SUMPRODUCT(N(LoanPrices[Mark Date]=[@Date]),
    LoanPrices[Initial Amount])
    ```

    This formula returns the average price of the marks for a given day weighted by each loan's initial amount.

33. In cell C2, under the "% Change" column, use the following formula and then drag it down:

    ```
    =([@All]-C3)/C3
    ```

    This formula calculates the daily percent price change by comparing the value in the All column to the value from the previous day. Note that the last row will return an error because there is not a previous day's price to compare.

34. Under Healthcare, enter the following formula:

    ```
    =SUMPRODUCT(N(LoanPrices[Mark Date]=[@Date]),
    N(LoanPrices[Industry]="Healthcare"),LoanPrices[Initial Amount],
    LoanPrices[Evaluated Price])/
    SUMPRODUCT(N(LoanPrices[Mark Date]=[@Date]),
    N(LoanPrices[Industry]="Healthcare"),LoanPrices[Initial Amount])
    ```

This formula is the same as that in step 32, which calculates the weighted average daily loan price, but this formula only includes Healthcare loans.

35. Under Retail, enter the following formula:

```
=SUMPRODUCT(N(LoanPrices[Mark Date]=[@Date]),
N(LoanPrices[Industry]="Retailing"),LoanPrices[Initial Amount],
LoanPrices[Evaluated Price])/
SUMPRODUCT(N(LoanPrices[Mark Date]=[@Date]),
N(LoanPrices[Industry]="Retailing"),LoanPrices[Initial Amount])
```

This formula is the same as that in step 34, except that it includes only Retail loans.

36. Under Oil & Gas, enter the following formula:

```
=SUMPRODUCT(N(LoanPrices[Mark Date]=[@Date]),
N(LoanPrices[Industry]="Oil & Gas"),LoanPrices[Initial Amount],
LoanPrices[Evaluated Price])/
SUMPRODUCT(N(LoanPrices[Mark Date]=[@Date]),
N(LoanPrices[Industry]="Oil & Gas"),LoanPrices[Initial Amount])
```

This is the same formula as the last two columns except it includes only loans from Oil and Gas companies.

The resulting table should look like Figure 8-3.

	A	B	C	D	E	F	G
1	Date	Count	All	% Change	Healthcare	Retail	Oil & Gas
2	2/17/2017	6,020	99.47	0.02%	99.09	98.63	97.81
3	2/16/2017	6,031	99.46	0.00%	99.08	98.65	97.82
4	2/15/2017	6,027	99.45	-0.03%	99.08	98.69	97.89
5	2/14/2017	6,014	99.48	0.00%	99.09	98.66	98.42
6	2/13/2017	6,012	99.48	0.01%	99.07	98.68	98.58
7	2/10/2017	6,019	99.47	0.06%	99.04	98.72	98.59
8	2/9/2017	6,016	99.40	-0.01%	99.03	98.72	98.57
9	2/8/2017	6,000	99.41	-0.01%	99.01	98.80	98.59
10	2/7/2017	5,969	99.42	0.04%	99.02	98.82	98.61
11	2/6/2017	6,013	99.38	0.56%	98.66	98.85	97.55
12	2/3/2017	5,998	98.82	-0.59%	99.02	98.83	98.37
13	2/2/2017	5,992	99.41	-0.02%	99.03	98.79	98.37
14	2/1/2017	5,975	99.43	0.04%	99.02	98.85	98.35
15	1/31/2017	5,956	99.39	#DIV/0!	99.05	98.93	98.08

Figure 8-3. Daily loan price summary

You can use the breakdown of daily loan prices by industry and how those prices changed over time to identify areas of the market that are stressed or particularly in demand.

You can track daily price changes for the entire market to quickly summarize statistics for individual loans with a lot less work than BDH functions. The following steps will demonstrate how to summarize historical prices for specific loans:

37. In row 1, across columns I through Q, add the following column headers: **LoanX ID**, **Deal Name**, **Current Price**, **Max Price**, **Max Date**, **Min Price**, **Min Date**, **Count**, **StdDev**.

38. Under the LoanX ID column, place the LoanX identifiers for the loans to summarize from the LoanXFacility worksheet. Place one identifier in each row under the LoanX ID column header.

39. Convert the Excel range into a table.

40. Under the Deal Name column header, enter the following formula:

    ```
    =INDEX(LoanFacilities[Deal Name],MATCH([@[LoanX ID]],
    LoanFacilities[LoanX ID],0))
    ```

    This formula uses the INDEX and MATCH functions to pull the Deal Name column from the LoanFacilities table for the given LoanX ID.

41. In the Current Price column, enter the following formula:

    ```
    =SUMPRODUCT(N(LoanPrices[Mark Date]=MAX(LoanPrices[Mark Date])),
    N(LoanPrices[LoanX ID]=[@[LoanX ID]]),LoanPrices[Evaluated Price])
    ```

    This formula returns the latest loan price for the given LoanX ID by filtering the Mark Date by the latest Mark Date in the LoanPrices table.

42. In the Max Price column, enter the following formula:

    ```
    =MAXIFS(LoanPrices[Evaluated Price],LoanPrices[LoanX ID],[@[LoanX ID]])
    ```

    This formula returns the highest price in LoanPrices for a given LoanX ID.

43. In the Max Date column, enter the following formula:

    ```
    =MAXIFS(LoanPrices[Mark Date],LoanPrices[LoanX ID],[@[LoanX ID]],
    LoanPrices[Evaluated Price],[@[Max Px]])
    ```

    This formula uses the MAXIFS function to return the latest date on which the loan had the highest price.

44. In the Min Price column, enter the following formula:

    ```
    =MINIFS(LoanPrices[Evaluated Price],LoanPrices[LoanX ID],[@[LoanX ID]])
    ```

    Similar to step 42, this formula returns the minimum price in LoanPrices for a given LoanX ID.

45. In the Min Date column, enter the following formula:

```
=MAXIFS(LoanPrices[Mark Date],LoanPrices[LoanX ID],
  [@[LoanX ID]],LoanPrices[Evaluated Price],[@[Min Px]])
```

Similar to step 43, this formula returns the latest date on which the loan had the lowest price.

46. Under the Count column header, enter the formula:

```
=COUNTIF(LoanPrices[LoanX ID],[@[LoanX ID]])
```

This formula simply returns the number of dates with a price for the given loan.

47. In the StdDev column, enter the following array formula:

```
=STDEV(IF(LoanPrices[LoanX ID]=[@[LoanX ID]],LoanPrices[Evaluated Price]))
```

This formula returns the standard deviation of the loan prices for a given loan. As discussed in the previous chapter, standard deviation is a measurement of volatility and risk. Note that because this formula is an array formula, you must press Ctrl-Shift-Enter after typing it.

The resulting table should look like Figure 8-4. Knowing the standard deviation and the loan's high and low prices is important to consider when making an investment, even though past performance is not a guarantee of future performance. Knowing the dates of the highs and lows helps to discern whether the loan price movement was more of a function of the overall market rather than the loan itself. The dates can also inform you as to whether the loan is currently or was recently at its highest or lowest price.

	LoanX ID	Deal Name	Current Px	Max Px	Max Date	Min Px	Min Date	Count	StdDev
2	LX143540	Community Health 3/1	99.36	99.55	10/14/2016	98.76	1/4/2017	34	16%
3	LX148423	Nelson Education 10/	57.75	57.83	2/9/2017	52.67	10/14/2016	34	89%
4	LX157886	EW Scripps 12/16 Cov	100.75	100.75	2/17/2017	100.56	1/3/2017	33	6%

Figure 8-4. Loan price summary

Paths 2 and 3: Access and C#

Because the data used in this chapter is already in the database, there isn't a need to write C# code. Instead, this section will cover how to analyze the Markit loan data using Microsoft Access regardless of whether the data was imported using the CSV import in Access or through C#. Like previous chapters, this section focuses on implementation of the concepts covered in the Excel (Path 1) section. Because Access is better suited for querying data, the implementation in this section is a lot simpler.

New Issue Loan Analysis

The following query results in the same output as the Excel table shown in Figure 8-1:

```
SELECT
DateSerial(Year([close date]),Month([close date]),1) AS MonthlyDate,
Count(*) AS [Count],
format(Sum(x.[Initial Amount]),"#,##0") AS TotalSize,
format(Sum(x.[Initial Amount])/Count(*),"#,##0") AS AvgSize,
format(Sum(term*[initial amount])/Sum([initial amount]),"0.00") AS WtdTerm,
format(Sum([initial spread]*[initial amount])/Sum([initial amount]),"0.00") AS
WtdSprd,

format(
Sum(iif([Industry]='Healthcare',[Initial Spread]*[initial amount],0))/
Sum(iif([Industry]='Healthcare',[initial amount],0))  ,"#,##0") AS
WtdHealthcareSpread,

format(
Sum(iif([Industry]='Retailing',[Initial Spread]*[initial amount],0))/
Sum(iif([Industry]='Retailing',[initial amount],0))
 ,"#,##0") AS WtdRetailSpread,

format(
Sum(iif([Industry]='Oil & Gas',[Initial Spread]*[initial amount],0))/
Sum(iif([Industry]='Oil & Gas',[initial amount],0))
 ,"#,##0") AS WtdOilGasSpread


FROM LoanXFacilityUpdates AS x
WHERE
 (((x.Currency)='us dollar')
And ((x.[LoanX Facility Category])='Institutional')
And ((x.Status)='Active') And ((x.[Initial Spread])>0))
GROUP BY DateSerial(Year([close date]),Month([close date]),1);
```

The MonthlyDate column uses the DATESERIAL function to convert every date to the first day of the month by constructing a new date using the year and month of the date stored in the database. This same function is used in the GROUP BY statement to aggregate all of the values on a monthly basis.

The Count, TotalSize, and AvgSize columns use the standard COUNT and SUM functions to aggregate the rows by the MonthlyDate column. The WtdTerm column weights the Term column by the Initial Amount column to return a weighted average term for the loans in each month. Similarly, the WtdSprd column returns a weighted average spread for the loans in each month.

The WtdHealthcareSpread column uses the same calculation as the WtdSprd column, except that it uses the IIF function to include only loans for which the Industry is

Healthcare. Likewise, the WtdRetailSpread and WtdOilGasSpread include only Retail and Oil & Gas loans, respectively.

Refinancings

The following query results in the same output as the Excel table shown in Figure 8-2:

```
SELECT
DateSerial(Year([Inactivation Date]),Month([Inactivation Date]),1) AS MonthlyDate,
Count(*) AS [Count],
format(Sum(x.[Initial Amount]),"#,##0") AS TotalSize,

format(
(Sum(   iif([Repl Maturity Date] >= [Maturity Date],
(datediff("d",[Maturity Date],[Repl Maturity Date])) *[initial amount],0))
/Sum(iif([Repl Maturity Date] >= [Maturity Date],
[initial amount],0)))/365
,"0.00") AS YrsExt,

format(Sum([initial spread]*[initial amount])/Sum([initial amount]),"0.00")
AS OrigSprd,
format(Sum([Repl initial spread]*[initial amount])/Sum([initial amount]),"0.00")
AS NewSprd,
format(Sum(([Repl initial spread]-[initial spread])*[initial amount])/
Sum([initial amount]),"0.00") AS SprdDiff,

format(
Sum(iif([Industry]='Healthcare',
([Repl initial spread]-[initial spread])*[initial amount],0))
/Sum(iif([Industry]='Healthcare',
[initial amount],0))
,"0.00") AS WtdHealthcareSpreadChg,

format(
Sum(iif([Industry]='Retailing',([Repl initial spread]-
[initial spread])*[initial amount],0))
/Sum(iif([Industry]='Retailing',[initial amount],0))  ,"0.00") AS
WtdRetailSpreadChg

FROM LoanXRecUpdates AS x
WHERE [inactivationreason]='Refinanced'
and [Repl Initial Spread] > 0
and [Initial Spread] > 0
GROUP BY DateSerial(Year([Inactivation Date]),Month([Inactivation Date]),1);
```

Like the previous query, the MonthlyDate column is constructed by using the date of refinancing (contained in the Inactivation Date) and is used in the GROUP BY statement to aggregate the rows by month. The Count and TotalSize columns return the number of rows and total amount of refinancings in each month.

The YrsExt column, which returns the weighted average of extended years from a maturity amendment, is a bit more complicated. The statement divides the weighted differences between the old and new Maturity Date (contained in the Repl Maturity Date) by 365 to get the number of years. The IIF function is used to limit the numerator and denominator by loans that kept or extended their maturities. The DATEDIFF function is used to return the number of days between the current and replacement Maturity Dates.

The OrigSprd and NewSprd columns return the weighted average initial and replacement spread. The SprdDiff returns the weighted average difference between the initial and replacement spread. Similarly, the WtdHealthcareSpreadChg and WtdRetailSpreadChg use the same logic as the SprdDiff column, except that they include only Healthcare and Retail loans, respectively.

Price History

The following query results in the same output as the Excel table shown in Figure 8-3:

```
SELECT
[Mark Date],
Count(*) AS [Count],
Format(sum([initial amount] * [evaluated price])/sum([initial amount]),"0.00") AS
WtdPx,

Format(
sum([initial amount] * [evaluated price])/sum([initial amount]) /
(SELECT top 1 sum(x2.[initial amount] *
m2.[evaluated price])/sum(x2.[initial amount])
  FROM LoanXMarks AS m2
  INNER JOIN LoanXFacilityUpdates AS x2 ON x2.[loanx id]=m2.[loanx id]
  where m2.[mark date] < m.[mark date]
  group by m2.[mark date]
  order by m2.[mark date] desc )-1
,"0.00%") AS PctChg,

format(
Sum(iif([Industry]='Healthcare',[evaluated price]*[initial amount],0))/
Sum(iif([Industry]='Healthcare',[initial amount],0))  ,"0.00") AS
WtdHealthcarePx,

format(
Sum(iif([Industry]='Retailing',[evaluated price]*[initial amount],0))  /
Sum(iif([Industry]='Retailing',[initial amount],0))
,"0.00") AS WtdRetailPx,

format(
Sum(iif([Industry]='Oil & Gas',[evaluated price]*[initial amount],0))
/Sum(iif([Industry]='Oil & Gas',[initial amount],0))  ,"0.00") AS WtdOilGasPx
```

```
FROM LoanXMarks AS m
INNER JOIN LoanXFacilityUpdates AS x ON x.[loanx id]=m.[loanx id]
GROUP BY [Mark Date]
ORDER BY [mark date] DESC;
```

As this resulting table shows data on every date, Mark Date is selected and contained in the GROUP BY statement. The Count and WtdPx columns return the number of rows and the price weighted by size, respectively.

The PctChg column, which shows the percentage daily change, is a complicated formula because, unlike Excel, you cannot simply reference the row beneath. Instead, this column uses a subquery to return the percentage change for the prior day. Although most examples of percent change in this book divide the difference between current value and original value by the original value, another formula for percentage change is dividing the current value by the original value and subtracting one. The first part of the PctChg statement uses the same logic as the WtdPx column but then divides by the WtdPx of the prior day and subtracts one. The subquery returns the prior row's WtdPx by selecting the first row from LoanXMarks for which the date is less than the current row's date. The subquery can cause the query to run slower and should be removed to improve performance.

The WtdHealthcarePx, WtdRetailPx, and WtdOilGasPx columns use the same logic as the WtdPx column, but they use the IIF statement to return only Healthcare, Retail, and Oil and Gas companies, respectively.

This query also INNER JOINs the LoanXFacilityUpdates table because the Initial Amount and Industry columns aren't part of the LoanXMarks table.

The next query results in the same output as the Excel table shown in Figure 8-4:

```
SELECT
[LoanX ID],
[Deal Name],

format(
(select top 1 [evaluated price]
 from LoanXMarks m
 where m.[loanx id]=x.[loanx id]
 order by [mark date] desc
)   ,"0.00") AS CrrPx,

format(
(select top 1 max([evaluated price])
 from LoanXMarks m
 where m.[loanx id]=x.[loanx id]
 group by [evaluated price]
 order by [evaluated price] desc
),"0.00") AS MaxPx,

(select top 1 max([mark date])
```

```
    from LoanXMarks m
    where m.[loanx id]=x.[loanx id]
    group by [evaluated price]
    order by [evaluated price] desc) AS MaxDt,

    format(
    (select top 1 max([evaluated price])
     from LoanXMarks m
    where m.[loanx id]=x.[loanx id]
    group by [evaluated price]
    order by [evaluated price] )
    ,"0.00") AS MinPx,

    (select top 1 max([mark date])
     from LoanXMarks m
    where m.[loanx id]=x.[loanx id]
    group by [evaluated price]
    order by [evaluated price]
    ) AS MinDt,

    (select count(*)
     from LoanXMarks m
    where  m.[loanx id]=x.[loanx id]
    ) AS [Count],

    format(
    (select stdev([evaluated price])
     from LoanXMarks m
    where  m.[loanx id]=x.[loanx id])
    ,"0%") AS StdDev

    FROM LoanXFacilityUpdates AS x
    WHERE x.[loanx id] in ('LX143540','LX148423','LX157886');
```

This query selects rows from LoanXFacilityUpdates for a set of distinct LoanX IDs and uses several subqueries instead of INNER JOIN because it needs to aggregate the LoanXMarks data in different ways. The first subquery, that returns the current price (CrrPx), selects the first price from LoanXMarks for the specific LoanX ID ordered by most recent price.

The next subquery (MaxPX) returns that highest price for a given LoanX ID by selecting the first price from LoanXMarks ordered by highest to lowest price. Access differs from Microsoft SQL Server in that it requires the MAX function be used in conjunction with a GROUP BY to ensure that the subquery returns only one row, despite the inclusion of the TOP statement.

The MaxDt subquery is the same as the MaxPX subquery except that it returns the date of the row with the highest price. The MaxPX and MaxDt logic is replicated to query the MinPX and MinDt columns except that the rows in the subquery are ordered from lowest to highest price.

The Count and StdDev subqueries use the Access COUNT and STDEV aggregate functions to return the number of marks and their standard deviation, respectively. The query uses the IN statement in the WHERE clause to specify the list of LoanX IDs to include.

A Step Further

This section contains additional queries that aren't covered under Path 1 to demonstrate more complex techniques in Access.

Loans currently above $90 that were below $80

One of the more interesting analyses to perform when working with large datasets, like Markit's loan data, is to look for anomalies that could result in investment ideas. One such analysis is to look at loans that were recently trading below $80 but have made large gains and are currently trading above $90:

```
SELECT
m.[LoanX ID],
x.[Deal Name],
m.[Evaluated Price],
n.MinPx,

(select max(m3.[mark date])
 from LoanXMarks m3
 where m3.[loanx id]=m.[loanx id]
 and m3.[evaluated price]=n.minPx
) AS DateOfMinPrice

FROM (LoanXMarks AS m
            INNER JOIN LoanXFacilityUpdates AS x ON x.[loanx id]=m.[loanx id])
            INNER JOIN (
              SELECT
              m2.[LoanX ID],
              Min(m2.[Evaluated Price]) AS MinPx
              FROM LoanXMarks AS m2
              WHERE m2.[evaluated price] < 80
              and m2.[mark date] > dateadd("d",-90,now())
              GROUP BY m2.[LoanX ID])  AS n ON n.[LoanX ID]=m.[LoanX ID]

WHERE m.[mark date] = (select max([mark date]) from LoanXMarks) and
m.[evaluated price] > 90;
```

In the previous query, the LoanX ID and Evaluated Price columns are selected from the LoanXMarks table, whereas the Deal Name column is from the INNER JOINed LoanXFacilityUpdates table.

The MinPx column is from the subquery also INNER JOINed. The subquery selects the LoanX ID and minimum price from LoanXMarks for each LoanX ID for which the price is below $80 and it was within the last 90 days. Another way Access differs from SQL Server is that it allows you to INNER JOIN only one table, unless you group them with extra parentheses.

The DateOfMinPrice column uses a subquery to return the most recent date on which the loan had the minimum price below $80.

The WHERE clause uses a subquery to filter out marks from dates that aren't the latest in the LoanXMarks table. Additionally, it filters out all loans that aren't currently marked above $90. The query results should look like Figure 8-5.

Figure 8-5. Query results showing loans that have rallied

Another useful query is one that returns all the loans that have had more than a 10 percent price change in the past two weeks. You can easily modify the following query with different price limits over a different period:

```
SELECT
m.[LoanX ID],
[Deal Name],
format(m.[Evaluated Price],"0.00") AS TodayPrice,
format(twoweeksago.[Evaluated Price],"0.00") AS TwoWeeksAgo,
twoweeksago.[mark date],
format( (m.[Evaluated Price]-twoweeksago.[Evaluated Price])/
twoweeksago.[Evaluated Price],"0.00%") AS PctChg
FROM
(LoanXMarks AS m
 INNER JOIN LoanXFacilityUpdates AS x ON x.[loanx id]=m.[loanx id])
INNER JOIN (
 SELECT m2.[LoanX ID],
        m2.[Mark Date],
        m2.[Evaluated Price]
        FROM LoanXMarks AS M2 WHERE m2.[Mark Date] =(select

max(m3.[mark date])

from LoanXMarks m3
```

```
where m3.[mark date] < dateadd("d",-14,now())

)
) AS twoweeksago ON twoweeksago.[LoanX ID]=m.[LoanX ID]
WHERE
m.[mark date] = (select max([mark date]) from LoanXMarks)
and m.[evaluated price] > 0
and twoweeksago.[evaluated price] >0
and abs((m.[Evaluated Price]-twoweeksago.[Evaluated Price])/
twoweeksago.[Evaluated Price]) > 0.1
ORDER BY (m.[Evaluated Price]-twoweeksago.[Evaluated Price])/
twoweeksago.[Evaluated Price];
```

This query is a bit complicated because it INNER JOINs a subquery that contains another subquery. The outer subquery in the INNER JOIN statement selects the LoanX ID, Mark Date, and Evaluated Price from LoanXMarks for which the date is the most recent date in LoanXMarks that is at least 14 days before today (the NOW function returns today's date).

The table alias "m" represents the most current price information for each loan because the WHERE clause filters out rows where the mark date isn't the newest date in the LoanXMarks table using a subquery. The table alias "twoweeksago" represents the data on the same loan two weeks earlier. As such the PctChg column returns the percentage change from the earlier date (displayed in the Mark Date column) to the most current price.

The WHERE clause also uses the ABS function to display only loans that have an absolute percentage change of more than 10 percent. The resulting query should look like Figure 8-6.

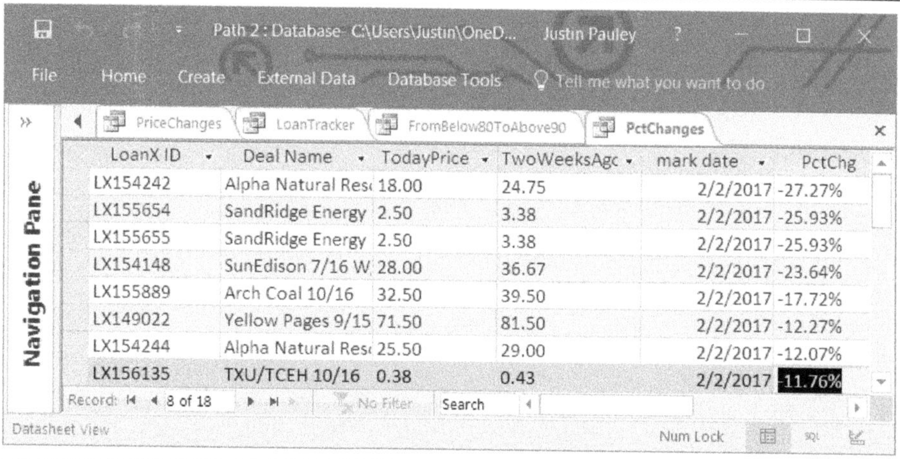

Figure 8-6. Price changes over 10%

Summary

Tunnel vision is one of the more dangerous traps analysts fall into. It is easy to focus on their corner of the world and not be concerned with trends in other sectors or areas of the market. It is important that analysts have a sense of the trends in the overall market because there is no such thing as isolated markets that aren't affected at least in part by changes in other markets. This chapter covered how to use Markit's data on the loan market to identify broader trends with the ability to dig deep into the underlying information. This chapter is the final chapter in the Financial Data Analysis section; the next section covers how to display the results of the analysis in various reports.

CHAPTER 9

Creating Reports

If I can't picture it, I can't understand it.
—Albert Einstein

This section makes use of most of the lessons from earlier chapters to demonstrate building two-page analytic ("Tear Sheet") reports for individual companies including historical financials, comparative analysis, and relative value. Designing reports is a bit of an art form; this chapter walks you through different techniques and helpful examples, but people have very different ideas and preferences on how reports should look. The term *tear sheet* refers to Standard & Poor's one-page reports on public companies back when brokers tore them out of a book, but today there are numerous online sources of one-page analytic reports. Bloomberg has some useful ones in its Excel Template Library (XLTP <GO>).

However, the entire point of this book is to give you an edge by enabling you to create your own reports, with data from multiple sources combined with your views and insights, laid out exactly the way you want. Your input on how companies should be categorized, which index is an appropriate comparison, incorrect or incomplete data that you've overridden or enhanced, and the comments you've recorded will make the reports designed in this chapter a much more powerful tool than the ones that every other investor uses. Moreover, there are thousands of pieces of financial data, including multiple ways of calculating earnings. Deciding which fields and calculations are appropriate is as personal and hotly debated as pizza toppings.

Currently, all of the financial data and analysis constructed in previous chapters exists in a single row for each company. As this chapter will demonstrate, although this view is great for comparison, creating a single page report makes the information a lot easier to digest. Like earlier chapters, this chapter is broken into three paths: Microsoft Excel, Access, and C#. Each section will demonstrate how to create a tear sheet report and automatically populate it by specifying a CompanyID. Excel is a great tool for creating reports because it has a lot of features, extensive charts, and is very simple to use. Access, on the other hand, is frustratingly difficult and nonintuitive. Although this chapter covers the reporting tools in Access, I recommend that you use Excel or the C# option, SQL Server Reporting Services (SSRS). In the following sections, the layout, colors, charts, fields, and so on can all be adjusted to your preference; the goal is to provide different techniques and helpful hints that will make customizing a report a lot easier.

Path 1: Excel

This section covers the steps to create a two-page company report in Excel that can switch between companies by using a simple drop-down list. The first steps are creating a new worksheet that we'll call CompanyReport, setting the page layout, and adjusting the view to make it easier to visualize the resulting report:

1. Create a new worksheet called **CompanyReport**, change your view to Page Break Preview.

2. In Excel, on the ribbon, on the Page Layout tab, click the Orientation button, and then select Landscape.

3. Select cells A1 through M68. Again, on the Page Layout tab, click Print Area, and then choose Set Print Area.

   The resulting cells with a white background represent the available space for the report. You can use the gray cells outside the box marked "Page 1" for calculating report items.

4. Still on the Page Layout tab, but in the Sheet Options group, in the Gridlines section, clear the check mark adjacent to View.

5. Change the font size of every cell to 8.

   Size 11 font is bigger than most people need.

   The basic structure of the report will consist of six sections that will be separated by section headers or thick outside cell borders. The next steps set up the basic skeleton of the report.

6. Merge the cells in row 3 from columns A through M, change the background color and font color of the merged cell, and label it **Company Description**.

7. Repeat step 6, but merge the cells in row 6 and label it **Overview**.

8. Merge the cells in row 13 from column A through H, alter the background color and font color, and label it **Relative Value**.

9. Merge the cells to the right of Relative Value on row 13 (columns I through M) and label it **Comments**.

The next steps add the drop-down functionality that will let you switch quickly between companies.

10. On the Formula tab, in the Defined Names group, click Name Manager.

11. Click New, and then, in the text box, type **Ticker**. In the "Refers to" list box, select:

    ```
    =Company[CompanyID]
    ```

    A defined name needs to be created for the drop-down list created in the next steps.

12. Label cell A7 **Ticker**, select cell B7, and then, on the Data tab, click Data Validation.

13. In the Data Validation dialog box, on the Settings tab, in the Allow list box, choose List, and then type **=Ticker** in the Source box.

    After you click OK, a list box appears in which you can select any CompanyID from the company worksheet, as demonstrated in Figure 9-1.

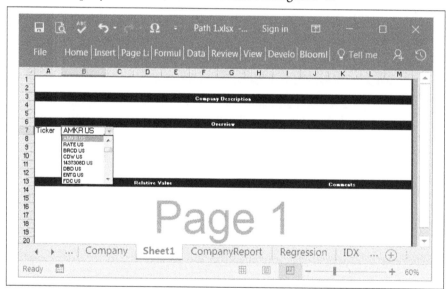

Figure 9-1. Report skeleton with drop-down list

The next steps add the Company Name to the report header based on the selected CompanyID. The header will include both the date on which the report was created as well as the date when the financial information was updated. These dates are important, especially on printouts, because they give context to the information found in the report.

14. Merge cells A1 through H2, and then enter the following formula:

```
=INDEX(Company[CompanyName],MATCH($B$7,Company[CompanyID],0))
```

This uses the INDEX/MATCH functions to pull the Company Name from the Company table for which the CompanyID matches the one in cell B7. This same formula will be used multiple times on this report to pull fields from the Company worksheet.

15. Label cell I1 **Financials As Of**, and then, in cell J1, enter the following formula:

```
=INDEX(Company[Latest Financials],MATCH($B$7,Company[CompanyID]))
```

This formula pulls the date of the latest financial record date from the Company Worksheet.

16. Label cell I2 **Report Date**, and then, in cell J2, enter the following formula:

```
=TODAY()
```

The Report Date is always Today because the comments and equity prices are being updated daily.

The next steps populate the Company Description section with the full description from Bloomberg. Because this can be a large description, you must use the BDS function to pull it.

17. Label cell N1 **BBID**, and then, in cell O1 enter the following formula:

```
=INDEX(Company[BBID],MATCH($B$7,Company[CompanyID]))
```

These cells are not going to appear on the report, but pulling the BBID from the Company worksheet into this cell will avoid having to do it multiple times in the future.

18. Merge cells A4 through M5, and then enter the following formula:

```
=BDS($O$1,"CIE_DES_BULK","aggregate=y")
```

This formula pulls the full company description from Bloomberg. The extra argument forces the entire description to be placed into a single cell instead of spanning multiple rows.

19. Format the merged cell, and then, on the Home tab, in the Alignment group, click Wrap Text.

The next steps populate the Overview section of the report with information from the Company worksheet. The steps only walk through a handful of fields and should be expanded based on your preference. Furthermore, different fields have various size labels and values and might require merging to fit everything.

20. Under Ticker, in column A, label rows 8 through 12: **Current Price**, **Moody's Rating**, **S&P Rating**, **Private**, and **EBIT**. Bold these labels.

21. In the cell next to each label, in column B, use the INDEX/MATCH functions like step 14 to pull the respective columns. For instance, use the following formula to pull Price:

```
=INDEX(Company[Price],MATCH($B$7,Company[CompanyID]))
```

The result of steps 20 and 21 should be column labels and corresponding data from the Company Worksheet.

22. Align all cells to the left, and then repeat steps 20 and 21 to create multiple columns of label and value combinations.

23. Set the background color on alternating rows in the Overview section to a light gray to make the individual rows easier to see.

24. Either include the units of each value in the label, such as "Total Revenue ($MM)" or adjust the cell format to identify the units. For instance, "Short Interest/% Float" format can be set to a custom format of: 0.00"%";(0.00"%"), which adds the percent sign after the value.

It is important to include units because this isn't always clear. You can also use the custom format #,##0.00x;(#,##0.00x) to add an "x" after a value, such as with Interest Coverage.

The resulting top three sections should look like Figure 9-2.

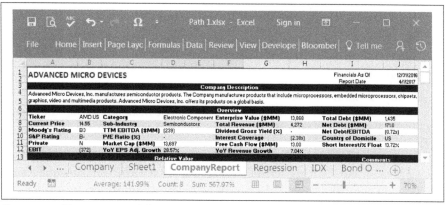

Figure 9-2. Top sections of the Company Report

The next steps build out the Relative Value section of the report. The Relative Value section of the report compares the company's performance to both its peers and the overall market using the Category and Index from the Company worksheet. Depending on the column widths and sizes, you might need to merge some cells or skip a column.

25. Label cells from A15 to A21: **52-Week High (% Chg)**, **52-Week Low (% Chg)**, **12-Month Total Return**, **YTD Price Change**, **3M Price Change**, **Total Debt/ EBITDA**, **FCF/Total Debt**. Bold these cells.

26. Label cell C14 "**Value**", and place formulas in cells C15 through C21 to pull the corresponding data from the Company table. For instance, use the following formula in cell C15 to pull the 52-Week High value:

    ```
    =INDEX(Company[52 Week High],MATCH($B$7,Company[CompanyID]))
    ```

27. In D14, enter the following formula:

    ```
    ="Median "&INDEX(Company[Category],MATCH($B$7,Company[CompanyID]))
    ```

    This formula displays "Median" followed by the company's category.

28. In the cells under the header (D15 through D21), place formulas to pull the median values from the Company table. For instance, to pull the median 52-Week High value, use the following formula:

    ```
    =INDEX(Company[Median 52 Week High],MATCH($B$7,Company[CompanyID]))
    ```

    Each of the columns should have a corresponding Median column value in the Company table.

29. In G14, enter the following formula:

    ```
    =INDEX(IDX[Name],MATCH(INDEX(Company[IndexID],
    MATCH($B$7,Company[CompanyID],0)),IDX[IndexID],0))
    ```

    This formula pulls the full name of the Index from the IDX table using the IndexID from the Company worksheet which, in turn, is pulled using the CompanyID in cell B7.

30. In the cells under the Index header (G15 through G19), place formulas to pull the Index values from the Company worksheet. For instance, to pull the Index's 52-Week High, use the following formula:

    ```
    =INDEX(Company[Index 52 Week High],MATCH($B$7,Company[CompanyID]))
    ```

    Cells G20 and G21 are left blank because Total Debt/EBITDA and FCF/Total Debt do not make sense to display for an index of companies.

31. Like step 24, format the cells containing values.

32. Set the background color in alternating rows to make them easier to see.

33. Add bold to the header rows in row 14 and increase the thickness of the bottom border to create a line beneath. If it makes it clearer, format the header cells using Wrap Text and increase the row height of row 14.

    The next steps create a box to display your comments on the company. These comments come from the Company Comments column on the Company worksheet.

34. Merge cells I14 through M21, and then set the format to Wrap Text.

This allows the comment to fill the box across multiple rows and columns.

35. Set the formula for the new set of cells to the following:

```
=INDEX(Company[Company Comments],MATCH(B7,Company[CompanyID]))
```

The Relative Value and Comments section should look like Figure 9-3.

Figure 9-3. Middle section of the Company Report

You cannot have a good-looking report without at least one chart. Charts are great at conveying a lot of information very quickly. This next set of steps adds a chart to the report that compares the daily price of the company's stock to its corresponding index and the consensus price target (fair value) provided by analysts covering the company.

36. Label cell N2 "**Index BBID**", and then, in cell O2, enter the following formula:

```
=INDEX(IDX[BBID],MATCH(INDEX(Company[IndexID],
MATCH($B$7,Company[CompanyID],0)),IDX[IndexID],0))
```

This formula returns the BBID from the IDX worksheet for the corresponding Index for the company.

37. Label cell N3 "**Start Date**", and then, in cell O3, enter the following formula:

```
=TODAY()-365
```

This sets the beginning date for the price history to a year ago from today.

38. Label cell N4 "**End Date**", and then, in cell O4, enter the following formula:

```
=TODAY()
```

39. In cells R1 and W1, enter the following formula:

```
=O1
```

This formula copies the Bloomberg ID for the company into these cells, which will serve as the header row for the price history in future steps.

40. Label cell R2 "**Date**", and then, in cell S2, enter the following formula:

```
=B7&" (Rt Axis)"
```

The formula in S2 displays the Ticker with " (Rt Axis)" to indicate that it will be on the right axis of the chart.

41. In cell R3, enter the following formula:

```
=BDH(R1,"PX_LAST",O3,O4,"FX",P1,"PER=CD","FILL=PNA","CDR=US")
```

This formula pulls the price for the company's stock from the Start Date to the End Date for each calendar day using the US calendar, filling missing dates with the period before.

42. In cell T4, enter the following formula, and then copy it down for each date in column R:

```
=(S4-S3)/S3
```

This formula calculates the daily price change

43. In cell U1, enter the following formula:

```
=O2
```

This displays the Index's Bloomberg ID as the column header above the price history.

44. In cell U2, enter the following formula:

```
=INDEX(Company[IndexID],MATCH($B$7,Company[CompanyID]))&" (Lft Axis)"
```

This formula returns Index ID from the Company worksheet and appends "Lft Axis" next to it to indicate that it will be displayed on the chart's left axis.

45. In cell U2, enter the following formula:

```
=BDH(U1,"PX_LAST",O3,O4,"FX",P1,"PER=CD","FILL=PNA","CDR=US","DTS=H")
```

This formula does the same as the one in step 41, except it pulls a history for the Index and it doesn't display the dates.

46. In cell V4, enter the following formula, and then copy it down for each row that contains a price:

```
=(U4-U3)/U3
```

Like step 42, this calculates the daily price index price change.

47. Label cell W2 "Target."

48. In cell W3, enter the following formula:

```
=BDH(W1,"BEST_TARGET_PRICE",O3,O4,"FX",P1,"PER=CD","FILL=PNA",
"CDR=US","DTS=H")
```

This formula is the same as step 41, except that BEST_TARGET_PRICE returns the consensus price target for the stock and also does not display the dates.

49. Add a line chart that is sized to fill cells A22 through F43, leaving one row of cells beneath.

50. Add the price history in columns S, U, and W to the line chart. Keep the price target and company's price on the same axis, but put the Index on a secondary axis. Format this to your preference.

51. Label cell N5 **Correlation**, and then, in cell O5, enter the following formula:

    ```
    =CORREL(T:T,V:V)
    ```

    This formula returns the correlation between the daily price changes in the company's stock and the index.

52. Label cell N6 **Beta**, and then, in cell O6, enter the following formula:

    ```
    =SLOPE(T:T,V:V)
    ```

    This formula returns the Beta between the daily price changes in the company's stock and the index.

53. Label cell N7 **R-Squared**, and then, in cell O7, enter the following formula:

    ```
    =RSQ(T:T,V:V)
    ```

    This formula returns the R-Squared between the daily price changes in the company's stock and the index.

54. Underneath the chart, in row 44, across columns A through F, add labels and link cells to the Correlation, Beta, and R-Squared values from steps 51 through 53.

    The next steps add a pie chart of the consensus buy and sell recommendations.

55. Label cells N15 through N17: **Buy**, **Sell**, and **Hold**.

56. In cell O15, enter the following formula:

    ```
    =INDEX(Company[Buy Recommendations],MATCH($B$7,Company[CompanyID]))
    ```

    This formula pulls the Buy Recommendations from the Company worksheet.

57. In cell O16, enter the following formula:

    ```
    =INDEX(Company[Sell Recommendations],MATCH($B$7,Company[CompanyID]))
    ```

58. In cell O17, enter the following formula:

    ```
    =INDEX(Company[Hold Recommendations],MATCH($B$7,Company[CompanyID]))
    ```

59. Add a pie chart using the labels in N15 through N17 and the values in O15 through O17. Format this to your preference.

    Page 1 of the report should look like Figure 9-4.

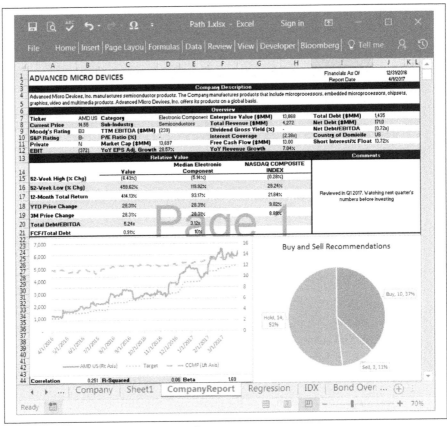

Figure 9-4. Company Report in Excel—page 1

The second page of the report will contain historical financials for the company. The report must be flexible enough to switch between Yearly, Semi-annually, and Quarterly financials by using a drop-down box. The following steps add the drop-down box and add the associated dates to the report using Bloomberg.

60. Select cell N46 (outside the printable area). On the ribbon, on the Data tab, click the Data Validation button.

61. In the Allow list box, select List, and then, in the Source text box, type **Yearly,Semi-Annual,Quarterly**, and then click Okay.

   This should place a drop-down box in cell N46. For now, select "Yearly."

62. In cell C45, enter the following formula:

   ```
   ="-0F"&LEFT($N$46,1)
   ```

   This displays "-0FY" (when cell "Yearly" is selected in cell N46), which we will use as an input to the BDP function to retrieve the latest fiscal year.

---

63. In the cell to the right of cell C45, enter the same formula but adjust the **0** to **1** through **3** such that row 45 reads **-0FY, -1FY, -2FY, -3FY**.

64. Select the cells in row 45 that contain the results of steps 62 and 63, and then set the font color to white to make them invisible.

We're doing this because although we will reference these cells in formulas, we do not need them to be displayed on the report.

65. In cell C46, enter the following formula:

```
=BDP($O$1,"BEST_PERIOD_END_DATE","BEST_FPERIOD_OVERRIDE",C45)
```

This formula returns the fiscal period end date of Bloomberg's estimate data for the fiscal period contained in cell C45.

66. Copy the formula in C45 (step 65) into the four cells to the right.

Depending on the format of the report, you might want to merge some cells together so that the dates fit on the page correctly.

The next set of steps adds the labels and corresponding Bloomberg Fields to the report. Keep in mind that these are just examples of some of the thousands of fields from which you can choose (see Chapter 3).

67. In cells A47 through A54, add the following labels: **Market Cap**, **Enterprise Value**, **Revenue**, **Adj**, **Gross Profit**, **Adj**, **EBITDA**, **Adj**, **Net Income**, **Adj**, **EPS**, **Adj**, and **Free Cash Flow**.

68. In cells N47 through N54, add the following labels containing Bloomberg Fields: **HISTORICAL_MARKET_CAP**, **ENTERPRISE_VALUE**, **SALES_REV_TURN**, **GROSS_PROFIT**, **EBITDA**, **EARN_FOR_COMMON**, **IS_DIL_EPS_CONT_OPS**, and **CF_FREE_CASH_FLOW**.

For more details on these fields, refer to the Bloomberg FLDS screen.

69. In cell C47, enter the following formula:

```
=BDP($O$1,$N47,"EQY_FUND_RELATIVE_PERIOD",C$45,"Fill=-","EQY_FUND_CRNCY",
$P$1)
```

This formula retrieves the field (HISTORICAL_MARKET_CAP) located in column N, for the period (-0FY) found in row 45, using the currency found in cell P1.

70. Copy the formula created in step 69 into each column with a date header, down to row 54.

71. Add a couple of charts of the most useful time series of data.

Page 2 of the report should look like Figure 9-5. Adjusting the drop-down cell N46 to Quarterly will instantly update the historical financials and charts.

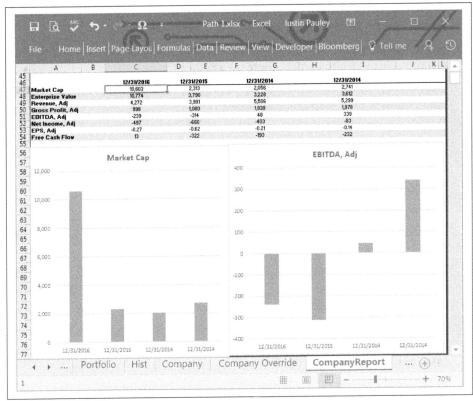

Figure 9-5. Company Report in Excel, page 2

Take a moment to digest the numbers on the report. I also recommend that you add conditional formatting on any cells that should be highlighted when a resulting number exceeds an upper or lower limit. To change between companies, simply use the drop-down list in cell B7 and watch the entire spreadsheet update. And, if the Index or comments change on the Company worksheet, the report will update automatically.

Path 2: Microsoft Access

Access is a great tool for querying large sets of data, but there are a few drawbacks to using its reporting tools. The primary issue is that the interface is not nearly as intuitive as Excel or other reporting tools. In addition, because Access cannot connect to Bloomberg directly, some data, such as historical prices and company descriptions needs to be persisted in the Excel workbook ahead of creating a report. As such, Excel is the recommended reporting platform, even if you are using Access to do your data analysis. Caveats aside, because financial data isn't always available in Bloomberg or might be too large to work with in Excel, it is useful to understand how to create a report in Microsoft Access. This section demonstrates how to create a one-page report on a single company using the Company table that is linked to the Excel worksheet.

The first step is to add a query that collects the data needed for the report for a given CompanyID:

1. Create a new query called **Company Report Query** by using the following:

```
SELECT *
FROM Company
WHERE CompanyID=[CID];
```

   The [CID] column isn't a column from the Company table and, as such, Access will prompt for a CompanyID when you run the query or report. The query will result in every column from the Company table for a given CompanyID.

   The next steps create the report and add fields to the report.

2. On the ribbon, on the Create tab, click Report Design to create a new blank report.

3. On the Page Setup tab, click Landscape.

4. On the Design tab, select Property Sheet. On the Data tab, click the Record Source button, and select the query Company Report Query that was created in step 1.

   This step binds the data from the query to the report.

5. Again, on the Design tab, select Add Existing Fields.

   This displays a Field List box with a list of the columns from the Company table.

6. Drag fields from the Field List onto the report in your preferred layout.

   When you drag a field onto the report, it generates two items: a box containing the name of the column that can be modified as the label, and another box (typically on the right and darker font) that will display the actual value of the field when the report is viewed. You can delete unnecessary labels. Fields dragged into the Page Header section will be repeated on every page.

   The next set of steps walks through how to add additional labels and modify cell formats. On the Design tab, there are two types of useful Controls that can be added to the report. The first is a Text Box that can include a formula and refer to other fields. The other type is a Label that you can format to help organize the report. To add either of these controls to the report, on the Design tab, select them from the Controls, and then drag to an area in which you want to place the control.

7. Add a Text Box to the report. Click inside the Text Box and place the following formula:

```
="Report Date " & Date()
```

When the report is viewed, this Text Box will display "Report Date" followed by today's date.

8. Add a few Labels to the report (such as **Overview**, **Relative Value**, or others like the report created in the Excel version at the beginning of this chapter). Use the options on the Format tab to alter the background color, font color, and to add bold to the labels.

9. Select all of the fields, Labels, and Text Boxes on the report, and then, using the options on the Format tab, set a consistent font size. It is also recommended that you set the control's border to Transparent (in the Control Formatting group, click Shape Outline, and then select Transparent).

10. The Align options on the Arrange tab can be helpful with arranging the different fields on the report.

11. To adjust number formats, right-click a field, and then, on the shortcut menu, point to Properties, and choose a format. You can also type in a custom format like: `0.00\x` to display a number like "2.35x."

Charting the price history of a company against an index, as shown in Figure 9-4, is more difficult in Access. The primary issue is getting the data into the database for every index and company and then transforming the data into a form that the Access chart tool can use. Without writing code, there aren't any elegant solutions. The next set of steps walks through creating a workaround that works but is not ideal.

12. In Excel, create a new worksheet called **PriceHistory**.

13. Label cell A1 **Date**.

14. In row 1, place the BBIDs from each Company and Index from the Company and IDX worksheets. For instance, cell B1 might read "ACIW US Equity" and cell C1 might read "CCMP Index."

15. In cell A2, enter the following formula:

```
=BDH(B$1,"PX_LAST",TODAY()-365,TODAY(),"FX=USD","PER=CD","FILL=PNA",
"CDR=US","DTS=0")
```

This formula populates column A with the calendar dates over the last year.

16. In cell B2, enter the following formula, and then copy it across columns in row 2:

```
=BDH(B$1,"PX_LAST",TODAY()-365,TODAY(),"FX=USD","PER=CD","FILL=PNA",
"CDR=US","DTS=H")
```

This populates the columns with the price history of the BBID in row 1.

17. In Access, on the ribbon, on the External Data tab, link the worksheet created in step 12 by clicking the Excel button.

18. Create a new query called "PriceHistQuery" as follows:

```
SELECT Date,
switch(
c.BBID='AMD US Equity',d.[AMD US Equity],
c.BBID='ACIW US Equity',d.[ACIW US Equity],
c.BBID='AMKR US Equity',d.[AMKR US Equity],
) AS Company,
switch(
c.IndexID='CCMP',d.[CCMP Index],
c.IndexID='S5INFT',d.[S5INFT Index]
) AS [Index]
FROM PriceHistory AS d, Company AS c
WHERE c.CompanyID=[CID];
```

The switch statement selects the appropriate column from the PriceHistory table to return based on the BBID and IndexID in the Company table for the given CompanyID. Unfortunately, this solution requires that every Company BBID and Index ID is listed in the two switch statements, respectively.

19. On the Access Report, on the Design tab, click Controls and then select Chart. Place the Chart on the report as desired. After you place the Chart, the Chart Wizard opens.

20. On the first page of the wizard, select PriceHistQuery. On the second page, copy over the Date, Company, and Index columns into the "Fields for Chart." On the third page, select a line chart. On the fourth page, drag the Index field from the right side of the window under SumOfCompany, and then click Finish.

21. Double-click the new chart to format it to your preference, including setting the second series to the secondary axis.

Note that when you view the report, it will prompt you for the CID (CompanyID) twice (which is another reason I dislike Access Reports). This can be combined into a single prompt using an Access Form. The resulting Access report should look like Figure 9-6.

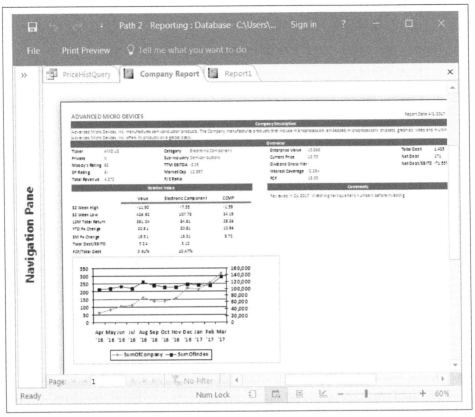

Figure 9-6. The Company Report in Access

Path 3: C# and SSRS

This section demonstrates how to create automated reports using C# and SQL Server Reporting Services (SSRS). SSRS is an advanced and dynamic reporting tool that comes in two flavors: server side and client side. As the name implies, the server-side flavor means the reports (RDL files) are hosted on a remote server and are accessed through a web portal, scheduled emails, or from applications. The client-side version are reports (RDLC files) that are rendered locally in an application; it does not require a SQL Server. Nevertheless, since both flavors use the same engine, report files can be converted from RDLC to RDL, and vice versa. This chapter focuses on the client-side reports, given that many analysts do not have access to a SQL server.

Before we get underway, you need to install SQL Server Data Tools (SSDT). To begin, in your Windows Control Panel, click Change on Microsoft Visual Studio. When the Visual Studio window opens, select Modify, and then, in the Windows and Web Development section, check the box labeled Microsoft SQL Server Data Tools.

SSRS is my favorite reporting tool because it has a comprehensive set of features and is a lot easier to use than the report builder in Access. This section walks you through creating a C# Windows Form Application that will combine data from our Access database and the Bloomberg API to create a report that can be easily exported to PDF or Excel. However, because there are already a lot of online resources on how to build SSRS reports, this chapter will focus on creating a very simple report and binding it to a C# application, not on the intricacies of the report builder tool.

The first set of steps creates the new project and adds a DataSet that will store the data used in the report.

1. Begin by creating a new Windows Form Application and adding a reference to the Bloomberg API.

2. Add a DataSet called **ADS.xsd** to the new project.

   The DataSet passes data from our Access database and Bloomberg API to our report.

3. In the ADS DataSet add a new TableAdapter called **Company** with a connection to the Access Database. Use the following query:

```
SELECT
c.CompanyID,
c.BBID,
c.CompanyName,
c.IsPrivate,
c.Sector,
c.Industry,
c.SubIndustry,
c.SPRating,
c.MoodyRating,
c.MarketCap,
c.TotalDebt,
c.NetDebt,
c.EV,
c.EBITDA,
c.TotalRevenue,
c.TotalDebtToEBITDA,
c.InterestCoverage,
c.FCF,
c.FCFToTotalDebt,
```

```
c.Price,
c.YrHi,
c.YrLow,
c.CDS5YrTicker,
c.NetDebtToEBITDA,
c.CDSSpread5Yr,
c.Category,
c.CompanyComments,
c.PERatio,
c.DVDYield,
c.TotalReturn12M,
c.PxChgYTD,
c.PxChg3M,
c.IndexID,
c.RecBuy,
c.RecSell,
c.RecHold,
i.IndexName,
i.Price AS IdxPx,
i.YrHi AS IdxHi,
i.YrLow AS IdxLow,
i.PxChgYTD AS IdxPxChgYTD,
i.PxChg3M AS IdxPxChg3m,
i.TotalReturn12M AS IdxTotalReturn12M,
s.YrHi as MedYrHi,
s.YrLow AS MedLow,
s.PxChgYTD AS MedPxChgYTD,
s.PxChg3M AS MedPxChg3m,
s.TotalReturn12M AS MedTotalReturn12M,
s.TotalDebtToEBITDA as MedTotalDebtToEBITDA,
s.FCFToTotalDebt as MedFCFToTotalDebt
FROM    ((Company c LEFT OUTER JOIN
               [Index] i ON i.IndexID = c.IndexID) LEFT OUTER JOIN
               MedianCompanyStats s ON s.Category = c.Category)
WHERE  (c.CompanyID = ?)
```

This query combines the columns from the Company table with the MedianStats and Index tables to pull together all the information needed for the report. We use the ? in the WHERE clause to filter by a CompanyID.

4. Right-click Company DataTable and add a column called "FullDescription"

   This field will be populated using the Bloomberg API.

5. Add another TableAdapter called **CompanyList** to the ADS DataSet by using the following query:

```
SELECT CompanyID, CompanyName
FROM    Company
```

This query returns a list of Company Names and IDs that will be used in a ComboBox, thus allowing the user to select the Company for the report using a convenient drop-down list.

6. Add a new DataTable to the ADS DataSet called **PriceHistory** with the following columns: **Ticker**, **Date**, **Value**, **IndexName**, and **IndexValue**. Change the DataType on the Date column to `DateTime` and the DataType on Value and IndexValue to `Double`.

   This DataTable will be populated using the Bloomberg API and will store the price history for the company and corresponding index's price.

   The next steps add the report to the project and connect it to the ADS DataSet.

7. Add a Report item to the project called **CompanyReport**.

8. Open the new report and, in the Datasets section of the Report Data window (Ctrl+Alt+D), right-click and select Add DataSet. Under Data source, select ADS, and under Available datasets, select Company, and then click OK.

   This binds the Company DataTable in ADS DataSet as "DataSet1" in the report.

9. Repeat step 8, except select PriceHistory under Available datasets.

   This binds PriceHistory from the ADS DataSet as "DataSet2" in the report.

   The next steps walk you through adding a few labels, a table, and a chart to the report.

10. In the Toolbox, select Text Box and drop it on the report. Right-click the Text Box and select Expression. In the Expression box enter the following:

    ```
    =First(Fields!CompanyName.Value, "DataSet1")
    ```

    This displays the Company Name from the Company table. The reason the field is surrounded by `First` and ends with `DataSet1` is because the Text Box is not bound to a specific DataSet, and although we know that the DataSet will contain only one row (so First() or Last() will be the same), using an aggregate function lets us reference the DataSet.

11. In the Toolbox, select a Table and drop it on the report. In the Properties window of the Table, set the DataSetName to **DataSet1**.

    The top row of the Table is the table header, the middle is the detail section that will be repeated for each row in the DataSet, and the bottom row is the footer that will appear after the detail section and is a good place to total values in the detail section.

12. Right-click the detail row (middle) and the footer row (bottom) and select Delete Rows.

    Because there is only one row in the Company DataSet, we don't need a details section.

13. Click the icon on the righthand side of one of the cells in the remaining row that appears when you mouse-over the cell. Then, choose a column to appear in that cell.

14. Repeat step 13 as many times as desired to add as many columns from the Data-Set to the report. You can right-click any cell to add additional columns or rows to the report.

15. From the Toolbox, add a Chart to the report, and then, when the Chart window opens, select a line chart.

16. Click the Chart. In the dialog box that opens, on the Category Groups tab, in the DataSet2 list box, select Date.

17. In the Values section, click the green plus symbol (+), and then choose Value. Click the plus symbol again, and then select IndexValue.

18. Select the down arrow next to IndexValue, and then choose Series Properties. In the Axes and Chart section, for the Vertical axis, select Secondary.

You can continue to add tables, charts, and play around with formatting to come up with a report like that shown in Figure 9-7.

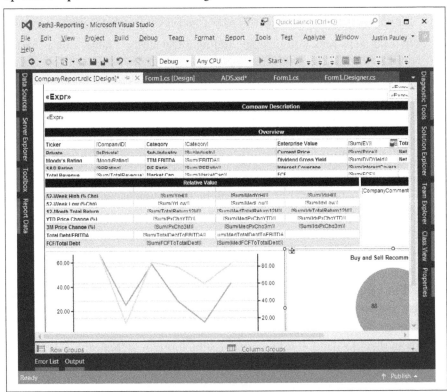

Figure 9-7. The SSRS Company Report in Design mode

The next steps add controls to the Windows form Form1 that will be used to select a company, view a report, and export it to either PDF or Excel.

19. On the Designer for Form1, begin by adding two panels, docking one to the top and the other, beneath it, to fill.

20. In the top panel, add a ComboBox (cmbCompanyList), a Load button (btnLoad), a PDF button (btnPDF), and an Excel button (btnExcel).

21. In the bottom panel, add a Report Viewer (rptView) control. Set its dock to fill, and then select the CompanyReport from the Report View tasks list box.

    This also adds a few objects to your form: an instance of the ADS DataSet, an instance of the CompanyTableAdapter, and a BindingSource for Company and PriceHistory.

Finally, we get to the code portion of this project. In *Form1.cs*, add the following using directives for Bloomberg:

```
using Event = Bloomberglp.Blpapi.Event;
using Element = Bloomberglp.Blpapi.Element;
using Message = Bloomberglp.Blpapi.Message;
using Name = Bloomberglp.Blpapi.Name;
using Request = Bloomberglp.Blpapi.Request;
using Service = Bloomberglp.Blpapi.Service;
using Session = Bloomberglp.Blpapi.Session;
using DataType = Bloomberglp.Blpapi.Schema.Datatype;
using SessionOptions = Bloomberglp.Blpapi.SessionOptions;
using InvalidRequestException =
        Bloomberglp.Blpapi.InvalidRequestException;
```

Next, in the Form1 class, add the Name instances for Bloomberg, like previous code projects:

```
private static readonly Name SECURITY_DATA = new Name("securityData");
private static readonly Name SECURITY = new Name("security");
private static readonly Name FIELD_DATA = new Name("fieldData");
private static readonly Name RESPONSE_ERROR = new Name("responseError");
private static readonly Name SECURITY_ERROR = new Name("securityError");
private static readonly Name FIELD_EXCEPTIONS = new Name("fieldExceptions");
private static readonly Name FIELD_ID = new Name("fieldId");
private static readonly Name ERROR_INFO = new Name("errorInfo");
private static readonly Name CATEGORY = new Name("category");
private static readonly Name MESSAGE = new Name("message");
private static readonly Name DATE = new Name("date");
```

Next, define the Form1_Load event that populates the CompanyList DataTable in the ADS DataSet (instance created in step 21) and binds it to the ComboBox. When the program starts, the ComboBox (cmbCompanyList) is populated with a list of Company names from the Access database:

```
private void Form1_Load(object sender, EventArgs e)
{
    // Populate the Company List DataTable from Access database
    using (ADSTableAdapters.CompanyListTableAdapter ta =
    new ADSTableAdapters.CompanyListTableAdapter())
    {
        ta.Fill(this.ADS.CompanyList);
        ta.Connection.Close();
    }
    // Bind the CompanyList to the ComboBox.
    this.cmbCompanyList.DataSource = this.ADS.CompanyList;
    this.cmbCompanyList.ValueMember = "CompanyID";
    this.cmbCompanyList.DisplayMember = "CompanyName";
}
```

Next, define the btnLoad_Click event that fires when the Load button is clicked. This
method uses the Company query to load a Company based on the CompanyID
selected in the cmbCompanyList. Then, it appends the full description of the company along with historical stock and index prices from the Bloomberg API to the
ADS dataset and loads the report in the Report Viewer. The report is bound to the
rptView object in the designer.

```
private void btnLoad_Click(object sender, EventArgs e)
{
    // Populate the Company table in the Dataset using the
    // CompanyID from the ComboBox
    this.CompanyTableAdapter.Fill(this.ADS.Company,
    this.cmbCompanyList.SelectedValue.ToString());
    ADS.CompanyRow company = this.ADS.Company[0];

    //Get the full description from Bloomberg
    company.FullDescription = GetFullDescription(company.BBID);

    this.ADS.PriceHistory.Clear();
    //Get 1yr price history from Bloomberg
    Dictionary<DateTime, double> history =
    GetHistory(company.BBID, "PX_LAST", DateTime.Now.AddYears(-1));
    //Insert price history into PriceHistory Datatable
    foreach (DateTime dt in history.Keys)
    {
        this.ADS.PriceHistory.AddPriceHistoryRow(company.CompanyID, dt,
        history[dt], null, 0);
    }

    if (company.IsIndexIDNull() == false)
    {
        //If the IndexID on the Company row is populated, get its price history
        //as well.
        history = GetHistory(company.IndexID + " Equity", "PX_LAST",
        DateTime.Now.AddYears(-1));
        foreach (DateTime dt in history.Keys)
        {
```

```
            ADS.PriceHistoryRow row = this.ADS.PriceHistory.FindByDate(dt);
            if (row != null)
            {
                row.IndexName = company.IndexID;
                row.IndexValue = history[dt];
            }

        }
    }
    //Refresh the report.
    this.rptView.RefreshReport();
}
```

The next two methods handle sending the Bloomberg request to retrieve the company's full description (CIE_DES_BULK) and then process the response. The code should look like previous programs in this book:

```
private string GetFullDescription(string security)
{
    string description = "";
    SessionOptions sessionOptions = new SessionOptions();
    Session session = new Session();
    bool sessionStarted = session.Start();
    if (!sessionStarted)
    {
        System.Console.Error.WriteLine("Failed to start session.");
        return null;
    }
    if (!session.OpenService("//blp/refdata"))
    {
        System.Console.Error.WriteLine("Failed to open //blp/refdata");
        return null;
    }

    Service refDataService = session.GetService("//blp/refdata");
    Request request = refDataService.CreateRequest("ReferenceDataRequest");

    Element securities = request.GetElement("securities");
    securities.AppendValue(security);
    Element fields = request.GetElement("fields");
    //CIE_DES_BULK is the full description of a company.
    fields.AppendValue("CIE_DES_BULK");

    try
    {
        session.SendRequest(request, null);
    }
    catch (InvalidRequestException e)
    {
        System.Console.WriteLine(e.ToString());
    }
```

```
    bool done = false;
    while (!done)
    {
        Event eventObj = session.NextEvent();
        if (eventObj.Type == Event.EventType.PARTIAL_RESPONSE)
        {
            description += ProcessResponse(eventObj);
        }
        else if (eventObj.Type == Event.EventType.RESPONSE)
        {
            description += ProcessResponse(eventObj);
            done = true;
        }
        else
        {
            foreach (Message msg in eventObj)
            {
                System.Console.WriteLine(msg.AsElement);
                if (eventObj.Type == Event.EventType.SESSION_STATUS)
                {
                    if (msg.MessageType.Equals("SessionTerminated"))
                    {
                        done = true;
                    }
                }
            }
        }
    }
    session.Stop();
    return description;
}
private string ProcessResponse(Event eventObj)
{
    string description = "";
    foreach (Message msg in eventObj)
    {

        if (msg.HasElement(RESPONSE_ERROR))
        {
            Element error = msg.GetElement(RESPONSE_ERROR);
            Console.WriteLine("Request failed: " +
            error.GetElementAsString(CATEGORY) +
            " (" + error.GetElementAsString(MESSAGE) + ")");
            continue;
        }

        Element securities = msg.GetElement(SECURITY_DATA);
        for (int i = 0; i < securities.NumValues; ++i)
        {
            Element security = securities.GetValueAsElement(i);

            if (security.HasElement("securityError"))
```

```
        {
            Element error = security.GetElement(SECURITY_ERROR);
            Console.WriteLine("Security Error: " +
            error.GetElementAsString(CATEGORY) +
            " (" + error.GetElementAsString(MESSAGE) + ")");

            continue;
        }

        Element fieldExceptions = security.GetElement(FIELD_EXCEPTIONS);
        if (fieldExceptions.NumValues > 0)
        {
            for (int k = 0; k < fieldExceptions.NumValues; ++k)
            {
                Element fieldException =
                    fieldExceptions.GetValueAsElement(k);

                Element error = fieldException.GetElement(ERROR_INFO);
                Console.WriteLine("Field Exception: " +
                fieldException.GetElementAsString(FIELD_ID) + " " +
                error.GetElementAsString(CATEGORY) +
                " (" + error.GetElementAsString(MESSAGE) + ")");

            }
        }

        Element fieldElements = security.GetElement(FIELD_DATA);
        if (fieldElements.NumElements > 0)
        {

            for (int j = 0; j < fieldElements.NumElements; ++j)
            {
                Element field = fieldElements.GetElement(j);
                for (int k = 0; k < field.NumValues; k++)
                {
                    // Description will be broken down into multiple values
                    // found in the field.
                    description +=
                    field.GetValueAsElement(k).GetElement(0).
                    GetValueAsString(0) + " ";
                }
            }
        }


    }
}
return description;
}
```

The next two methods are the same ones used in previous applications to pull historical prices from Bloomberg:

```
private Dictionary<DateTime, double> GetHistory
(string security, string field, DateTime startDate)
{

    Dictionary<DateTime, double> date2value = new Dictionary<DateTime, double>();
    SessionOptions sessionOptions = new SessionOptions();
    Session session = new Session();
    bool sessionStarted = session.Start();
    if (!sessionStarted)
    {
        System.Console.Error.WriteLine("Failed to start session.");
        return null;
    }
    if (!session.OpenService("//blp/refdata"))
    {
        System.Console.Error.WriteLine("Failed to open //blp/refdata");
        return null;
    }

    Service refDataService = session.GetService("//blp/refdata");
    Request request = refDataService.CreateRequest("HistoricalDataRequest");

    Element securities = request.GetElement("securities");
    securities.AppendValue(security);
    Element fields = request.GetElement("fields");
    fields.AppendValue(field);

    request.Set("startDate", startDate.ToString("yyyyMMdd"));
    request.Set("periodicityAdjustment", "ACTUAL");
    request.Set("periodicitySelection", "DAILY");
    request.Set("nonTradingDayFillOption", "ALL_CALENDAR_DAYS");
    request.Set("nonTradingDayFillMethod", "PREVIOUS_VALUE");


    try
    {
        session.SendRequest(request, null);
    }
    catch (InvalidRequestException e)
    {
        System.Console.WriteLine(e.ToString());
    }

    bool done = false;
    while (!done)
    {
        Event eventObj = session.NextEvent();
        if (eventObj.Type == Event.EventType.PARTIAL_RESPONSE)
        {
            ProcessHistoryResponse(eventObj, date2value);
        }
        else if (eventObj.Type == Event.EventType.RESPONSE)
```

```csharp
        {
            ProcessHistoryResponse(eventObj, date2value);
            done = true;
        }
        else
        {
            foreach (Message msg in eventObj)
            {
                System.Console.WriteLine(msg.AsElement);
                if (eventObj.Type == Event.EventType.SESSION_STATUS)
                {
                    if (msg.MessageType.Equals("SessionTerminated"))
                    {
                        done = true;
                    }
                }
            }
        }
    }
    session.Stop();
    return date2value;

}
private void ProcessHistoryResponse(Event eventObj,
Dictionary<DateTime, double> date2value)
{
    foreach (Message msg in eventObj)
    {
        if (msg.HasElement(RESPONSE_ERROR))
        {
            Element error = msg.GetElement(RESPONSE_ERROR);
            Console.WriteLine("Request failed: " +
            error.GetElementAsString(CATEGORY) +
            " (" + error.GetElementAsString(MESSAGE) + ")");
            continue;
        }


        Element securityData = msg.GetElement(SECURITY_DATA);
        string security = securityData.GetElement(SECURITY).GetValueAsString();
        Console.WriteLine(security);

        Element fieldData = securityData.GetElement(FIELD_DATA);

        for (int i = 0; i < fieldData.NumValues; i++)
        {
            Element element = fieldData.GetValueAsElement(i);
            DateTime date = element.GetElementAsDatetime(DATE).ToSystemDateTime();
            double? value = null;
            for (int f = 0; f < element.NumElements; f++)
            {
                Element field = element.GetElement(f);
```

```
                if (!field.Name.Equals(DATE))
                {
                    if (field.Datatype == DataType.FLOAT32)
                        value = Convert.ToDouble(field.GetValueAsFloat32());
                    else if (field.Datatype == DataType.FLOAT64)
                        value = field.GetValueAsFloat64();
                }
            }
            if (value != null)
                date2value.Add(date, value.Value);
        }


    }
}
```

The next method, Export, takes a string parameter, ext, that contains either PDF or XLS, which determines the file type to export. The code uses the Reporting Services API to export an Excel or PDF report into a temporary file and then launch that file:

```
private void Export(string ext)
{
    Warning[] warnings;
    string[] streamids;
    string mimeType;
    string encoding;
    string extension;

    //Temp file location
    string file =
    System.Environment.GetFolderPath(Environment.SpecialFolder.InternetCache) +
    "\\" + Guid.NewGuid().ToString() + "." + ext;

    string type = null;
    if (ext.ToUpper() == "XLS")
        type = "Excel";
    else
        type = "PDF";

    //Render report as byte array
    byte[] bytes = this.rptView.LocalReport.Render(
        type, null, out mimeType, out encoding,
        out extension,
        out streamids, out warnings);

    // Save byte array to a file.
    FileStream fs = new FileStream(file, FileMode.Create);
    fs.Write(bytes, 0, bytes.Length);
    fs.Close();

    //Open file
```

```
    System.Diagnostics.Process.Start(file);
}
```

The final two methods connect the PDF and Excel buttons to the Export method:

```
private void btnPDF_Click(object sender, EventArgs e)
{
    Export("PDF");
}

private void btnExcel_Click(object sender, EventArgs e)
{
    Export("XLS");
}
```

Once completed, the final product should look like Figure 9-8.

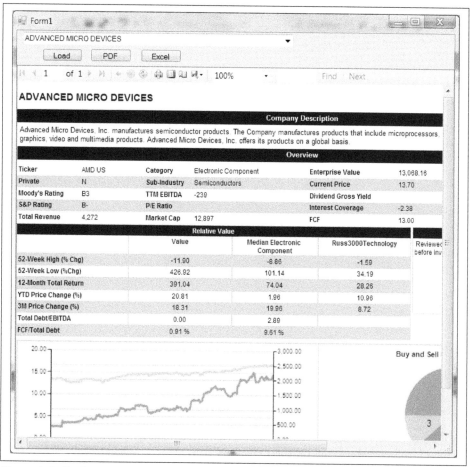

Figure 9-8. C# Reporting Application

Summary

This chapter introduced you to three different reporting tools and, more important, demonstrated how to combine the lessons from earlier chapters and produce a useful report to help make investment decisions. I encourage you to spend time looking at the report you created for a few companies, contemplate what the information implies about the value of the company, and what information or analysis you could add to improve the report. For instance, you could expand these reports to include details about the underlying securities (bonds and loans) issued by the company. Chapter 10 builds upon this chapter's techniques to create portfolio-level reports.

Portfolio Reports

Although previous chapters focused on using financial data to make investment decisions, this chapter focuses on measuring the performance and risks of your portfolio. It also demonstrates how to calculate monthly returns, annualized returns, annualized standard deviations, and the Sharpe Ratio for a portfolio of investments. Additionally, this chapter walks you through how to create a two-page tear sheet report that highlights key portfolio metrics and compares the portfolio's time-weighted and risk-adjusted returns to different benchmarks. And though the techniques shown in this chapter are intended for measuring the performance of your portfolio, you can also use them to measure the performance of other money managers, funds, or portfolios.

This chapter begins by taking two inputs (monthly profit and loss [P&L] and monthly starting balances) and calculates the different types of returns. Calculating and aggregating returns can be more complicated than many assume; simply Googling "how to calculate portfolio returns" will return various confusing methods. When aggregating returns, you must take into consideration compounding by using a time-weighted geometric return. The time-weighted return (also referred to as a cumulative return, compounded return, or geometric return) incorporates gains and losses from prior periods.

Monitoring Performance and Risk

Consider the following example: you invest $1 million and then lose $500,000 (–50 percent return) the very first month. The next month, you have $500,000 invested and you manage to earn back the half million you lost last month ($500,000 on $500,000 invested is a 100 percent return). If you simply added the two monthly returns together, you'd show a 50 percent return. If you averaged the returns together, you would show a 25 percent return. However, in reality and shown by calculating the geometric return, you returned 0 percent (conceptually $1,000,000 – $500,000 + $500,000 = $1,000,000 and a 0 percent return: we discuss the actual geometric return formula later). Although there are some complicated methods for calculating a time-weighted return involving Microsoft Excel `Array` functions, this chapter demonstrates a much simpler technique.

Next, we cover annualizing the returns since inception as a basis for comparison with different benchmarks or other funds. By annualizing, you can reverse the compounding and scale down a return from a period greater than a year into a 12-month period. In other words, annualizing a four-year compounded return produces a one-year return that, when compounded over four years, would result in the original return. Annualizing is important when comparing returns because the effect of compounding can have a large impact.

 Even though the formula for annualizing returns will work to extrapolate returns shorter than one year, it is not recommended given its limited sample size. Furthermore, Global Investment Performance Standards (GIPS) requirements prohibit annualizing returns for periods of less than one year. However, you can use the formula to annualize partial years (such as 16 months, etc.).

Chapter 7 covered calculating the Sharpe Ratio for your current portfolio using either forecasted or historical returns for each position in the portfolio; however, this chapter demonstrates how to calculate the Sharpe Ratio using historical portfolio returns. The key difference is that, in Chapter 7, the Sharpe Ratio was forward looking and based on the current composition of the portfolio, whereas this chapter uses historical performance to calculate the Sharpe Ratio. In this instance, we can use the Sharpe Ratio to measure the portfolio's average risk-adjusted return relative to other portfolios or investments.

Finally, this chapter builds upon lessons from Chapter 9 to create a two-page tear sheet report in Excel and SSRS that lays out the calculations covered here as well as the Portfolio Breakdown section in Chapter 7. Like most chapters, the calculations and explanations are detailed in the Excel section (Path 1). Of course, you can link the Excel tables created in Path 1 to Microsoft Access. The Path 3 section contains a full implementation in C# and SSRS.

Path 1: Microsoft Excel

This section begins by creating a new worksheet ("Returns") that will store the monthly P&L, assets under management (AUM), Sharpe Ratio, and return calculations for your portfolio. In addition, this worksheet calculates the corresponding returns and Sharpe Ratio for the S&P 500 index and the Bloomberg Barclays US

Aggregate Bond Index (Barclays Agg). Whereas the S&P 500 is an index of 500 stocks, the Barclays Agg is a composite of investment grade, fixed-rate bonds that contains far less risk and return than equities. Then, this section details how to create a basic portfolio report displaying some of the key values calculated on the Returns worksheet.

Calculating Returns

For this section, you will need monthly P&L and starting market value for each month of some portfolio.

After creating a new worksheet called Returns, follow the subsequent steps to create the Excel Returns table that will contain the return information for your portfolio and benchmark indices.

1. Label the cells M1 to Y1: `Date`, `Monthly PNL`, `Starting AUM`, `Monthly Return`, `Value of $100`, `Monthly Risk Free`, `Return–RF`, `S&P 500`, `S&P 500 Pct`, `S&P–RF`, `Barclays Aggregate`, `Barclays Pct`, `Barclays–RF`.

2. In the Date, Monthly PNL, and Starting AUM columns, place the last day of the month for each month, the amount in dollars gained or lost that month, and the starting market value of investments in the portfolio. Place the dates in ascending order.

   For instance, if the first full month of portfolio returns was January 2015, place "1/31/2015" in cell M2 under the Date header. If, during January 2015, the portfolio was up $300,000, enter "300,000" in cell N2. If, at the beginning of January 2015, the beginning market value of the portfolio was $30 million, enter "30,000,000" in cell O1 under the Starting AUM header.

3. Convert the entire range used from M1 through the last-used cell in column Y to an Excel range and name it "Returns."

4. In column P (Monthly Return), enter the following formula in the cells:

   ```
   =[@[Monthly PNL]]/[@[Starting AUM]]
   ```

   This formula calculates the monthly return by dividing the total monthly P&L by the month's starting balance.

   The following step populates a "Value of $100" column with a formula that will track the current value of a $100 investment on day one of the portfolio. For instance, if, in the first month since inception, the portfolio returned 3% the first row in "Value of $100" would read $103 ($100 + 3% of $100 = $103). If the portfolio gained 4 percent the following month, the "Value of $100" would read $107.12 ($103 + 4% of $103 = $107.12). This column is used to track the impact of compounding returns and to calculate the portfolio's time-weighted return.

5. Place the following formula in the "Value of $100" column:

```
=IF([@Date]=MIN([Date]),100*(1+[@[Monthly Return]]),
Q1*(1+[@[Monthly Return]]))
```

For the current value, this formula checks whether the current row's date is the earliest date in the Excel table and, if it is, uses $100; otherwise, it uses the value from the previous row. The formula multiplies the current value by the monthly return plus 1 which is the same as: current value + (current value × monthly return).

Follow the next steps to pull monthly prices from Bloomberg for the S&P 500, Barclays Agg (now Bloomberg Barclays Aggregate), and the three-month London Interbank Offered Rate (LIBOR) rate that will be used as the risk-free rate to calculate the Sharpe Ratio.

6. Label cells A1 and B1 "Date" and "SPX Index," respectively.

7. In cell A2, enter the following formula:

```
=BDH(B1,"PX_LAST",EDATE(MIN(Returns[Date]),-1),"-0cm","FX=USD",
"PER=AM","FILL=P","DAYS=A")
```

This formula pulls the latest month-end price for the S&P 500 index (SPX Index <GO>) between the earliest date in the Returns table to the latest month end available. It will always include the last day of the month because of the "DAYS=A" argument. This formula should result in columns A and B populated with S&P 500 price history.

8. Copy the following formula down, starting in C3:

```
=(B3-B2)/B2
```

This formula calculates the monthly total return of the S&P 500 by dividing the difference between months by the starting month.

9. Repeat steps 6 through 8 to pull in the Barclays Agg in columns E and F using "LBUSTRUU Index" in cell F1 and calculating the monthly total returns in column G.

10. Repeat steps 6 through 7 to pull in three-month LIBOR in columns I and J using "US0003M Index" in cell J1.

Using the same BDH formula in step 7 pulls down the annualized three-month LIBOR rate using the same date range as the monthly returns.

11. In column K, enter the following formula, starting in cell K2, and copy it down:

```
=J2/100/12
```

This formula takes the three-month LIBOR rate, divides it by 100 to convert it to a percentage, and then divides it by 12 to get the monthly rate.

The following steps take the monthly market data retrieved from Bloomberg in the prior steps and adds them to the Excel Returns table.

12. In the Monthly Return column, enter the following formula:

```
=VLOOKUP([@Date],I:K,3,FALSE)
```

This formula pulls the three-month LIBOR rate for the given month using a VLOOKUP.

13. In the Return-RF column, enter the following formula:

```
=[@[Monthly Return]]-[@[Monthly Risk Free]]
```

This formula simply reduces the monthly return by the risk-free rate (three-month LIBOR).

14. In the S&P 500 column, enter the following formula:

```
=VLOOKUP([@Date],A:C,2,FALSE)
```

This formula pulls the ending value of the S&P 500 for each month using a VLOOKUP.

15. In the S&P 500 Pct column, enter the following formula:

```
=VLOOKUP([@Date],A:C,3,FALSE)
```

This formula pulls the monthly return for the S&P 500 using a VLOOKUP.

16. In the "S&P-RF" column, enter the following formula:

```
=[@[S&P 500 Pct]]-[@[Monthly Risk Free]]
```

This reduces the S&P 500 return by the risk-free rate.

17. Repeat steps 14 through 16 to populate the Barclays Aggregate columns using the following formulas:

```
=VLOOKUP([@Date],E:G,2,FALSE),
=VLOOKUP([@Date],E:G,3,FALSE),
=[@[Barclays Pct]]-[@[Monthly Risk Free]]
```

The resulting Returns table should look like Figure 10-1.

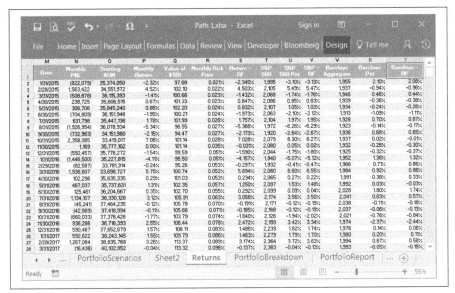

	Date	Monthly PNL	Starting AUM	Monthly Return	Value of $100	Monthly Risk Free	Return - RF	S&P 500	S&P 500 Ret	S&P - RF	Barclays Aggregate	Barclays Ret	Barclays RF
2	1/31/2015	(822,079)	35,374,050	-2.32%	97.68	0.021%	-2.345%	1,995	-3.10%	-3.13%	1,955	2.10%	2.08%
3	2/28/2015	1,563,422	34,551,972	4.52%	102.10	0.022%	4.503%	2,105	5.49%	5.47%	1,937	-0.94%	-0.96%
4	3/31/2015	(508,878)	36,115,393	-1.41%	100.66	0.023%	-1.432%	2,068	-1.74%	-1.76%	1,946	0.46%	0.44%
5	4/30/2015	238,725	35,606,515	0.67%	101.33	0.023%	0.647%	2,086	0.85%	0.83%	1,939	-0.36%	-0.38%
6	5/31/2015	306,706	35,845,240	0.86%	102.20	0.024%	0.832%	2,107	1.05%	1.03%	1,934	-0.24%	-0.26%
7	6/30/2015	(704,809)	36,151,946	-1.95%	100.21	0.024%	-1.973%	2,063	-2.10%	-2.12%	1,913	-1.09%	-1.11%
8	7/31/2015	631,798	35,447,136	1.78%	101.99	0.026%	1.757%	2,104	1.97%	1.95%	1,926	0.70%	0.67%
9	8/31/2015	(1,926,954)	36,078,934	-5.34%	96.55	0.027%	-5.368%	1,972	-6.26%	-6.29%	1,923	-0.14%	-0.17%
10	9/30/2015	(732,963)	34,151,980	-2.15%	94.47	0.027%	-2.173%	1,920	-2.64%	-2.67%	1,936	0.68%	0.65%
11	10/31/2015	2,358,085	33,419,017	7.06%	101.14	0.028%	7.028%	2,079	8.30%	8.27%	1,937	0.02%	-0.01%
12	11/30/2015	1,169	35,777,102	0.00%	101.14	0.035%	-0.031%	2,080	0.05%	0.02%	1,932	-0.26%	-0.30%
13	12/31/2015	(550,457)	35,778,272	-1.54%	99.59	0.051%	-1.590%	2,044	-1.75%	-1.80%	1,925	-0.32%	-0.37%
14	1/31/2016	(1,446,500)	35,227,815	-4.11%	95.50	0.051%	-4.157%	1,940	-5.07%	-5.12%	1,952	1.36%	1.32%
15	2/29/2016	(82,587)	33,781,314	-0.24%	95.26	0.053%	-0.297%	1,932	-0.41%	-0.47%	1,966	0.71%	0.66%
16	3/31/2016	1,936,607	33,698,727	5.75%	100.74	0.052%	5.694%	2,060	6.60%	6.55%	1,984	0.92%	0.86%
17	4/30/2016	102,296	35,635,335	0.29%	101.03	0.053%	0.234%	2,065	0.27%	0.22%	1,991	0.38%	0.33%
18	5/31/2016	467,037	35,737,631	1.31%	102.35	0.057%	1.250%	2,097	1.53%	1.48%	1,992	0.03%	-0.03%
19	6/30/2016	125,461	36,204,667	0.35%	102.70	0.055%	0.292%	2,099	0.09%	0.04%	2,028	1.80%	1.74%
20	7/31/2016	1,134,107	36,330,128	3.12%	105.91	0.063%	3.058%	2,174	3.56%	3.50%	2,041	0.63%	0.57%
21	8/31/2016	(45,241)	37,464,235	-0.12%	105.78	0.070%	-0.191%	2,171	-0.12%	-0.19%	2,038	-0.11%	-0.18%
22	9/30/2016	(42,569)	37,418,994	-0.11%	105.66	0.071%	-0.185%	2,168	-0.12%	-0.19%	2,037	-0.06%	-0.13%
23	10/31/2016	(660,033)	37,376,426	-1.77%	103.79	0.074%	-1.840%	2,126	-1.94%	-2.02%	2,021	-0.76%	-0.84%
24	11/30/2016	936,286	36,716,393	2.55%	106.44	0.078%	2.472%	2,199	3.42%	3.34%	1,974	-2.37%	-2.44%
25	12/31/2016	590,467	37,652,679	1.57%	108.11	0.083%	1.485%	2,239	1.82%	1.74%	1,976	0.14%	0.06%
26	1/31/2017	592,622	38,243,145	1.55%	109.79	0.086%	1.463%	2,279	1.73%	1.70%	1,980	0.20%	0.11%
27	2/28/2017	1,267,084	38,835,768	3.26%	113.37	0.093%	3.174%	2,364	3.72%	3.63%	1,994	0.67%	0.58%
28	3/31/2017	(16,436)	40,102,852	-0.04%	113.32	0.096%	-0.137%	2,363	-0.04%	-0.13%	1,993	-0.05%	-0.15%

Figure 10-1. Returns Excel table

The following steps create another table that summarizes the values for the portfolio and benchmarks for key dates.

18. Label cells AA1 through AE1: Range, Date, Portfolio, S&P, Barclays.

19. In column AA, under the Range header, place the following labels on sequential rows: Latest, QTD, YTD, Last 12 Months, ITD.

These are the row headers that will correspond to a date; the values will appear under the last three column headers.

20. In cell AB2, under the Date header and next to Latest, enter the following formula:

```
=MAX(Returns[Date])
```

This formula pulls the latest date from the Returns.

21. In cell AB3, under the Date header and next to QTD, enter the following formula:

```
=EOMONTH(DATE(YEAR(AB2),FLOOR(MONTH(AB2)-1,3)+1,1),-1)
```

QTD stands for Quarter-to-Date. This formula calculates the starting date of the quarter based on the latest month (from step 20) and then uses the EOMONTH function to get the last day of the prior month. We use the date from the prior month because we want the closing value of the day before the quarter starts.

22. In cell AB4, under the Date header and next to YTD, enter the following formula:

```
=DATE(YEAR(AB12)-1,12,31)
```

YTD stands for Year-to-Date. This formula returns December 31 of the year prior to the latest return.

23. In cell AB5, under the Date header and next to Last 12 Months, enter the following formula:

    ```
    =EDATE(AB2,-12)
    ```

    This formula returns the last day of the month for 12 months before the latest return date.

24. In cell AB6, under the Date header and next to ITD, enter the following formula:

    ```
    =EOMONTH(MIN(M:M),-1)
    ```

    ITD stands for Inception-to-Date. This formula returns the last day of the month prior to the first monthly return. Note that ITD refers to the portfolio's inception, not the inception of S&P 500 or the Barclays Agg.

25. In column AC, under the Portfolio column header, in cell AC6, enter **100** and then, in cell AC2, enter the following formula and copy it down to AC5:

    ```
    =INDEX(Returns[Value of $100],MATCH(AB2,Returns[Date],0))
    ```

    This formula uses the dates from steps 20 to 24 to pull the corresponding "Value of $100." Naturally, the ITD for the portfolio starting number (cell AC6) should be $100.

26. In column AD, under the S&P column header, place the following formula and copy it down:

    ```
    =VLOOKUP(AB2,A:B,2,FALSE)
    ```

    This formula returns the S&P value for the given date in the Date column.

27. In column AE, under the Barclays column header, enter the following formula and copy it down:

    ```
    =VLOOKUP(AB2,E:F,2,FALSE)
    ```

    This formula returns the Barclays Agg value for the given date in the Date column.

Now that we have a table containing the values, we need one final table that will contain the returns for the given date ranges in a format that will be easy to turn into a chart. The next steps will create a new table below the one created in steps 18 through 27 that will contain the time-weighted returns and annualized standard deviation for each period. Because the table created in steps 18 through 27 used the "Value of $100," which incorporates compounding, we can calculate the time-weighted return simply by dividing the difference between the current value and the starting value by the starting value: (current value–starting value) / starting value. If you prefer not to use the "Value of $100" column, you can also calculate the time-weighted return using an array formula; to calculate the ITD time-weighted return, use the array formula (Ctrl-Shift-Enter) `=PRODUCT(1+Returns[Monthly Return])-1`. However, the "Value of $100" has the added benefit of sharing the same return calculations as the S&P 500 and Barclays Agg.

28. Starting in cell AA11, repeat steps 18 through 24 to re-create the column and row headers.

29. Under the Portfolio column header, in cell AC12, enter the following formula:

    `=INDEX(Returns[Monthly Return],MATCH(AB12,Returns[Date],0))`

    This formula returns the latest monthly return using the date in AB12.

30. Under the S&P column header, in cell AD12, enter the following formula:

    `=INDEX(Returns[S&P 500 Pct],MATCH(AB12,Returns[Date],0))`

    This returns the latest S&P 500 monthly return.

31. Under the Barclays column header, in cell AE12, enter the following formula:

    `=INDEX(Returns[Barclays Pct],MATCH(AB12,Returns[Date],0))`

    This returns the latest Barclays Agg monthly return.

32. Under the Portfolio column header, in the row below the cell used in step 29 (cell AC13), enter the following formula and copy it down to AC16:

    `=(AC$2-AC3)/AC3`

    This formula references the table created earlier to calculate the time-weighted return using the Latest date as the current value and each row's range as the starting value.

33. Copy the formula from step 32 (cells AC13 through AC16) to the two adjoining columns (AD and AE) such that the same formula should be in cells AC13 through AE16.

    The same formula used to calculate the time-weighted return for the portfolio is used to calculate the time-weighted return for S&P 500 and Barclays Agg.

    The following steps annualize the Inception-to-Date returns for the portfolio and two benchmarks. As a reminder, you should not use the annualization unless there are at least 12 months of returns. Figure 10-2 shows the basic formula for annualizing a return. If you Google "How to annualize monthly returns," you will get a long list of formulas with a varying degree of merits, but the formula used here is one of the more accurate solutions.

$$\text{Annualized Return} = (1 + \text{Total Return})^{\frac{365}{\# \text{ of days}}} - 1$$

Figure 10-2. The formula to calculate annualized return

34. Label cell AA17 "ITD Annualized."

35. In cell AB17, enter the following formula:

    ```
    =EOMONTH(MIN(M:M),-1)
    ```

    This formula is the same as the one next to the ITD row header.

36. In cell AC17, under the Portfolio column header, enter the following formula:

    ```
    =(1+AC16)^(365/($AB$12-$AB16))-1
    ```

    This formula annualizes the ITD time-weighted return using the formula presented in Figure 10-2.

37. Copy the formula used in step 36 (cell AC17) to cells AD17 and AE17 to annualize the S&P 500 and Barclays Agg return.

    The next set of steps adds annualized standard deviation for each period to the table. Unfortunately, there is not a consensus on which Excel standard deviation function is the appropriate one to use (STDEV.S or STDEV.P). STDEV.S assumes a sample population, whereas STDEV.P assumes the entire population. I have heard valid arguments for both, but for this scenario, I have chosen to use STDEV.S because it appears to be common practice. There are also a lot of arguments about the accuracy of using the square root of 12 to annualize the standard deviation of returns, but it is still an industry standard.

38. Across columns AF through AH in row 11, add the following labels: Portfolio, S&P 500, Barclays Agg.

39. Under the Portfolio column header on the QTD row (cell AF13), place the following array formula and copy it down to cell AF16. Because this is an array formula, you need to press Ctrl-Shift-Enter:

    ```
    =STDEV.S(IF(Returns[Date]>AB13,Returns[Monthly Return]))*(12^0.5)
    ```

    This formula takes the standard deviation of monthly returns after and including the date in the AB column. The standard deviation is annualized by multiplying by the square root of 12.

40. Repeat step 39 in columns AG and AH to calculate the annualized standard deviation for S&P 500 and the Barclays Agg using the array formulas

    ```
    =STDEV.S(IF(Returns[Date]>AB13,Returns[S&P 500 Pct]))*(12^0.5)
    ```

and:

```
=STDEV.S(IF(Returns[Date]>AB13,Returns[Barclays Pct]))*(12^0.5)
```

With the annualized standard deviations calculated, we can calculate the ITD Sharpe Ratio. We calculate the Sharpe Ratio by dividing the product of the average returns and 12 by the annualized standard deviation. There are also a few different implementations of the Sharpe Ratio available online, but this one is common.

41. Label cell AA20 "ITD Sharpe Ratio."

42. Label cells AC19 through AE19: Portfolio, S&P 500, Barclays Agg.

43. In cell AC20, enter the following formula, under the Portfolio column header:

```
=AVERAGE(Returns[Return - RF])*12/AF16
```

This formula calculates the Sharpe Ratio by averaging all the returns, annualizing it by multiplying by 12, and dividing by the Portfolio's annualized standard deviation since inception.

44. Under the S&P 500 column header (cell AD20), enter the following formula:

```
=AVERAGE(Returns[S&P - RF])*12/AG16
```

This returns the Sharpe Ratio for the S&P 500 over the same period as the portfolio's inception.

45. Like steps 43 and 44, under the Barclays column header, enter the following formula:

```
=AVERAGE(Returns[Barclays - RF])*12/AH16
```

It is important to take a moment to look at the results, ensure that they make sense, and see if there are any interesting outcomes (results should look like Figure 10-3). As you would expect, the S&P 500 has higher returns and risk (standard deviation) than the Barclays Agg. In the example shown in Figure 10-3, the S&P 500 has a higher annualized return (6.31 percent compared to portfolio's 5.72 percent annualized return) but because the S&P 500 had a higher standard deviation it ended up with a slightly lower Sharpe Ratio (0.54 versus 0.56). As a reminder, the Sharpe Ratio measures risk-adjusted return, and thus the higher the number, the better.

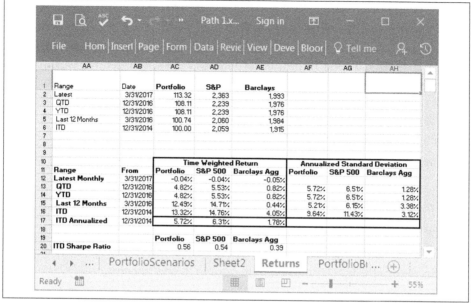

Figure 10-3. Returns summary table

Portfolio Report

This section covers how to create a two-page tear sheet report using the summary of returns and the tables created in the Portfolio Breakdown section of Chapter 7. Keep in mind that there are no fixed rules for creating reports; you should customize them to fit your needs. The first page of the report contains some key data points (portfolio size, Sharpe Ratio, date of last return, and the date the report was created). Additionally, the first page contains four charts that give the reader a high-level view of the portfolio's performance, growth, risk-adjusted return, and composition. The second page illustrates additional portfolio composition details using four charts derived from the summary data from the Portfolio Breakdown worksheet.

The following steps create a new worksheet for the report, setting the page layout and adjusting the view to make it easier to visualize the report.

46. Create a new worksheet called "PortfolioReport," and then change your view to Page Break Preview.

47. On the ribbon, on the Page Layout tab, in the Page Setup group, click the Orientation button, and then select Landscape.

48. Select cells A1 through M96, and then, on the Page Layout tab, in the Page Setup group, click Print Area, and then select Set Print Area.

    This shows the canvas for the two-page report.

49. Still on the Page Layout tab, in the Gridlines section, clear the View checkbox.

50. Change the font size of every cell to 8.

The next set of steps organizes some of the data used in the report off to the side. The first set pulls the historical Portfolio MV from the Returns worksheet to show a chart of growth. Linking the Portfolio MV from the Returns worksheet into the PortfolioReport worksheet makes it easier to customize which dates are shown.

51. Label cell O1 "Date" and cell P1 "Portfolio MV."

52. Under the "Date" header in cell O2, enter the following formula:

```
=MAX(Returns[Date])
```

This returns the latest return date for the portfolio.

53. Directly beneath that cell, in cell O3, enter the following formula:

```
=EOMONTH(O2,-1)
```

This returns the last day of the month prior to the cell above it.

54. Drag the formula in cell O3 down such that the entire return history is covered.

55. Under the "Portfolio MV" header, in cell P2, enter the following formula, and then drag it down to match the rows from step 54:

```
=INDEX(Returns[Starting AUM],MATCH(O2,Returns[Date],0))
```

This uses the INDEX/MATCH functions to pull the Starting AUM from the Excel Returns table for which the dates match. The result should be two columns (O and P) containing the history of the portfolio MV.

The next set of steps creates another table off to the side that will contain the annualized return, annualized standard deviation, and Sharpe Ratio for the portfolio, the S&P 500, and the Barclays Agg. In addition, this table includes the current standard deviation, forecasted returns, and Sharpe Ratio of the portfolio created in Chapter 7, which we then use to compare expected and historical risk-adjusted returns of the portfolio.

56. Across row 1, in columns S through V, enter the following labels: ITD Portfolio, Current Portfolio, S&P 500, Barclays Agg.

57. In column R, down rows 2 through 4, place the following labels: Return, Standard Deviation, Sharpe.

The result of steps 56 and 57 should be a table that will store information about the returns that will be populated in the next steps.

58. On row 2, under the ITD Portfolio header (cell S2), link to the annualized ITD portfolio return from the Returns worksheet by using the following formula:

```
=Returns!AC17
```

59. Link the cells on row 2, under the S&P 500 and Barclays Agg, to their respective annualized ITD returns from the Returns worksheet using `=Returns!AD17` and `=Returns!AE17`, respectively.

60. On row 2, under the Current Portfolio, link to the portfolio return calculation in the PortfolioStats worksheet created in Chapter 7 by using the following formula:

    `=PortfolioStats!E2`

61. In row 3, across columns S through V, link the annualized standard deviation of the historical returns, current portfolio, S&P 500, and Barclays Agg by using the following formulas, respectively:

    `=Returns!AF16, =PortfolioStats!E1, =Returns!AG16, =Returns!AH16`

62. In row 5, across columns S through V, link the Sharpe Ratio by using the following formulas:

    `=Returns!AC20, =PortfolioStats!E3, =Returns!AD20, =Returns!AE20`

In the next set of steps, we begin designing the report, starting with the header. The following steps add a title, market value, Sharpe Ratio, and key dates to the top of the first page.

63. Merge cells A1 through C2, and then label it "Chapter 10" in size 18 font.

64. Merge cells H1 through K1, and then place the following formula in the cell:

    `=TEXT(P2/1000000,"$#,##0.00") & "MM Market Value"`

This cell takes the portfolio market value on latest return date and converts the format. If the latest portfolio market value were 123,456,789, it would display it as "$123.46MM Market Value."

65. Merge cells H2 through K2, and then place the following formula in the cell:

    `=TEXT(S4,"0.00") & " Sharpe Ratio"`

This formats the portfolio's Sharpe Ratio to two decimal places.

66. Label cell L1 "Latest Return," and then, in cell M1, enter the following formula:

    `=O2`

This just displays the latest date from the Portfolio MV column.

67. Label cell L2 "Report Date," and then, in cell M2, enter the following formula:

    `=TODAY()`

68. Change the background color of cells A3 through M3 to create separation between the report header and the contents below.

The next couple of steps add charts to the report that compare the relative returns of the portfolio to the two benchmark indices and the AUM growth of the portfolio.

69. In the upper-left quarter of the remaining space on the first page, add a column chart using the data in the range =Returns!$AA$11:$AE$17, which contains the returns summary table created in steps 28 through 37. Under the Horizontal Axis Labels, clear the ITD category checkbox because it makes more sense just to list the ITD Annualized category. Label the chart "Time Weighted Return."

70. In the upper-right quarter of the first page next to the "Time Weighted Return" chart, add a line chart using the data in columns O and P from steps 51 through 55. Label the chart "Portfolio MV."

Format the charts to your personal taste; the top of the report should look like Figure 10-4. These two charts can quickly convey relative performance and growth.

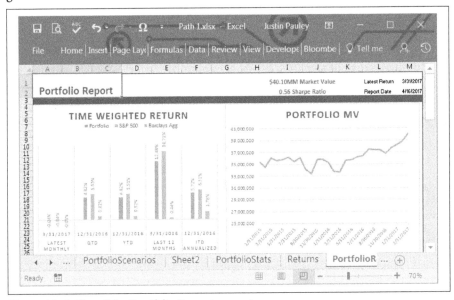

Figure 10-4. Top of the Portfolio Report, page 1

The next set of steps adds another two charts to the bottom of the Portfolio Report. The first chart is a scatter plot that compares risk (standard deviation) to return of the portfolio, the two benchmarks, and the forecasted portfolio (from Chapter 7). The second chart breaks down the portfolio composition by asset class.

71. In the lower-left quarter of the first page, add a scatter plot chart using the data from R1 through V4 created in steps 56 through 62. Label the chart "Risk vs Return."

72. In the lower-right quarter of the first page, add a pie chart using the data on the PortfolioBreakdown worksheet containing the breakdown by asset type (=Portfo lioBreakdown!$A$1:$C$4).

Format these charts as you like. The bottom of the first page should look like Figure 10-5. The "Risk vs Return" chart can quickly demonstrate which funds are getting the best risk-adjust return. Ideally, a fund or portfolio would be in the upper-left quadrant of the "Risk vs Return" chart because that is the most return for the least risk. Conversely, the lower-right of the chart indicates a fund with a lot of risk and low return.

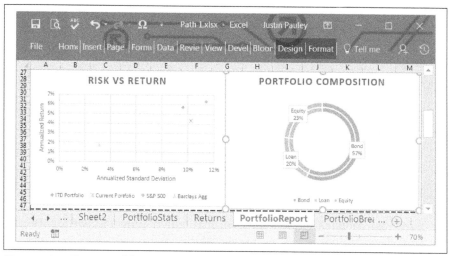

Figure 10-5. Bottom of the Portfolio Report, page 1

The next couple of steps adds two pie charts to the top of the second page that will display the composition of the portfolio by company rating and category.

73. Add a pie chart directly below the blue dashed line that separates pages of the report, in the upper-left quarter. Use the "% of Portfolio" from the table in the PortfolioBreakdown worksheet that breaks the portfolio down by Portfolio Corp Rating. Label the report "By Company Rating."

74. In the upper-right quarter of the second page, add a pie chart using the Category breakdown table in the PortfolioBreakdown worksheet. Label the chart "By Category."

After formatting those charts, the top of the second page should look like Figure 10-6. These charts are quick ways to answer common questions about the portfolio's composition, but you can replace them with other charts that better suit your needs.

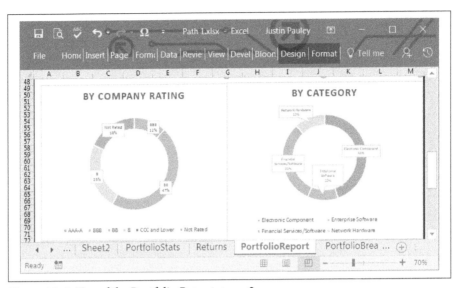

Figure 10-6. Top of the Portfolio Report, page 2

The final two steps add combination column and line charts to the bottom of the second page of the report. These charts demonstrate how to show both the total market value and percentage of portfolio for a range.

75. In the lower-left quarter of the second page, add a column chart labeled "Market Cap" that contains the Market Cap distribution from the PortfolioBreakdown worksheet. Include a column for the Market value and "% of Portfolio." Right-click the Market Value columns in the chart, and then select "Change chart type," change the Market Value series to a line chart on the secondary axis.

76. Repeat step 75 to add a chart labeled "Fixed Income Price Distribution" using the price distribution of the fixed income assets from the PortfolioBreakdown worksheet.

After formatting, the bottom half of page 2 should look like Figure 10-7. These charts can quickly inform someone about a percentage and a total market value of a distribution.

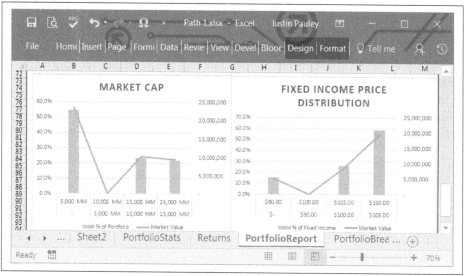

Figure 10-7. Bottom of the Portfolio Report, page 2

Path 3: C# and SSRS

This section covers making modifications in Visual Studio to the Windows Form application created in Chapter 9 to view reports. The modifications add an additional button that will display an SSRS Portfolio report in a separate tab of the application. The application covers the same calculations as the Excel section of this chapter and creates most of the same charts. Because the queries for the Portfolio Breakdown were covered in Chapter 7, those charts are not included in this chapter. Before beginning, be sure to add a reference to MathNet.Numerics used in other projects in this book. This chapter assumes a new table ("Returns") was created and populated in the Access database containing the monthly P&L and starting AUM using the schema in Table 10-1. Note that the Period column is the Primary Key.

Table 10-1. Returns table schema

Field name	Data type
Period*	Date
MonthlyPNL	Number (Double)
StartingAUM	Number (Double)

In the Visual Studio solution created in Chapter 9, the first modifications occur in the *ADS.xsd* DataSet. In addition to adding the Returns TableAdapter, three additional DataTables need to be added to pass the calculation results to the report (RDLC). The first of the three DataTables is the ReturnCalcs that will resemble the Returns Excel table and will store calculated returns from Bloomberg. The second DataTable is ReturnSummary that contains the time-weighted returns and standard deviations for different periods. Finally, a DataTable called Header will contain the portfolio's Sharpe Ratio, date of last return, and latest market value to populate the header of the report.

1. Add a TableAdapter called **Returns** that selects every column from the Returns table.

2. Add a ReturnsCalc DataTable containing the following columns: **Date, Month lyPNL, StartingAUM, MonthlyReturn, ValueOf100, MonthlyRF, ReturnRF, SP500, SPRF, Barclays**, and **BarclaysRF**. Set Date as a primary key and its DataType to DateTime. The other columns should all be set to Double.

3. Add a ReturnSummary DataTable containing the following columns: **Range, Date, PortfolioReturn, SP500Return, BarclaysReturn, PortfolioStdDev, SP500StdDev**, and **BarclaysStdDev**. Set Range as a primary key with a String DataType, set Date to a DateTime DataType, and set the rest to Double.

4. Add a Header DataTable containing the following columns: **Sharpe, LatestMV**, and **Date**. This DataTable does not require a primary key. Set Date to DateTime DataType and the others to Double.

When completed, the resulting DataSet should have the additional tables, as shown in Figure 10-8.

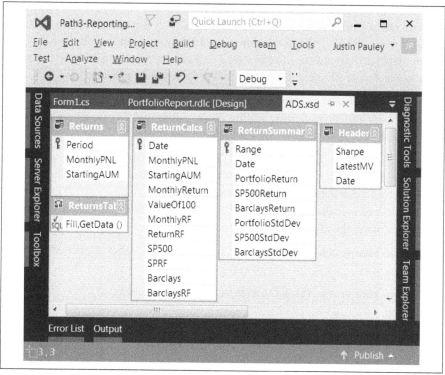

Figure 10-8. New DataTables in ADS

The following steps add a new SSRS report to the project and add an additional ReportViewer to the form:

5. Add a new SSRS report to the project called PortfolioReport.rdlc.

6. In the Report Data window, right-click Datasets, and then, one at a time, add the following Datasets: Returns, header, ReturnSummary

7. On the Windows Form (Form1.cs) Designer, add a tab controller in panel2, set its dock to fill, place the original ReportViewer control in the first tab, and then add a new ReportView to the second tab.

8. Set the Report property of the new ReporterViwer (named rptPortfolio) to the PortfolioReport that was created in step 5. This will also automatically add BindingSources and TableAdapters for the different tables created in steps 1 through 4.

9. Add a new button called **btnPortfolio** and label it **Portfolio**.

10. In the Form1.cs, remove the rptPortfolio.RefreshReport() that was also automatically added to the Form_Load event.

The entire code for this enhancement is in the btnPortfolio_Click event. The code that follows begins by fetching the Bloomberg history for S&P 500, Barclays Agg, and three-month LIBOR. Then, it combines the BloombergHistory with the Returns data to populate the ReturnCalcs DataTable. The ReturnCalcs DataTable is essentially the same as the Returns Excel table and they share the same calculations.

Next, the code begins by populating the ReturnSummary DataTable with the different period ranges and their corresponding dates. Although this does require two loops through the ReturnSummary, I find it cleaner than trying to do everything at once.

Then, as soon as the ReturnSummary DataTable has the ranges and dates, it loops through again, referencing the relevant rows in the ReturnCalcs DataTable for the given date and calculating returns for the various periods except "ITD Annualized." The annualized calculation is left until the next step because it references calculations of other periods, specifically the ITD row.

Finally, the Sharpe Ratio is calculated and the ADS DataSet is sent to the portfolio report:

```
private void btnPortfolio_Click(object sender, EventArgs e)
{

    // Populate the Returns table
    this.ReturnsTableAdapter.Fill(this.ADS.Returns);


    // Find inception date and latest return date
    DateTime inception = this.ADS.Returns.OrderBy(x => x.Period).First().Period;
    DateTime latest =
    this.ADS.Returns.OrderByDescending(x => x.Period).First().Period;

    // Get S&P 500, Barclays, and 3M Libor history
    // The method returns daily prices, which is overkill
    // it can be adjusted to return monthly.
    // The 31 days are subtracted because we
    // need to calculate monthly return on the first month
    Dictionary<DateTime, double> sp500 =
    GetHistory("SPX Index", "PX_LAST", inception.AddDays(-31));
    Dictionary<DateTime, double> barclays =
    GetHistory("LBUSTRUU Index", "PX_LAST", inception.AddDays(-31));
    Dictionary<DateTime, double> libor =
    GetHistory("US0003M Index", "PX_LAST", inception.AddDays(-31));

    //Populate ReturnCalcs Table
    double valueof100 = 100;
    foreach (ADS.ReturnsRow row in this.ADS.Returns.OrderBy(x => x.Period))
    {
        // Figure out the last day of the prior month
        // if you just subtract 1 month, it will break when the month
        // is February since it would return January 28.
```

```csharp
        DateTime endOfPriorMonth =
        new DateTime(row.Period.Year, row.Period.Month, 1).AddDays(-1);
        ADS.ReturnCalcsRow calc = this.ADS.ReturnCalcs.NewReturnCalcsRow();
        calc.Date = row.Period;
        calc.MonthlyPNL = row.MonthlyPNL;
        calc.StartingAUM = row.StartingAUM;
        calc.MonthlyReturn = (calc.MonthlyPNL / calc.StartingAUM);
        calc.ValueOf100 = valueof100 * (1 + calc.MonthlyReturn);
        valueof100 = calc.ValueOf100;
        calc.MonthlyRF = libor[calc.Date] / 100 / 12;
        calc.ReturnRF = calc.MonthlyReturn - calc.MonthlyRF;
        calc.SP500 =
        (sp500[calc.Date] - sp500[endOfPriorMonth]) / sp500[endOfPriorMonth];
        calc.SPRF = calc.SP500 - calc.MonthlyRF;
        calc.Barclays =
        (barclays[calc.Date] - barclays[endOfPriorMonth]) /
        barclays[endOfPriorMonth];
        calc.BarclaysRF = calc.Barclays - calc.MonthlyRF;
        this.ADS.ReturnCalcs.AddReturnCalcsRow(calc);
    }


    //Add Ranges to ReturnsSummary
    List<string> ranges = new List<string>()
    {
        "Latest Monthly",
        "QTD",
        "YTD",
        "Last 12 Months",
        "ITD",
        "ITD Annualized"
    };
    // This loops through and adds Ranges and their
    // corresponding dates.
    foreach (string range in ranges)
    {
        ADS.ReturnSummaryRow srow = this.ADS.ReturnSummary.NewReturnSummaryRow();
        srow.Range = range;
        switch(range)
        {
            case "Latest Monthly":
                srow.Date = latest;
                break;
            case "QTD":
                // This gets the day before the start of the quarter
                // based on the latest return.
                srow.Date =
                new DateTime(latest.Year, 3 * ((latest.Month + 2) / 3) - 2, 1).
                AddDays(-1);
                break;
            case "YTD":
                srow.Date = new DateTime(latest.Year - 1, 12, 31);
                break;
```

```
            case "Last 12 Months":
                srow.Date = latest.AddMonths(-12);
                break;
            case "ITD":
                //returns the last day of the month prior to inception
                srow.Date =
                new DateTime(inception.Year, inception.Month, 1).AddDays(-1);
                break;
            case "ITD Annualized":
                //returns the last day of the month prior to inception
                srow.Date =
                new DateTime(inception.Year, inception.Month, 1).AddDays(-1);
                break;
        }
        this.ADS.ReturnSummary.AddReturnSummaryRow(srow);
}

//Iterate through ReturnSummary and
//Calculate Returns and StandardDev
foreach(ADS.ReturnSummaryRow srow in this.ADS.ReturnSummary)
{
    ADS.ReturnCalcsRow curr = this.ADS.ReturnCalcs.FindByDate(latest);
    ADS.ReturnCalcsRow prev = this.ADS.ReturnCalcs.FindByDate(srow.Date);
    if (srow.Range=="Latest Monthly")
    {
        srow.PortfolioReturn = prev.MonthlyReturn;
        srow.SP500Return = prev.SP500;
        srow.BarclaysReturn = prev.Barclays;
    }
    else if (srow.Range== "ITD Annualized")
    {
        //ITD Annualized isn't added here
        //because it is dependent on other rows
        continue;
    }
    else
    {
        //ITD always starts with a price of 100 for
        // ValueOf100
        if(srow.Range=="ITD")
            srow.PortfolioReturn= (curr.ValueOf100 - 100) / 100;
        else
            srow.PortfolioReturn =
            (curr.ValueOf100 - prev.ValueOf100) / prev.ValueOf100;

        srow.SP500Return =
        (sp500[latest] - sp500[srow.Date]) / sp500[srow.Date];
        srow.BarclaysReturn =
        (barclays[latest] - barclays[srow.Date]) / barclays[srow.Date];

        //Populate List Objects
        // with returns that are after
```

```
                // the ReturnSummary starting date
                List<double> monthlyReturns = new List<double>();
                List<double> sp500Returns = new List<double>();
                List<double> barclaysReturns = new List<double>();
                foreach (ADS.ReturnCalcsRow calc in this.ADS.ReturnCalcs)
                {
                    if (calc.Date > srow.Date)
                    {
                        monthlyReturns.Add(calc.MonthlyReturn);
                        sp500Returns.Add(calc.SP500);
                        barclaysReturns.Add(calc.Barclays);
                    }
                }
                srow.PortfolioStdDev =
                Statistics.StandardDeviation(monthlyReturns) * Math.Sqrt(12);
                srow.SP500StdDev =
                Statistics.StandardDeviation(sp500Returns) * Math.Sqrt(12);
                srow.BarclaysStdDev =
                Statistics.StandardDeviation(barclaysReturns) * Math.Sqrt(12);
            }
        }
        ADS.ReturnSummaryRow ITDRow = this.ADS.ReturnSummary.FindByRange("ITD");

        // Once every other row is populated,
        // populate the ITD Annualized row.
        ADS.ReturnSummaryRow annualRow =
        this.ADS.ReturnSummary.FindByRange("ITD Annualized");
        double daycount =
        (latest - new DateTime(inception.Year, inception.Month, 1).
        AddDays(-1)).TotalDays;
        annualRow.PortfolioReturn =
        Math.Pow(1 + this.ADS.ReturnSummary.FindByRange("ITD").PortfolioReturn,
        (365 / daycount)) - 1;
        annualRow.SP500Return =
        Math.Pow(1 + this.ADS.ReturnSummary.FindByRange("ITD").SP500Return,
        (365 / daycount)) - 1;
        annualRow.BarclaysReturn =
        Math.Pow(1 + this.ADS.ReturnSummary.FindByRange("ITD").BarclaysReturn,
        (365 / daycount)) - 1;
        //Using the same StdDev as the non-annualized rows.
        annualRow.PortfolioStdDev = ITDRow.PortfolioStdDev;
        annualRow.SP500StdDev = ITDRow.SP500StdDev;
        annualRow.BarclaysStdDev = ITDRow.BarclaysStdDev;

        //Fields needed for report header.
        ADS.HeaderRow header = this.ADS.Header.NewHeaderRow();

        header.Sharpe =
        this.ADS.ReturnCalcs.Average(x => x.ReturnRF) * 12/ITDRow.PortfolioStdDev;
        header.LatestMV =
        this.ADS.Returns.OrderByDescending(x => x.Period).First().StartingAUM;
        header.Date = latest;
```

```
this.ADS.Header.AddHeaderRow(header);


    this.rptPortfolio.RefreshReport();
}
```

In the Portfolio Report, the Header Dataset is used to populate the text boxes at the top, such as the Portfolio MV:

```
="$"&Format(Sum(Fields!LatestMV.Value/1000000, "Header"),"#,##0.00")
& "MM Market Value"
```

The ReturnSummary Dataset is used to populate a column chart containing the time-weighted returns. The Returns Dataset is used to populate a line chart in the upper-right corner containing a history of the portfolio's market value.

Finally, the ReturnSummary Dataset is used again to populate a scatter plot chart on the bottom that compares annualized returns and standard deviations. The chart has a filter set to include only rows for which the Range is equal to ITD Annualized. Even though this scatter plot does not contain the portfolio's current standard deviation or forecasted return that was calculated in Chapter 7, you can use the code from that chapter to append the ReturnSummary DataTable.

When you're finished, the program output should look like Figure 10-9.

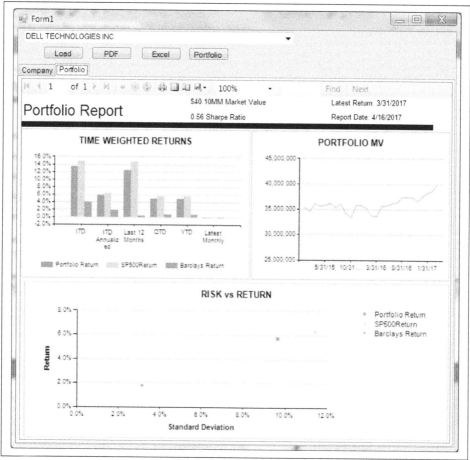

Figure 10-9. Windows Form with Portfolio Report

Summary

You can use the calculations and charts covered in this chapter to measure the performance, growth, and relative value of your portfolio or a portfolio of investments. This chapter also explained why it is important to take compounding into consideration. Although Excel and database tables are useful for analyzing information, transforming numbers into charts makes it a lot easier to identify trends and spot issues.

CHAPTER 11

Conclusion

This book has walked you through how to find and retrieve financial information from Bloomberg and Markit, analyze the data, and generate custom reports. The lessons have emphasized the need to add your own views at each step to create something truly valuable and unique. The real goal, however, was not to simply re-create the spreadsheets, databases, or code that came with the book. The goal was to teach, by example, how to build your own platform for analysis and reporting. I have no doubt that many of you wondered why I didn't include some field, calculation, or report element that seems critical to you. My hope is that, whatever it is that you are trying to build, this book gave you the framework for achieving your goals.

As next steps, I would suggest reaching for the moon. I always find it useful to sketch out what the ideal spreadsheet, report, or application would look like and build it one piece at a time. Begin by identifying all the different data needed and finding the best source for that data. Remember, sometimes the best or only source of good data is you. Ensure that you really understand the data and its nuances (accuracy, reliability of the source, etc.). Remember third normal form from Chapter 2, and make sure the data is stored properly. Ensure that you put the data into context, otherwise it is meaningless. Always take a moment to confirm that everything makes sense; too many people just trust their calculations and don't double-check the results. Finally, get creative and have fun with the reporting.

Thank you for reading, and feel free to drop me a note at *Justin.Pauley@gmail.com.*

—Justin

Table Reference

The tables throughout the book have been compiled here for easy reference.

Table A-1. Pricing source summary (Table 3-1)

Pricing source	Description
BGN	A real-time composite based on quotes from multiple contributors
BVAL	Combines direct market observations with quantitative pricing models
MSG1	Bloomberg mines prices from your inbox
TRAC	TRACE is FINRA's Corporate and Agency Bond price Dissemination Service. Access to real-time bond price information requires permission and a subscription fee. Nonsubscribers view pricing information on a four-hour delay.

Table A-2. Excel options for BDS (see "Pulling Bulk Data (BDS)" on page 29)

Parameter	Description
DIRECTION	Specifies how the returned values are arranged, either horizontally across columns or vertically across rows
SORTASC/SORTDESC	Parameters that control the order of the returned data
HEADERS	Displays headers
STARTROW, ENDROW, STARTCOL, and ENDCOL	Parameters to limit the data that is returned
AGGREGATE/SEPARATOR	AGGREGATE combines the BDS results into a single cell; SEPARATOR customizes the way the data is aggregated
PCS	Changes the pricing source
ARRAY	Returns values that can be used in the Excel Aggregate function

Table A-3. Bloomberg date types (Table 3-2)

Type	Daily	Weekly	Monthly	Quarterly	Semi-Annual	Annual
Fiscal	—	—	—	FQ	FS	FY
Calendar	CD	CW	CM	CQ	CS	CY
Actual	AD	AW	AM	AQ	AS	AY

Table A-4. Excel options for BDH (see "Pulling Historical Data (BDH)" on page 31)

Parameter	Description
Fill	Indicates missing dates set to Previous, Error, Blank, NA, PNA (previous date), F (next available), or custom text
PERIOD	Displays the data at a frequency other than daily
CAPCHG	Changes the way Bloomberg adjusts for spin-offs, stock splits/consolidations, stock dividends/bonuses, and rights offerings/entitlements
FX	Adjusts the currency of the returned values
POINTS	Controls the maximum number of dates to return
SORT	Set to D for descending
DIRECTION	Specify how the returned values are arranged, either horizontally across columns or vertically across rows
ARRAY	Returns values that can be used the the Excel Aggregate function
PCS	Changes the pricing source
DATES	Set to HIDE to return only values
QUOTETYPE	Set to "P" for price when PC_LAST returns yield

Table A-5. Bond worksheet columns and Bloomberg map (Table 3-3)

Column	Input into row 1	Input into row 2	Description
A	[Intentionally blank]	BondID	
B	[Intentionally blank]	BBID	
C	BOND_TO_EQY_TICKER	CompanyID	Bond issuer's equity ticker
D	SECURITY_DES	Security Description	Bloomberg description of security
E	CPN_TYP	Coupon Type	Type of interest (Fixed, Floating)
F	CPN	Fixed Coupon	Current interest rate
G	MATURITY	Maturity	Maturity date of bond
H	RTG_MOODY	Moody's Rating	Moody's rating
I	RTG_SP	S&P Rating	S&P rating
J	QUOTED_CRNCY	Currency	Quoted currency
K	PAYMENT_RANK	Rank	Payment rank (Senior Unsecured, Secured, etc.)
L	PX_LAST	Price	Last price
M	CHG_PCT_YTD	YTD Px Chg	Year-to-date price change (percent)
N	CHG_PCT_3M	3M Px Chg	Three-month price change (percent)
O	YAS_YLD_SPREAD	YAS Spread	At current price, the difference in basis points (bps) between the bond's yield and its default benchmark yield. Default settings controlled by YASD <GO> screen.

Column	Input into row 1	Input into row 2	Description
P	YAS_BOND_YLD	YAS Yield	At current price, the bond's yield. Default settings controlled by YASD <GO> screen
Q	CALLABLE	Callable?	Can the bond be called/redeemed?
R	NXT_CALL_DT	Next Call Date	Next date bond can be redeemed by issuer
S	NXT_CALL_PX	Next Call Price	The price the bond can be redeemed at on next call date
T	[Intentionally blank]	Bond Comments	

Table A-6. Loan worksheet columns and Bloomberg map (Table 3-4)

Input into row 1	Input into row 2	Description
[Intentionally blank]	LoanID	Contains the unique identifier for each loan
[Intentionally blank]	BBID	Contains the full Bloomberg Identifier
ISSUER_PARENT_EQY_TICKER	CompanyID	Loan issuer's equity ticker
SECURITY_DES	Security Description	Bloomberg description of security
LN_CURRENT_MARGIN	Margin	Margin or spread above benchmark in coupon
INDEX_FLOOR	Floor	Floor on index if applicable
RESET_IDX	Index	Benchmark index for coupon
MATURITY	Maturity	Maturity date
RTG_MOODY	Moody's Rating	Moody's rating
RTG_SP	S&P Rating	S&P rating
PX_LAST	Price	Last price
CHG_PCT_YTD	YTD Px Chg	Year-to-date price change (percent)
DISC_MRGN_ASK	DM	Discount margin (DM) based on current ask price
YLD_YTM_ASK	Yield	Yield to maturity based on ask price
CALLABLE	Callable?	Can the bond be called/redeemed?
NXT_CALL_DT	Next Call Date	Next date bond can be redeemed by issuer
NXT_CALL_PX	Next Call Price	The price the bond can be redeemed at on next call date
[Intentionally blank]	Loan Comments	

Table A-7. IDX worksheet columns and Bloomberg map (Table 3-5)

Input into row 1	Input into row 2	Description
[Intentionally blank]	IndexID	Contains the unique identifier for each loan
[Intentionally blank]	BBID	Contains the full Bloomberg Identifier
NAME	Name	Name of the index
PX_LAST	Price	Last price
CHG_PCT_HIGH_52WEEK	52 Week High	Percent difference between current price and highest price in last 52 weeks
CHG_PCT_LOW_52WEEK	52 Week Low	Percent difference between current price and lowest price in last 52 weeks
CHG_PCT_YTD	YTD Px Change	Percent price change year to date
CHG_PCT_3M	3M Px Change	Percent price change over last three months
CURRENT_TRR_1YR	12M Total Return	One-year total return; dividends are reinvested

Table A-8. Company worksheet columns and Bloomberg map (Table 3-6)

Input into row 2	Input into row 3	Description
[Intentionally blank]	CompanyID	Contains the unique identifier for each Company
[Intentionally blank]	BBID	Contains the full Bloomberg Identifier
NAME	CompanyName	The name of the company
COMPANY_IS_PRIVATE	Private	Indicates if the company is private
GICS_SECTOR_NAME	Sector	Global Industry Classification Standard (GICS) sector classification
GICS_INDUSTRY_NAME	Industry	Global Industry Classification Standard (GICS) industry classification
GICS_SUB_INDUSTRY_NAME	Sub-Industry	Global Industry Classification Standard (GICS) subindustry classification
RTG_SP_LT_LC_ISSUER_CREDIT	S&P Rating	S&P long-term obligation issuer rating
RTG_MDY_LT_CORP_FAMILY	Moody's Rating	Moody's long-term corporate family rating
CRNCY_ADJ_MKT_CAP*	Market Cap	Currency adjusted market capitalization
SHORT_AND_LONG_TERM_DEBT*	Total Debt	Sum of short-term and long-term debt (in millions)
NET_DEBT*	Net Debt	Net debt of the company
CRNCY_ADJ_CURR_EV*	Enterprise Value	Currency adjusted enterprise value
TRAIL_12M_EBITDA*	TTM EBITDA	Trailing 12-month EBITDA
PE_RATIO	PE Ratio	P/E Ratio, ratio of the stock price and the company's earnings per share
EQY_DVD_YLD_IND	Dividend Gross Yield	The most recently announced gross dividend, annualized, divided by the current price
CURRENT_TRR_1YR	12M Total Return	One-year total return. Dividends are reinvested
CHG_PCT_YTD	YTD Px Change	Percent price change year to date
CHG_PCT_3M	3M Px Change	Percent price change over last three months
SALES_REV_TURN*	Total Revenue	Company's total operating revenues less various adjustments to Gross Sales
TOT_DEBT_TO_EBITDA	Total Debt/EBITDA	Total Debt divided by Trailing twelve-month EBITDA
INTEREST_COVERAGE_RATIO	Interest Coverage	Earnings before interest and taxes (EBIT) divided by total interest incurred
TRAIL_12M_FREE_CASH_FLOW*	FCF	Trailing twelve-month free cash flow
FCF_TO_TOTAL_DEBT	FCF/Total Debt	Trailing twelve-month free cash flow divided by Total Debt
CRNCY_ADJ_PX_LAST*	Price	Currency adjusted last price
CHG_PCT_HIGH_52WEEK	52 Week High Change	Percent difference between current price and highest price in last 52 weeks
CHG_PCT_LOW_52WEEK	52 Week Low Change	Percent difference between current price and lowest price in last 52 weeks
CDS_SPREAD_TICKER_5Y	5yr CDS Spread Ticker	Bloomberg ticker for five-year credit default swap par spread
TOT_BUY_REC	Buy Recommendations	Total number of research analyst buy recommendations
TOT_SELL_REC	Sell Recommendations	Total number of research analyst sell recommendations
TOT_HOLD_REC	Hold Recommendations	Total number of research analyst hold recommendations
[Intentionally blank]	Net Debt/EBITDA	

Input into row 2	Input into row 3	Description
[Intentionally blank]	5yr CDS Spread	
[Intentionally blank]	Category	
[Intentionally blank]	Company Comments	

Table A-9. Company table design (Table 3-7)

Field name	Data type
CompanyID*	Short Text
BBID	Short Text
CompanyName	Short Text
IsPrivate	Short Text
Sector	Short Text
Industry	Short Text
SubIndustry	Short Text
SPRating	Short Text
MoodyRating	Short Text
MarketCap	Number
TotalDebt	Number
NetDebt	Number
EV	Number
EBITDA	Number
TotalRevenue	Number
TotalDebtToEBITDA	Number
InterestCoverage	Number
FCF	Number
FCFToTotalDebt	Number
Price	Number
YrHi	Number
YrLow	Number
CDS5YrTicker	Short Text
NetDebtToEBITDA	Number
CDSSpread5Yr	Number
Category	Short Text
CompanyComments	Long Text
PERatio	Number
DVDYield	Number
TotalReturn12M	Number
PxChgYTD	Number
PxChg3M	Number
RecBuy	Number
RecSell	Number

Field name	Data type
RecHold	Number

Table A-10. Bond table design (Table 3-8)

Field name	Data type
BondID*	Short Text
BBID	Short Text
CompanyID	Short Text
SecurityDes	Short Text
CpnType	Short Text
FixedCpn	Number
Maturity	Date/Time
MoodyRating	Short Text
SPRating	Short Text
Currency	Short Text
Rank	Short Text
Price	Number
PxChgYTD	Number
PxChg3M	Number
YASSpread	Number
YASYield	Number
IsCallable	Short Text
NextCallDate	Date/Time
NextCallPrice	Number
BondComments	Long Text

Table A-11. Loan table design (Table 3-9)

Field name	Data type
LoanID*	Short Text
BBID	Short Text
CompanyID	Short Text
SecurityDesc	Short Text
CpnType	Short Text
Margin	Number
Floor	Number
Index	Short Text
Maturity	Date/Time
MoodyRating	Short Text
SPRating	Short Text
Currency	Short Text
Rank	Short Text

Field name	Data type
Price	Number
PxChgYTD	Number
PxChg3M	Number
DM	Number
Yield	Number
IsCallable	Short Text
NextCallDate	Date/Time
NextCallPrice	Number
LoanComments	Long Text

Table A-12. Index table design (Table 3-10)

Field name	Data Type
IndexID*	Short Text
BBID	Short Text
IndexName	Short Text
Price	Number
YrHi	Number
YrLow	Number
PxChgYTD	Number
PxChg3M	Number
TotalReturn12M	Number

Table A-13. Map table design (Table 3-11)

Field name	Data type
DestTable*	Short Text
DestCol*	Short Text
BloombergFLD	Short Text

Table A-14. Map table data (Table 3-12)

DestTable	DestCol	BloombergFLD
Company	CompanyName	NAME
Company	IsPrivate	COMPANY_IS_PRIVATE
Company	Sector	GICS_SECTOR_NAME
Company	Industry	GICS_INDUSTRY_NAME
Company	SubIndustry	GICS_SUB_INDUSTRY_NAME
Company	SPRating	RTG_SP_LT_LC_ISSUER_CREDIT
Company	MoodyRating	RTG_MDY_LT_CORP_FAMILY
Company	MarketCap	CRNCY_ADJ_MKT_CAP
Company	TotalDebt	SHORT_AND_LONG_TERM_DEBT
Company	NetDebt	NET_DEBT

DestTable	DestCol	BloombergFLD
Company	EV	CRNCY_ADJ_CURR_EV
Company	EBITDA	TRAIL_12M_EBITDA
Company	TotalRevenue	SALES_REV_TURN
Company	TotalDebtToEBITDA	TOT_DEBT_TO_EBITDA
Company	InterestCoverage	INTEREST_COVERAGE_RATIO
Company	FCF	TRAIL_12M_FREE_CASH_FLOW
Company	FCFToTotalDebt	FCF_TO_TOTAL_DEBT
Company	Price	CRNCY_ADJ_PX_LAST
Company	YrHi	CHG_PCT_HIGH_52WEEK
Company	YrLow	CHG_PCT_LOW_52WEEK
Company	CDS5YrTicker	CDS_SPREAD_TICKER_5Y
Company	PERatio	PE_RATIO
Company	DVDYield	EQY_DVD_YLD_IND
Company	TotalReturn12M	CURRENT_TRR_1YR
Company	PxChgYTD	CHG_PCT_YTD
Company	PxChg3M	CHG_PCT_3M
Company	RecBuy	TOT_BUY_REC
Company	RecSell	TOT_SELL_REC
Company	RecHold	TOT_HOLD_REC
Bond	CompanyID	BOND_TO_EQY_TICKER
Bond	SecurityDes	SECURITY_DES
Bond	CpnType	CPN_TYP
Bond	FixedCpn	CPN
Bond	Maturity	MATURITY
Bond	MoodyRating	RTG_MOODY
Bond	SPRating	RTG_SP
Bond	Currency	QUOTED_CRNCY
Bond	Rank	PAYMENT_RANK
Bond	Price	PX_LAST
Bond	PxChgYTD	CHG_PCT_YTD
Bond	PxChg3M	CHG_PCT_3M
Bond	YASSpread	YAS_YLD_SPREAD
Bond	YASYield	YAS_BOND_YLD
Bond	IsCallable	CALLABLE
Bond	NextCallDate	NXT_CALL_DT
Bond	NextCallPrice	NXT_CALL_PX
Loan	CompanyID	ISSUER_PARENT_EQY_TICKER
Loan	SecurityDesc	SECURITY_DES
Loan	CpnType	CPN_TYP
Loan	Margin	LN_CURRENT_MARGIN
Loan	Floor	INDEX_FLOOR

DestTable	DestCol	BloombergFLD
Loan	Index	RESET_IDX
Loan	Maturity	MATURITY
Loan	MoodyRating	RTG_MOODY
Loan	SPRating	RTG_SP
Loan	Currency	QUOTED_CRNCY
Loan	Rank	PAYMENT_RANK
Loan	Price	PX_LAST
Loan	PxChgYTD	CHG_PCT_YTD
Loan	PxChg3M	CHG_PCT_3M
Loan	DM	DISC_MRGN_ASK
Loan	Yield	YLD_YTM_ASK
Loan	IsCallable	CALLABLE
Loan	NextCallDate	NXT_CALL_DT
Loan	NextCallPrice	NXT_CALL_PX
Index	IndexName	NAME
Index	Price	PX_LAST
Index	YrHi	CHG_PCT_HIGH_52WEEK
Index	YrLow	CHG_PCT_LOW_52WEEK
Index	PxChgYTD	CHG_PCT_YTD
Index	PxChg3M	CHG_PCT_3M
Index	TotalReturn12M	CURRENT_TRR_1YR

Table A-15. API arguments for historical request (Table 3-13)

Argument	BDH equivalent	Comments
startDate	—	Start date in YYYYMMDD format
endDate	—	End date in YYYYMMDD format
periodicityAdjustment	—	ACTUAL, CALENDAR, or FISCAL
periodicitySelection	—	DAILY, WEEKLY, MONTHLY, QUARTERLY, SEMI_ANNUALLY, YEARLY
currency	FX	Three letter ISO code; for example, USD, GBP
overrideOption	Quote	Set to OVERRIDE_OPTION_GPA to use average price in quote calculation instead of closing price
pricingOption	QuoteType	PRICING_OPTION_PRICE for price, PRICING_OPTION_YIELD for yield
nonTradingDayFillOption	Days	NON_TRADING_WEEKDAYS, ALL_CALENDAR_DAYS, ACTIVE_DAYS_ONLY
nonTradingDayFillMethod	Fill	PREVIOUS_VALUE or NIL_VALUE for blank
adjustmentNormal	CshAdjNormal	Set to true or false
adjustmentAbnormal	CshAdjAbnormal	Set to true or false
adjustmentSplit	CapChg	Set to true or false
adjustmentFollowDPDF	UseDPDF	Set to true or false

Argument	BDH equivalent	Comments
calendarCodeOverride	CDR	For example, "US" or "JN"

Because Markit has a partnership with S&P, some of the columns in Table A-16 (denoted by an asterisk [*]) are accessible only to clients that also have an agreement with S&P. In addition, some columns (denoted by **) must be specifically requested from Markit (you can contact *support@markit.com*) before they will appear in the results. Columns denoted with *** require both an agreement with S&P and a specific request to Markit.

Table A-16. Facility update columns (Table 4-1)

Column	Description
LoanX ID	Unique Identifier for each loan.
PMD ID	Unique identifier associated with a particular issuer/tranche combination. This can be a positive or negative number.
PMD Trans ID*	Unique ID by which PMD/LCD identifies a Transaction, or loan package.
Issuer Name	Name of borrower or issuer.
Issuer ID*	A generated unique identifier associated with a particular issuer.
Deal Name	Name of borrower. This is usually the same as preceding cell but can include date and type of deal.
Facility Type	Specific loan type; TLB, bridge loan, etc.
LoanX Facility Type	Markit consolidates the PMD Facility Type into one of currently 16 standardized values.
Facility Status*	Specific instrument type: bridge, 364-day, subord, Term Loan Amortizing.
LoanX Facility Type Code*	Code representation of LoanX Facility Type + LoanX Facility Category.
LoanX Facility Category*	Markit simplifies the PMD Facility type to one of the following: Institutional, RC, TLA, Other.
Industry	Industry classification based on SIC code
Initial Amount	Facility amount in MM.
Initial Spread	Original LIBOR spread.
Maturity Date	Final maturity date.
Ticker***	The issuer's ticker symbol.
Currency***	Currency of the loan.
LoanX Currency Code*	Standardized currency abbreviation.
SP Org ID***	S&P's assigned Org ID.
Commitment Fee*	Commitment Fee.
Sponsor*	Sponsor of the loan.
LoanX Sponsor Code*	Sponsor name as a numeric code.
Launch Date*	Launch date of the loan.
Close Date*	Close date of the loan.
State*	State of issuer.
Country*	Country of issuer.
LoanX Country Code*	Standardized Country abbreviation.
Pro Rata Assignment*	Pro Rata Assignment Minimum.

Column	Description
Institutional Assignment*	Institutional Assignment Minimum.
Pro Rata Fee*	Pro Rata Fee.
Institutional Fee*	Institutional Fee.
Facility Fee*	Annual fee paid on the full amount of a facility.
Consent*	Agent, company, both.
Security*	Assets securing the loan.
LoanX Security Code*	Standardized Security abbreviation.
Lead Agent*	Lead agent.
LoanX Lead Agent Code*	A generated unique identifier associated with an agent name.
Admin Agent*	Administrative agent.
LoanX Admin Agent Code*	A generated unique identifier associated with an agent name.
Document Agent*	Documentation agent.
LoanX Doc Agent Code*	A generated unique identifier associated with an agent name.
Syndicate Agent*	Syndication agent.
LoanX Synd Agent Code*	A generated unique identifier associated with an agent name.
Initial SP Rating*	Initial S&P rating.
Industry Code*	Industry code.
SIC Code*	SIC code.
SIC Description*	SIC description.
Industry Segment ID*	Industry segment ID.
Industry Segment Description*	Industry segment description.
Status Code*	Code for internal status.
Status	Description of internal status.
Cancelled*	Flag to indicate the deal was cancelled.
Created Time	Date a facility record was created.
Modified Time	Date a facility record was modified.
Term*	Term of the loan, in years.
RC Term*	Term of the RC loan, in years.
TLA Term*	Term of the TLA loan, in years
TLB Term*	Term of the TLB loan, in years.
TLD Term*	Term of the TLD loan, in years.
OID*	Original offering price of the loan at issuance.
Libor Floor*	The minimum base rate paid in the event Libor is below the specified floor level.
Lien Type***	Seniority of the debt within the levels of borrower's capital structure.
Cov-Lite***	Flag to indicate the tranche is cov-lite.

Table A-17. Recommended Update columns (Table 4-2)

Column	Description
LoanX ID	Unique Identifier for each loan.
LCD ID	Identifier for S&P LCD Data.
Issuer Name	Name of borrower or issuer.
Dealname	Name of borrower. This is usually the same as preceding cell but can include date and type of deal.
Facility Type	Specific loan type; TLB, bridge loan, etc.
Industry	Industry classification based on SIC code.
Initial Amount	Facility Amount in MM.
Final Maturity	Final maturity date.
Initial Spread	Original LIBOR spread.
Facility Status	Active/ inactive status (A or I).
Inactive Date	Date of status change, always in the past.
Inactive Reason	Reason for status change.
Replacement LoanX ID	The LoanX ID for the replacement loan.
Replacement PMD ID	Replacement Unique identifier associated with a particular issuer/tranche combination. This can be a positive or negative number.
Replacement Issuer Name	Replacement Name of borrower or issuer.
Replacement Deal Name	Replacement Name of borrower; usually same as preceding cell, but can include date and type of deal.
Replacement Facility Type	Replacement Specific loan type; TLB, bridge loan, etc.
Replacement Industry	Replacement Industry classification based on SIC code
Replacement Initial Amount	Replacement Facility Amount in MM.
Replacement Final Maturity	Replacement Final maturity date.
Replacement Initial Spread	Replacement Original LIBOR spread.
Replacement Status	Replacement Facility Status.

Table A-18. Daily Rating columns (Table 4-3)

Column	Description
As of Date	Date the file was created
LoanX ID	Unique Identifier for each loan
Price Date	Date of the Bid and Offer provided
Moody's Rating	Rating provided by Moody's
Moody's Rating Date	Date the rating was last updated by Moody's
Moody's Watch	Watch list description from Moody's
Moody's Watch Date	Date the watch list was last updated
Moody's Outlook	Outlook provided by Moody's
Moody's Outlook Date	Date the outlook was last updated by Moody's
S&P Rating	Rating provided by S&P
S&P Rating Date	Date the rating was last updated by S&P

Column	Description
S&P Watch	Watch list description from S&P
S&P Watch Date	Date the watch list was last updated
S&P Outlook	S&P's outlook value
S&P Outlook Date	Date the outlook was last updated by S&P

Table A-19. LoanID Updates columns (Table 4-4)

Column	Description
Identifier	An industry-standard unique identifier associated with a particular issuer/tranche combination (typically stores the CUSIP)
Identifier Type	Specifies the source of the Identifier (e.g., "CUSIP")
LoanX ID	Unique identifier for each loan
Valid From	Date the Identifier was mapped to the LoanX ID
Valid To	Date the Identifier was unmapped from the LoanX ID
Modified Time	Date the Identifier Mapping was edited

Table A-20. Marks column descriptions (Table 4-5)

Column	Description
LoanXID	Unique identifier for each loan.
Mark Date	Date of price.
Evaluated Price	Midpoint of close bid/close offer.
Bid	Average bid for facility on mark date subject to change through the trading day.
Offer	Average offer for facility on mark date subject to change through the trading day.
Depth	Depth is generally the count of the contributing dealers.
Close Bid	Closing bid captured at 4 PM Eastern time. This will not change.
Close Offer	Closing offer captured at 4 PM Eastern time. This will not change.
Close Date	Date of Close bid and offer.
Contributed	Returns "Yes" if your company contributed to the average mark.

Table A-21. Financial Statement columns (Table 4-6)

Column	Description
SP_COMPANY_ID	S&P Capital IQ identifier
Currency	Currency of the financial data
Year	Year of the financial statement
Quarter	Quarter of the financial statement
Is_Annual	Indicator of annual data
Is_Latest	Indicator of the most recent information available
Total_Sr_Secured_EBITDA	Total senior secured debt/EBITDA
Sr_Debt_EBITDA	Senior debt/EBITDA
Sr_Sub_Debt_EBITDA	Senior subordinated debt/EBITDA
Jr_Sub_Debt_EBITDA	Junior subordinated debt/EBITDA

Column	Description
Sub_Debt_EBITDA	Subordinated debt/EBITDA
Total_Debt_EBITDA	Total debt/EBITDA
Net_Debt_EBITDA	(Total debt – cash and ST investments)/EBITDA
Total_Assets	Total assets
Revenue	Revenue
EBITDA	Earnings before interest, tax, depreciation, and amortization
Retained_Earnings	Retained earnings
EBITDA_INT	EBITDA/interest expense
Quick_Ratio	(Total cash and short-term investments + accounts receivables)/total current liabilities
Current_Ratio	Total current assets/total current liabilities
Total_Debt_Capital	Total debt/total capital
Total_Debt_Equity	Total debt/total equity

Table A-22. Primary Keys for Markit tables (Table 4-7)

Table name	Primary Key(s)
LoanIDUpdates	Identifier, Modified Time
LoanPricingAndAnalytics	PricingAsOf, LoanX ID
LoansDailyRatings	Date, LoanX ID
LoanXFacilityUpdates	LoanX ID, Modified Time
LoanXMarks	LoanX ID, Mark Date
LoanXRecUpdates	LoanX ID, Inactivation Date
FinancialStatement	SP_COMPANY_ID, Year, Quarter
FinancialStatementMap	LXID

Table A-23. Portfolio table design (Table 5-1)

Field name	Data type
PositionID*	Number
Type	Short Text
SecurityID	Short Text
Size	Number
PurchasePx	Number
PurchaseDate	Date/Time
Position Comments	Short Text

Table A-24. Moody's Rating Factor (source: Moody's Investors Service, Inc.; Table 6-1)

Rating	Rating factor
Aaa	1
Aa1	10
Aa2	20
Aa3	40

Rating	Rating factor
A1	70
A2	120
A3	180
Baa1	260
Baa2	360
Baa3	610
Ba1	940
Ba2	1,350
Ba3	1,766
B1	2,220
B2	2,720
B3	3,490
Caa1	4,770
Caa2	6,500
Caa3	8,070
Ca	10,000
C	10,000

Table A-25. Comp table schema (Table 6-2)

Field name	Data type
HistDate	Date/Time (set as Primary Key)
X	Number (set Field Size to Double)
Y	Number (set Field Size to Double)

Table A-26. RF table schema (Table 6-3)

Field name	Data type
Rating (Primary Key)	Short Text
Factor	Number

Table A-27. MedianBondStats table schema (Table 6-4)

Field name	Data type
PeerGroup (Primary Key)	Short Text
Count	Number
PxChgYTD	Number (Field Size Double)
PxChg3M	Number (Field Size Double)
YASSpread	Number (Field Size Double)
YASYield	Number (Field Size Double)
FixedCpn	Number (Field Size Double)
MonthsUntilMaturity	Number (Field Size Double)
RF	Number

Table A-28. MedianLoanStats table schema (Table 6-5)

Field name	Data type
PeerGroup (Primary Key)	Short Text
Count	Number
PxChgYTD	Number (Field Size Double)
PxChg3M	Number (Field Size Double)
DM	Number (Field Size Double)
Yield	Number (Field Size Double)
Margin	Number (Field Size Double)
MonthsUntilMaturity	Number (Field Size Double)
RF	Number

Table A-29. MedianCompanyStats table schema (Table 6-6)

Field name	Data type
Category (Primary Key)	Short Text
Count	Number
MarketCap	Number (Field Size Double)
TotalDebt	Number (Field Size Double)
TotalDebtToEBITDA	Number (Field Size Double)
NetDebtToEBITDA	Number (Field Size Double)
FCFToTotalDebt	Number (Field Size Double)
YrHi	Number (Field Size Double)
YrLow	Number (Field Size Double)
PxChgYTD	Number (Field Size Double)
PxChg3M	Number (Field Size Double)
TotalReturn12M	Number (Field Size Double)

Table A-30. BondZWeights schema (Table 6-7)

Field name	Data type
PxChgYTD	Number (Field Size Double)
PxChg3M	Number (Field Size Double)
YASSpread	Number (Field Size Double)
YASYield	Number (Field Size Double)
FixedCpn	Number (Field Size Double)
MonthsUntilMaturity	Number (Field Size Double)
RF	Number (Field Size Double)

Table A-31. PortfolioScenarios schema (Table 7-1)

Field name	Data type
PositionID (Primary Key)	Number
BestReturn	Number (double)
AverageReturn	Number (double)
WorstReturn	Number (double)
BestProbability	Number (double)
AverageProbability	Number (double)
WorstProbability	Number (double)

Table A-32. Returns table schema (Table 10-1)

Field name	Data type
Period*	Date
MonthlyPNL	Number (Double)
StartingAUM	Number (Double)

Index

A

Access, 7, 8
  advantages and limitations of, 8
  creating reports in, 228-232
  importing Markit data into, 86
  importing Markit data using C#, 88-92
  linking Excel worksheets to, 103
  maintaining a history of Portfolio table,
    using C#, 109
  organizing financial data in tables, 17-20
    connecting data with queries, 19
  populating database tables using Bloomberg
    C# API, 63-74
    code, 64
    creating a typed dataset, 63
    preliminaries, 63
  setting up for use with C#, 48
  using for analysis on large datasets, 203
  using for market analysis, 207-216
    loans currently above $90 that were
      below $80, 213
    new issue loan analysis, 208
    price history for corporate loans, 210
    refinancings, 209
  using for portfolio risk analysis, 178-184
    generating warning signs, 183
    portfolio breakdown, 178
  using for relative value analysis, 130
    correlation and regression, 131
    median in Access, 132
  using to keep a history, 107-109
accessing financial data, 3
ADS.xsd dataset, creating, 64
analysis (see financial data analysis)
analytics on loans (IHS Markit), 83
annualizing returns, 248
  formula for calculating, 254
array functions (Excel), 31
autocomplete functionality (Excel), 16
AVERAGE function (Excel), 124, 128

B

backup.bat script, 106
bank loans (see corporate loans)
banks, custom indices on Bloomberg, 36
BasicExample method, Program class, 55
batch files, 106
BDH function (Excel), pulling historical data
  into Excel, 31, 119
BDP (Bloomberg Data Point) function, 25
  pulling a single field into Excel, 26
    Fill argument, 28
    Security argument, 27
  security identifiers returned by, 36
  using in Bond Override worksheet in Excel,
    48
  using in Company worksheet in Excel, 46
BDS function, 29
  pulling index's constituent list into Excel, 36
  retrieving securities' peers, 36
  security identifiers returned by, 36
Beta, 117, 225
Bloomberg Barclays Indices, 35
Bloomberg Barclays US Aggregate Bond Index
  (Barclays Agg) index, 249
  calculating portfolio returns against, 253
  calculating returns against in Excel, 250
Bloomberg Field Search (in Excel), 25

comma-separated values (CSV) files
  data requests for IHS Markit, 76
  facility data from IHS Markit, 76
  IHS Markit data, storing in Excel, 85
  IHS Markit loan facilities data, importing
    into Access, 86
Committee on Uniform Security Identification
  Procedures (see CUSIPs)
Comp table schema, 289
Company table (Access), 49, 279
Company worksheet (Excel), using Bloomberg
  data, 44, 278
comparable securities, 35-39
  finding using indices, 35
  peers, 36
  related securities in Bloomberg data, 37
composite key or composite primary key, 15
corporate bond and loan data, 2
corporate bonds, 3
  Bloomberg data on, 6
  Bond Override worksheet in Excel, 47
  Bond table in Access, 50
  Bond worksheet columns and Bloomberg
    map, 276
  Bond worksheet in Excel using Bloomberg
    data, 39
  Bonds table in Access, populating, 66
  IHS Markit data on, 84
  in portfolio breakdown, 167
corporate family ratings
  of all portfolio positions, 173
  warnings for CCC or lower ratings, 176
corporate loans, 3, 5
  creating Loan worksheet in Excel with
    Bloomberg data, 42
  IHS Markit data on, 75-84
    data requests, 76
    facility information, 76
    loan pricing, financials, and analysis, 81
    using in market analysis, 195
  in portfolio breakdown, 167
  Loan table in Access, 50
  Loan worksheet columns and Bloomberg
    map, 277
  loans above $90 that were below $80, analy-
    sis in Access, 213
  Loans table in Access, populating, 72
  new issue loan analysis in Access, 207
  new issue loan analysis in Excel, 196

price history analysis in Access, 210
  refinancings, examining in Access market
    analysis, 209
  refinancings, examining in Excel market
    analysis, 199
CORREL function (Excel), 119
  using OFFSET and MATCH functions with,
    157
correlation and regression
  correlation between daily price changes in
    company stock and index, 225
  correlation in portfolios, 152, 156
  calculating using C#, 192
  in Access, 131
  in C#, 134, 138
  in Excel, 114-120
    creating a correlation matrix, 119
    regression, 116
creating financial reports, 4
Credit Default Swap (CDS), 46
currencies
  in Bloomberg data on Excel, 27
  in Company worksheet (Excel) with Bloom-
    berg data, 44
CUSIPs, 27, 40, 55
  in IHS Markit LoanID Updates, 81

D

Daily Ratings channel (IHS Markit), 80
  Daily Rating columns, 286
data access (see accessing financial data)
data analysis (see financial data analysis)
data integrity, 96-99
  checking the data, 96
  outliers, 98
  sample size, 97
data validation
  Data Validation tool, 219
  in Excel, 16
Database Tools (Access), 18
DataSet, typed, creating in Visual Studio, 64
DATEDIFF function, 210
dates and time
  Bloomberg date types, 32, 275
  date in Program class, 59
  specifying date for ratings data, 80
discount margin (DM), 196
DMedian function, 134
Dow Jones Industrial Average, 35

E

F

About the Author

Justin Pauley is a Senior Structured Credit Analyst at Brigade Capital Management, an asset management firm based in New York. At Brigade, Justin's responsibilities include making investment recommendations, executing trades, and developing the systems used to analyze and value complex investments. Prior to joining Brigade, Justin headed CLO Strategy at the Royal Bank of Scotland where he published monthly reports to investors and developed bond analytic systems. Justin started his career in Wachovia's technology department, developing front-office applications for analysts and traders. He has been published in the *Journal of Structured Finance*, quoted in the *Wall Street Journal* and Bloomberg News, and has spoken on numerous panels at finance-related conferences.

Learn from experts.
Find the answers you need.

Sign up for a **10-day free trial** to get **unlimited access** to all of the content on Safari, including Learning Paths, interactive tutorials, and curated playlists that draw from thousands of ebooks and training videos on a wide range of topics, including data, design, DevOps, management, business—and much more.

Start your free trial at:
oreilly.com/safari

(No credit card required.)

9 781491 973257